Welfare, Ideology and Need

Welfare, Ideology and Need

Developing Perspectives on the Welfare State

Martin Hewitt
Lecturer in Social Policy, Hatfield Polytechnic

HARVESTER WHEATSHEAF
BARNES & NOBLE BOOKS

First published 1992 by
Harvester Wheatsheaf,
Campus 400, Maylands Avenue
Hemel Hempstead,
Hertfordshire, HP2 7EZ
A division of
Simon & Schuster International Group

First published in the United States of America in 1992 by
Barnes and Noble Books
8705 Bollman Place
Savage, Maryland 20763

Typeset in 10/12 pt Times
by Pentacor plc

Printed and bound in Great Britain by
BPCC Wheatons Ltd, Exeter

British Library Cataloguing in Publication Data

Hewitt, Martin
  Welfare, ideology and need: Developing
  perspectives on the Welfare State.
  I. Title
  361.6

  ISBN 0-7450-1076-8
  ISBN 0-7450-1077-6 pbk

Library of Congress Cataloging-in-Publication Data
are available from the Library of Congress

ISBN 0-389-20983-X

1 2 3 4   95 94 93 92

To my mother and to the memory of my father

Contents

Acknowledgements

I am indebted to many people who have helped directly or indirectly in the formation of this book, not all of whom received the acknowledgement they deserve. I am particularly grateful to the following for reading and commenting on various versions of early drafts that eventually formed chapters in the book: to John Alden, Digby Anderson, Christine Cousins, Hartley Dean, Peter Dews, Alan Hooper, Ian Parker, Martin Powell, Liz Shepherd, Peter Squires, Monika Temple and Paul Temple; to colleagues at Hatfield Polytechnic for listening to and discussing presentations of papers that developed into the book; and to Harvester-Wheatsheaf in the person of Clare Grist, my editor, and the two readers for supporting and encouraging this publication.

I owe a special and lasting gratitude to Ann for her support over several years of intellectual gestation – together with my occasional bouts of indigestion and general irritability – and to her, Daniel and Matthew for reminding me that there is a reality beyond ideology.

Chapter nine draws on an earlier paper published in *Theory, Culture and Society* and reprinted in Hewitt (1991).

1

Introduction

In the history of welfare studies the topic of ideology has dawned slowly into the daylight of critical examination. Only during the recent development of Marxist studies of welfare has this topic been fully acknowledged as playing a significant role in the formation, function and practice of social policy. Yet, during its development, the study of welfare has not been entirely blind to a formative presence requiring attention. This presence is now called ideology, the system of ideas and imagery through which people come to see the world and define their needs and aspirations. However, previously it passed under different guises as values, beliefs, norms and expectations, each bearing a family resemblance to ideology. The role of ideology in the formation of welfare is the primary concern of this book.

Today, ideology has become more than ever a salient feature of welfare in the context of social, political and economic developments, which together contribute towards the dissolution of the postwar consensus between the Labour and Conservative Parties. One of the major outcomes of this dissolution has been the current restructuring of the welfare state. Ideology is a key factor in explaining formative developments in the British welfare state during the second half of the twentieth century that have led to recent changes. The significance of ideology is seen in several ways.

First, the idea that postwar western societies were governed by a political consensus called for an understanding of the values and objectives by which this agreement was founded. The consensus was cemented by political parties of both Right and Left and underlaid by developments transcending political differences. These developments included the extensive influence exercised by science and technology, increasing state hegemony, government intervention in the economy, and the state's commitment to maintain the welfare of each citizen. The welfare state formed the institutional embodiment of this consensus, receiving practical support from the social and economic policies of Socialist and

Conservative governments alike, despite apparent differences in ideology. An understanding of these consensual values required their description and location *vis-à-vis* welfare policy. In British welfare studies, these values were supported by research into the implementation and appraisal of policy conducted in social administration, the field of study most concerned with welfare policy. In keeping with its Social Democratic and Fabian tradition, social administration has been at the forefront of the advancement of a consensual ideology about social justice and the abolition of want. This was despite the polemic that leading social administrators waged against 'the irresponsible society' of private advantage, and despite the Right's commitment to increasing the scope of selectivity and divisive means-testing (see Titmuss 1963, ch. 11; Townsend 1975, ch. 7). The ideology of consensus represented as much an ideal for the welfare state to build on as an achievement to hold on to against external assault. The welfare state was the basis on which to consolidate and advance consensus in postwar society. Several writers working within social administration, and a few branching out towards Marxism, sought to codify this ideology.

A second development pointing to the importance of ideology has been the need to appraise the practical achievements of welfare policy. The fact that practice often departed from the ideals used in policy formulation provided a gauge for appraising performance. Although this discrepancy was seen mainly as a matter of policy evaluation, it also provided important insights into ideological questions about the function of welfare services in setting goals and raising expectations that are far from fulfilled in reality (cf. Runciman 1966). The emergence of a Marxist perspective in social policy has brought such questions to the fore, leading to a reappraisal of the purposes of welfare policy in postwar capitalist society (O'Connor 1973; Habermas 1976a; Gough 1979; Offe 1984), and suggesting that welfare serves as a 'smokescreen' to disguise the 'real' objectives of policy: controlling deviance, disciplining labour, taming dissidence and policing resistance. A different appraisal influenced by Weberian sociology has recognised that the relationship between ideals and practice is not linear – i.e. setting policy objectives and then implementing policy in conformity with these objectives – but reflexive. For example, during the 1970s writers like Rein (1976) and Room (1979) stressed the cyclical process of policy formulation, whereby the setting of goals leads to interventions, which in turn influence the reappraisal of goals and practices – a conception that resembles 'muddling through' (Lindblom 1959), but with greater intent and purpose.

Thirdly, the reappraisal of the ideology of postwar welfare received its strongest impetus from the New Right and from policies bearing the imprint of Thatcherism in the United Kingdom and Reaganomics in the United States. Not surprisingly, the Marxist critique of the welfare state has seen the rise of Thatcherism as evidence of the vulnerability of the postwar consensus and a portent of its eventual demise, and has paid considerable attention to the ideological significance of the restructuring of the welfare state. Consequently, the ideologies of Thatcherism, the Right and the welfare state in transition are now important topics in welfare studies. In the midst of these changes, the welfare state stands as a kind of touchstone for assessing the veracity of statements made by government ministers and prime ministers. Given the uncertainties about Tory plans for the welfare state, the real intention behind government statements is gauged by what actually happens to welfare policy. For example, is the National Health Service safe in Conservative hands? Has the level of expenditure on the NHS and other services increased or decreased? Are we witnessing the demolition or the restructuring of the welfare state? (see Illife 1985/6; Robinson 1986.) What is happening to the welfare state after Thatcher? Underlying these questions is a more fundamental one, which hints at the increasingly illusory quality that ideology sheds over aspects of modern society: by what criteria – should any remain – are these questions to be answered?

One way of gauging what is really happening to the welfare state, adopted by some mainstream and Marxist analysts, is to hark back to standards set initially in the 1940s, as though these provide eternal truths by which to judge the welfare state in the late twentieth century. Yet, on the contrary, the difficulty now in answering the above, supposedly factual questions is that the task itself is obscured by the shadow ideology casts over the whole exercise, over the reform of welfare *and* its analysis. For the very criteria for appraising the welfare state have been lost under a welter of statistics, where each series is subject to constantly changing definitions of reality, of unemployment, poverty, public expenditure, standard of living, money, and so forth. The experience of constantly changing parameters in public life instils a sense of chaos, which researchers and administrators alike cannot easily adapt to – whatever ideological use it serves their political masters. The irony of this position cannot pass unnoticed. For in so far as Fabian and Marxist critics since the 1950s have implied that the welfare state has never achieved its founding ideals, these same critics are now referring to these ideals as criteria for appraising its present plight. This results in the elevation of a mythical welfare state, which serves as a perpetual standard of truth in symbolising a consensual and caring society. The oscillation between the illusory and the real status of the welfare state in the minds of its critics (social administration, Marxist *and* New Right) provides a further issue for the study of welfare ideology.

A fourth reason for studying ideology is that without the security of eternal truths, values and standards, a more profound questioning of ideology and culture is needed, which has implications for welfare policy. This questioning concerns the fate of modernity and the credence given today to Social Democracy and Marxism. For it has been these two grand narratives especially which have foretold the evolution of modern society through, respectively, the development of citizenship and the onward advance of the proletariat; and, more broadly, through the general development of civilisation and its institutions –

science, culture, state and welfare – from the close of the eighteenth century to the dawning of the twenty-first. The halting of this long march – under whichever ideological banner – has given rise to several accounts in recent years of 'the cultural contradictions of capitalism' (Bell 1976), 'the welfare state in crisis' (Mishra 1984), the death of grand narrative and the birth of 'the postmodern condition' (Lyotard 1984), 'the exhaustion of utopian energies' (Habermas 1985/6), and 'the end of history' (Fukuyama 1989); debates that together possess more than a passing resemblance to 'the end of ideology' debate of the 1950s, which ironically by comparison expressed technological optimism about the early postwar years.

More specifically, the crisis concerns the status of the universal expectations – for justice, citizenship and collective well-being – which the welfare state has underwritten in the public domain. These expectations are now being overtaken by an individualist dogma stressing competition, material success and market discipline. In issues of moral and spiritual life, this dogma has shifted the balance between public and private domains, between the state and civil society; that is, 'between the complex network of political institutions (including the military, legal, administrative, productive and cultural organs of the state) and the realm of social (privately owned, market- directed, voluntarily run or friendship-based) activities which are legally recognized and guaranteed by the state' (Keane 1988, p. 3). In the context of economic restructuring, widening social inequalities and new concentrations of political power, the management of these beliefs and expectations has become a major concern of the Right. This concern focuses on welfare services as the terrain for engineering a new ideological order that attempts to overcome several problems. Welfare services are expected to pick up the casualties of economic shake-down, while themselves being run down in relation to rising needs and increasing national wealth. They are expected to respond to a fickle public conscience – at least as portrayed by sections of the media – concerned about abused children and dependency generally, while being prepared to brand some dependants as social outcasts and scroungers. They are expected to support the enterprise culture – with its inducements to buy council houses, educate one's children in private schools, invest in private health care and entrust one's savings and future security into the hands of pension companies – while stemming the rising expectations that Keynes and Beveridge instilled in postwar generations. Finally, welfare services are required to sharpen the disciplinary edge of social security, employment training and further education. The political, economic and cultural manifestations of these contradictory changes make the welfare state ripe for nurturing a new ideology. Of course, the meaning of these developments and their crisis implications is subject to different interpretations (e.g. Golding and Middleton 1982; Hall 1984; Taylor-Gooby 1985; Jessop *et al.* 1988). But all are agreed on the key role ideology plays in these events.

Characterising welfare ideology

These are some of the significant postwar developments, which writers in social policy and other disciplines have used to thematise and contextualise ideology. For these writers, the welfare state is seen as more than a collection of social services. It is the social and political formation which most typifies postwar western industrial societies, and which plays a major role in the management of ideology. These accounts of the welfare state have characterised ideology in several ways: as systems of belief, institutional rationales, social practices and welfare discourse. We will identify each characterisation before introducing the theories of ideology associated with each.

Characterisations of ideologies informing the welfare state have produced ideal types of its core values. T. H. Marshall's seminal account, in *Citizenship and Social Class* (1963), of the emergence of citizenship culminating in the Beveridge welfare state, described a system of values that unified the contrary principles of private market and state collectivism into a welfare consensus. Later, Titmuss further codified the discussion by distinguishing between three separate models representing different ideologies of, and stages in, welfare formation: the *laissez-faire* Poor Law ('the residual model'), the postwar mixed economy ('the industrial-achievement-performance model'), and a stage where the state promotes core institutions responsible for the welfare of its citizens ('the institutional-redistributive model') (1974, ch. 2). Although designed for teaching purposes, this typology influenced the construction of further models of welfare values by writers in social administration (e.g. George and Wilding 1976; Room 1979), some of whom subsequently moved towards a Marxist approach (Taylor-Gooby and Dale 1981). Like Titmuss, they sought to typify different concepts of need, justifications for welfare, and welfare allocations between individual and state. They derived their constructions from historical and current patterns of welfare and from extrapolations drawn from existent and hypothetical welfare states. For Titmuss, the comparative elements in these models 'expose more clearly the value choices confronting society' (1974, p. 136); especially, it should be added, amid the welter of change and polemic surrounding different value approaches promoted in recent years. However, as characterisations, these studies limit the notion of ideology to a description of the ideas and conceptual linkages which exist, or ought to exist in logic, between the different value elements in each model; a somewhat rarefied and ideational view of ideology, which, as several writers have noted, does not address the linkages between the values and material bases of welfare existing at particular historical moments (e.g. Gough 1979, p. 172, n. 20; Taylor-Gooby and Dale 1981, p. 58). The consensus view of welfare is considered in Chapter 2.

With the advent in the 1970s of Marxist studies of welfare, the focus has shifted away from constructing typologies of ideology to an examination of the functions of welfare ideology in capitalist society. This perspective – the

Political Economy of Welfare – sees welfare as performing material and ideological functions for the state and for different social classes according to their relations to the means of production. For example, by providing benefits for the unemployed, retired and sick, state welfare functions to legitimate the state's universal claim to support different sectors of society, the poor as well as the rich, dependent as well as independent. At the same time, by policing and regulating the circumstances of the poor as a condition of benefit, the state is seen as legitimate in the eyes of the ruling classes concerned to make the poor more productive and limit the diversion of funds from capital to welfare. For some Marxists, however, welfare, whether for the able-bodied or sick, has few productive consequences; by branding some social minorities as deviant, the main function of state welfare is to maintain social cohesion among the majority. Whatever the case, functionalist accounts of ideology, far from providing a materialist analysis of the means of production, merely assume parallels between relations of production and welfare relations involving state and recipient. The assumption is that exploitative relations of production are replicated in welfare services. This proposition rests on analogy rather than empirical demonstration. While such analogies are instructive and germane, empirical studies have been slow to provide support for these contentions (an early exception is Ginsburg 1979). Further, this approach to ideology views with suspicion the non-controlling and positively enhancing functions of welfare, such as caring and giving (e.g. the 'gift relationship'), which are seen as ideological smokescreens disguising otherwise naked forms of oppression. Yet, whatever their ideological role, these functions may provide an important source of values for directing welfare policy towards achieving greater social justice. There remains a need for an account of ideology, which allows for the possibility that claims of this kind, based on some conception of normative truth, can be made concerning the purposes of welfare (cf. Habermas 1979, ch. 1), an issue developed in Chapter 6. The functions of ideology are further discussed in Chapters 5, 6 and 7 on Marxist theories of welfare.

A further development within Marxist studies of ideology, which possesses a potential to overcome the drawbacks of functionalism, is the study of ideology as practice. This approach holds out the promise of an empirical programme of work, which corrects the ideational emphasis in social administration's models of welfare ideology. The stimulus for this direction came from Althusser's influential essay on 'Ideological State Apparatuses and the Reproduction of Labour Power' (1971). However, despite the guidelines contained therein, there have been few studies of welfare procedures as ideological practices contributing to the reproduction of labour and social division. Studies that have tackled these questions using Althusser's approach, notably feminist studies, tend to define a broad problematic of welfare where social services function as one among other ideological state apparatuses, and simply adapt their accounts of the welfare terrain to Althusser's map. Such studies, however generative in potential, fall back on a level of abstractionism and functionalism shared with Althusser's initial account. (One recent exception is Dean's study (1991) of the partitioning of social security recipients).

The Political Economy and Althusserian approaches, which study the functions and practices of welfare ideology respectively, inform recent attempts seeking to understand the nature of the new hegemony replacing the postwar consensus. Gramsci's idea of hegemony as the 'political consciousness' of a social group that dominates other groups, suggests a developing ideology that positions social classes in a particular direction, draws into its momentum an increasing number of social groups, and thereby constitutes a particular structure of state and society (Gramsci 1971, p. 264). It implies the making of a consensus that is more than just a generally held system of ideals, as described in social administration. A hegemony operates as a dominant pattern of political interests, which articulates ideological assumptions and cultural norms in a political project transcending different class interests. Political ideology is thereby 'overdetermined' in relation to class forces determined by the economic means of production. It is a consensus operating at a higher power. Both the postwar welfare state consensus and the notion of Thatcherite 'authoritarian populism' provide examples of hegemony (Hall 1983; see Laclau and Mouffe 1985), which generate two opposing and powerful images of welfare. On the one hand, welfare is depicted as the universal extension of citizenship; on the other, it is the obverse, a social market that maximises individual freedom. In the latter, state welfare poses the growing threat of profligate mismanagement of the nation's resources. The ideological nature of these different hegemonies is discussed in Chapters 3 and 4 on New Right ideology and the prospects for a new consensus on the welfare state.

In suggesting a pervasive and cohesive political consciousness, the notion of hegemony implies a political project directed towards the attainment of social goals; a grand narrative that, drawing on collective memory, foretells the struggle of a nation, class or people towards a state of personal and social fulfilment. Although such narratives come in varying degrees of grandeur, ranging from Hegelian world history, through socialism's proletarian destiny, to more modest Social Democratic and welfare state theses, they all endow society, or sections of society, with a sense of purpose. The notion of collective welfare has been a major source for the past two centuries or so of the desire for social well-being and of state guarantees to meet human needs. We referred earlier to factors unsettling the rationality of such projects. One aspect of growing disillusionment in the idea of collective welfare is that the ideologies informing such narratives are themselves dissolving, removing from the grasp the handrails of truth and justice that traditionally supported the commitment to welfare. The welfare state faces a demise which could undermine the sense of collective responsibility for need, dismissing from public discourse the very notion of need itself, as Chapter 3 on the New Right seeks to demonstrate.

Without a public language, the experience of need can only be expressed in private and personal terms which divest social policy of its collective *raison d'etre*.

Several responses to this plight have emerged recently; some abandoning the notion of the collective and purposive subject, while others seek to recover a renewed sense of founding values for the human subject. For example, Foucault (1979a) provides an account of developments in punishment, discipline and welfare, which dispels collective notions of purpose defining individual and social subjects in history, and which dispenses with the idea of justice as a transcendental value guiding subjects in the fulfilment of human needs. This approach is examined in Chapter 9. Other writers, sharing similar concerns, see 'postmodern' society as liberated from the binding myths of truth and certainty, and open to new opportunities for creative activity in science, art and administration (e.g. Lyotard 1984). This approach is discussed in the final chapter. An alternative perspective, which reinstates the central notion of human purpose, permitting direction but not presupposing progress, is provided by Habermas (e.g. 1979), and is discussed in Chapters 6, 7 and 10. This perspective addresses the nature of social action which seeks to pursue collective ideals in the context of social and economic conditions often impeding human interests; this is the idea of 'collective will-formation'. Within this perspective, policies, contingent on limited material resources, none the less can express normative claims that orient people towards states of human welfare transcending these contingencies. In different areas of policy studies, the relations between policy ideals and contingencies are fundamentally problematic. In the present book, this problem leads to the conclusion that ideology resembles a thread, which ties together human projects in a conditional world and directs them towards the attainment of human ideals.

Conceptions of ideology

From the discussion of different characterisations of welfare ideology, it is clear that ideology appears under different concepts. Theories of ideology developed since the early 1970s attest to the multifaceted nature of ideology. Without examining each theory in detail – a task ably performed by several texts (e.g. Larrain 1979; Thompson 1984; Eagleton 1991) – we will identify and introduce three conceptions of ideology relevant to the study of the welfare state; namely, as social ideals and institutionalised values, social practice and discourse. This will serve as a preface to the studies of welfare ideology that are to follow.

In welfare studies, ideology is often portrayed as a system of ideas, beliefs and values that individuals and societies aspire towards. Social policies aim to achieve specific social norms and ideals which express particular value assumptions. Social norms concern society's or the state's expectations about its members' behaviour and achievements (e.g. that all children between the ages of five and sixteen should receive full-time education, whatever their ability). Collective ideals express the aspirations a society values in seeking to formulate and achieve policy objectives (that no member should be in poverty, or without appropriate health care and housing). Value assumptions refer to policy suppositions – not always explicit – about the way individuals behave and states operate (that individuals are normally self-reliant, honest and rational when claiming welfare, and that the state carries ultimate responsibility for the needs of its citizens). A model of ideology not only indicates the discrete values it contains, but also the internal logic of the value assumptions that shape policy statements, and bind its proposals into a coherent system. For example, the values of self-help, market competition and welfare deterrence, described in Titmuss's 'residual welfare' model (1974, p. 30), assume that individuals behave and interact according to their separate interests rather than collectively. These values are expressed in propositions located in textual sources such as government reports or statutes, or residing in the recesses of memory, convention or common sense. The typologies discussed earlier vary in the degree to which they authenticate the material sources of specific values. That some typologies provide little or no authentication removes the opportunity to study values in the context of specific social practices and modes of material production, and leads to a discussion of welfare ideas in the abstract.

The fact that values exist in the context of social institutions points to an important material expression of ideology. Values reside in specific social organisations formed to fulfil certain purposes, such as welfare and educational services. Many studies of welfare institutions refer to the particular values they embody, and attend closely to the difficulties in implementing these values. An example is seen in studies of state health services which, aiming to provide universal care for everyone, experience a serious lack of resources or excessive demand that cannot be met without providing services more selectively. However, an approach that sees values as enshrined in institutions and social relations is in danger of oversimplifying matters; in suggesting that organisations are established to achieve only the goals formally stated in the enabling charter or statute, and in ignoring the new and conflicting goals that groups inside and outside the organisation seek to introduce. Thus, the use of power and ideology is involved in the promotion, dominance and replacement of organisational goals. In the politics of organisational life, management practices can be justified in terms of goals that might not have been envisaged originally, but which new conditions, such as economic recession, demand. Moreover, managers will sometimes recite founding goals rhetorically to convince people that the organisation remains faithful to its original aims, when in fact new problems demand that it deviate from its original aims. Such *ad* and *post hoc* justifications are an important feature of the pragmatic and flexible conduct of policy implementation and appraisal (cf. Bittner 1974; Daudi 1986).

Institutions therefore cannot be seen as the repository of values without an understanding of the social practices that originate, sustain and adapt them – a second conception of ideology. Social practices refer to the concerted activities pursued by groups of individuals in producing products such as commodities, services, knowledge and political decisions. The activities, relations and products entailed are essentially material in nature. This means that the value placed on what is produced must be understood according to values analysed in a material context, rather than in an ideational context. These activities carry either use value in fulfilling human needs, or exchange value in being exchanged for other commodities through the medium of money. Moreover, in so far as production involves producing products, values and outcomes for some rather than for all groups in society, different judgements arise over the allocation of these products and the values placed on them. These differences, which lead to either conflict or makeshift compromises between competing groups, may require the presentation of sectional interests as if they are of universal interest to society. The production of value by a powerful group involves social practices that entail the production of ideology as well as products and services. This notion of social practice as entailing the construction of ideology in relation to material production has been developed in the influential work of Althusser (1971). He sought to expound a theory that addresses the subjective element of compliance in ideological relations and practices, by explaining why individuals who are subject to structures of state power and ideology become subjects who comply with this ideology, *as if* voluntarily.

Finally, ideology exists in the material form of policy texts, reports and discourse. For example, it is present when codified in the propositions stated in numerous texts – laws, regulations, orders, official reports, etc. – that articulate existing or desired states of affairs. Ideology is also present in interaction and dialogue between individuals sharing a common activity, communicating encouragement or discouragement, permission or prohibition, in a more expressive and less structured way by means of conversation and innuendo; for example, when a social worker interviewing a demoralised client seeks to give encouragement and support. Finally, ideology is present in the symbolic form evident in newspaper stories, advertisements and corporate logos, which rely on stereotypes and emblems rather than propositional statements. In welfare services, corporate logos give public identity to, for example, Legal Aid services, the Equal Opportunities Commission and public relations-conscious local authorities, and express values of justice, personal consideration, equality and consensus – even during times of severe cut-back. In each of these three types of text – policy statement, dialogue and symbol – ideology is evident in the way in which imaginary representations of social relations stand in place of real relations and impart normative ideals to these relations. In social policy, every aspect of welfare practice is rendered into some form of discourse. For example, various accounts are provided of states of need and dependency by researchers, social workers, social security officers, government committees of inquiry, and so forth, producing academic articles, 'social enquiry reports', case notes and official reports, all of which express ideology in some form or other. The complementing these accounts of need, likewise, welfare resources are routinely itemised and inventoried into financial statements, and matched to statements of need, measured in terms of outputs, and appraised for efficiency. The discourses of needs and resources constitute the discipline of social policy, defining policy objectives, targets and parameters, and shaping the policy process of identifying need and planning, implementing and appraising services.

Textual analysis of policy has in recent years become an interesting, though subsidiary, focus for policies studies. Initially this interest produced 'stories' (Rein 1976), 'readings' (Room 1979) and 'symbolic' accounts (Edelman 1977) of policy, which were suggestive, but avoided a close examination of texts and a revelation of the methods employed in such readings. Subsequently, further studies have given more attention to the methods and the texts read (e.g. Smith 1980; Williams 1981; Green 1983b), producing interesting analyses of particular policy texts and reforms (e.g. Trevillian 1988; Banton *et al.* 1985; Rojek *et al.* 1988). Parallel to these developments, studies of other types of policy have also turned their attention to text, in law and legal policy (Burton and Carlen 1979; Goodrich 1986), and in business and organisational policy (Daudi 1986).

Overview

In the 1980s, the renaissance of intellectual themes concerning ideology, rationality, modernity and need has enriched welfare studies. Yet while there have been several interesting theoretical developments in social policy, especially in texts published at the turn of the last decade (e.g. Gough 1979; Mishra 1981; Taylor-Gooby and Dale 1981), the terrain of social theory has been extended further and remains to be cultivated for welfare studies. The theme of ideology, for example, provides a rich seam that crosses a wide expanse, cutting into the other themes mentioned above and giving them a prominence in the context of current social and political developments. Against the background of this extended terrain, several of the texts on welfare theory inevitably begin to look dated. In addition to exploring welfare ideology, the present book has as its secondary aim to chart this terrain for students of welfare and of related disciplines, such as sociology, politics and political economy, which study the welfare state. In following this aim, I have sought to trace and situate the diverse influences and debates that the writers discussed have produced, often in areas outside welfare studies, in order to see where their arguments lead in investigating the welfare state, its ideological significance, and its interrelations with other social phenomena. This has led me to chart the contours, complexities and developments of the thoughts of various writers in some detail, and occasionally at some length, at the expenses of furnishing the reader with neat surveys and summaries.

To conclude, this book has three objectives. First, it seeks to examine the role played by ideology in conceptions of welfare advanced in different theories of its formation. Secondly, it attempts to explicate the ideological practices used in the argumentation of social policy. Thirdly, it draws on recent developments in the theory of ideology, to examine their contribution to welfare studies. In addition to these objectives, the book is guided by a normative concern – shared with modern Fabians and Critical Theorists alike – that there exists in social theory a powerful strand of welfare thought that requires articulation, and which when coupled with democratic theory can create a solidaristic philosophy to provide the only available protection against the anti-welfare and anti-democratic themes heard recently in political discourse.

Different studies of modern society – social administration, New Right, Marxist, Critical Theory and Foucauldian – have developed different accounts of welfare. In each account, ideology plays a formative role in the development and conception of welfare: consensus-forming, forming distorted accounts of needs and rights, controlling and disciplining, and enhancing human power and well-being. If we can understand how ideology is conceived in each account, we can better appreciate the contribution of each conception to the development of explanatory and normative perspectives in welfare studies. Yet the status of ideology in some accounts is not always explicit. In social administration and New Right thought, for example, it acts as a hidden resource which influences their perspectives on the specific functions attributed to welfare. Only in some, for example Marxist accounts, is ideology an explicit topic, understood in theoretical terms and applied in studying welfare and society. This means that to understand welfare ideology we must distinguish between two types of welfare theory. For theories such as Social Democratic and New Right, which address ideological phenomena without a developed conception of ideology, we will attempt to explicate the ideological resources shaping these theories. But for theories that possess an explicit conception of ideology, we will examine critically the role each assigns ideology in the formation of welfare.

In Part I, we discuss two ideologies of welfare. Chapter 2 addresses the notion of consensus that defines social administration's theory of welfare and the implicit ideological assumptions this theory holds. In particular, T. H. Marshall's and Richard Titmuss's ideas are examined. Their ideas provide the Social Democratic and Fabian foundations to the study of social administration. Subsequently, some writers such as Hadley and Hatch (1981) have developed Marshall and Titmuss's approach in understanding the meaning and ideology of welfare. Despite recent claims that these writers have capitulated to the Right, I argue that the latter-day Fabians have broadly kept faith with a Social Democratic ideology formed during the present century. Chapter 3 examines the New Right's view of the welfare state, expressed in its pro-market and anti-collectivist ideology. Chapter 4 explores recent debates about Thatcherism and the strength of its ideological legacy in building a new consensus on the welfare state.

In Part II, we examine the way Marxist theories of ideology have offered a more explicit understanding of welfare ideology. In Chapters 4, 5 and 6 the book explores contributions drawn, respectively, from the Marxist Political Economy of Welfare of O'Connor and Gough, for example; from the Critical Theory of Habermas and Offe; and from the Structural Marxism of Althusser and others.

The limitations ascribed to Marxist analyses of ideology and society have given rise in France to the work of Althusser, Foucault, Donzelot, Castel and other, which has influenced studies of social policy in Britain. The Althusserian and Foucauldian approaches to welfare studies are examined in Chapters 8 and 9, the first two chapters of Part III on the discursive dimension of welfare ideology. This development, in particular, has modified the global conception of ideology (with its connotations of a 'dominant ideology thesis' suggested by Abercrombie *et al.* 1980) in favour of a more localised and pluralist conception that sees ideology as a conjunction of discursive and political practices, of the 'Ideological State Apparatuses' or 'power/knowledge', that construct regimes of truth governing individual behaviour and outlook. However, in both cases these developments are not without difficulties, given the shades of functionalism they share and Foucault's contention about the *ubiquitous* relations of power characterising modern disciplinary societies and welfare systems. Foucault's approach in particular has directed attention to the discursive nature of ideology. His work can be seen as 'deconstructing' systems of ideology and power (Norris 1982) evident in material and epistemic formations of knowledge, for example, in hospital architecture, medical symptomatologies and treatment regimes.

Chapter 10 explores the ideological construction of human need, using a psychoanalytic perspective which attends to the unconscious processes influencing needing, its expression and signification. From this exploration emerges a more positive view of ideology and its role in the formation of collective ideals, such as those shaping public policy.

For, as the Conclusion argues, in Foucault's and Althusser's work, there is no place for ideology as a means of emancipation and as the prefiguration of states of welfare towards which society or social groups strive. The limitations of their work lead us to consider the role of ideology in the promotion of ideals that must be subject to reason, if their implementation is to be achieved in the practical context of constraints set by the contingencies of economic scarcity, demographic pressures of need, and political interests. The idea that ideology is part of a rational process which prefigures social ideals has a special salience for policy studies seeking to understand the formation of policy and welfare in society.

PART 1
Welfare state and ideology

The topic of ideology as discussed in the previous chapter has received at best passing attention in welfare studies. Although the 1980s have spawned several accounts of the ideology of Thatcherism, it remains the case that Social Democracy – the ideology of the postwar welfare state – has received comparatively scant attention. In seeking to redress this imbalance, the next three chapters discuss the ideologies of Social Democracy and the New Right, as they inform the perspectives respectively of social administration and the Hayekian and Thatcherite critiques of state welfare.

Three questions form the central concerns of these chapters. The first question concerns the understanding of ideology underpinning the Social Democratic perspective of social administration and the New Right critique of state welfare. What are their implicit or nascent theories of ideology and where do they stand in relation to their broader conceptions of society? The second question emerges when we consider that the values of each tradition – those of social cohesion, equality, individual autonomy and democratic accountability, on the one hand; and of self-sufficiency, competition and the market, on the other – are not all of a piece. Within each ideology, some values stand at variance with others: for example, in Social Democracy the beliefs in universal equality and individual autonomy; and in the New Right the ideas of aggressive individualism and market equilibrium. The tensions between these different values have formed a significant dynamic in the evolution of Social Democracy and the Right, creating various twists and turns in policy developments. These chapters therefore examine the question central in understanding ideology: how does each ideology conjoin different beliefs into a coherent system of ideas? The third question emerges when considering how social administration and rightist values operate in the practical and contingent world of policy. Social administration, for example, justifies its policies on the basis of values which fall broadly within the Social Democratic tradition. These values constitute the central beliefs of a consensus ideology that sees the welfare state as the principal means in society of securing social cohesion; an orientation that frequently justifies specific interventions in social problems. The question arises, therefore, as to how social administration's ideals are justified in the practical, problem-solving context of social and economic contingencies that have hitherto been impervious to control. For example, how can social administration's belief in egalitarian and universalist policies be justified given the widening gap between demands for welfare and available resources? Making ideals sound plausible (rather than abandoning them altogether) is for social administration – as for the Right – an ideological question.

In considering questions concerning the conjunctions between different ideals, and between ideals and contingencies, we will give some attention to the role of ideological language in articulating these conjunctions. For example, social administration has frequently deployed architectural metaphors referring to 'ceilings', 'floors', and so forth in income maintenance, and to 'base' and 'superstructures' to differentiate the functions of the welfare state generally. Moreover, the present 'crisis of the welfare state' has presented social administration with a challenge, to which it responds by resorting to this imagery in seeking an accommodation between its ideals and practical reality. For the grand narrative of postwar social reform, cogently expressed in Marshall's account of *Citizenship and Social Class* (1963), has been replaced by an alternative vision, based on values of individual effort and success (the so called 'Victorian ethic' of Thatcherism), which have dislodged the core values of collective welfare. These competing narratives represent opposing welfare ideologies expressed in social policy debates and informing official policy. Some writers (e.g. Kaye 1987) have argued that the crisis precipitated by an anti-welfare ideology calls for a new grand narrative, which will restore a positive model of welfare; one that replaces the ascendant 'public burden' model, avoids an undemocratic state administration and promotes greater sensitivity to individual needs.

This project is not new. It revives the challenge Marshall set for social policy in the late 1940s, of devising welfare systems that combine the contrary principles of individualism and collectivism. Social administration writers have responded to this challenge throughout the postwar decades. For this reason Marshall's thesis is used as a starting point, which defines an ideology of consensus and accommodates conflicting values (questions one and two above). Marshall and social administration writers are read to make explicit the ideology they embrace and, of more significance, to reconstruct the underlying problematic concerning the role of social ideals in the formulation of practical policies (question three above). This problematic provides a framework for integrating two distinct endeavours in social administration; a factual understanding of welfare and need, and a value orientation for policy. It is of course true, as several commentators have observed, that the two concerns lack logical coherence, leading to a gulf between fact and value (Mishra 1981, p. 12; Taylor-Gooby and

Dale 1981, p. 74; Hindess 1987, p. 83). However a conscious attempt at integrating fact and value is discerned in Marshall's and Titmuss's writings, an attempt that has characterised the tradition of twentieth century social administration.

2

Social administration and the welfare consensus

Social administration has consistently stressed the normative role of welfare in promoting social harmony over the discord and alienation caused by industrialisation. The material benefits, in cash and kind, promoted by welfare in lessening economic inequality and in compensating for multiple forms of deprivation were conceived in terms of the greater ideals of social justice and harmony. These normative objectives stood alongside the empirical, explanatory and material concerns of social administration: to measure the problems of inequality and deprivation; to explain the processes of diswelfare attending industrialisation and requiring corrective social welfare; and to create greater material equality.

Although the beliefs of social administration and its Social Democratic ideology have received extensive coverage, the idea that its foundations rest on an ethic of social integration has received only passing attention in recent years. Mishra, for example, has dismissed the unitary conception of welfare advanced by Titmuss – who located it in institutions promoting social integration – for its narrowness of focus (1981, p. 23). Casting doubt in a similar direction, Pinker sees social administration as less concerned with such normative ends and more with campaigning on a practical level against the normative tenets of classical political economy, grappling at close quarters with the effects of social problems, 'which precluded any overall approach or total critique', or the adoption of a coherent and systematic counter-ideology (1971, pp. 30, 84). Social administration arose from the practicalities of empirical investigation and problem-solving, whence normative principles emerged in piecemeal fashion. In the 1970s, the Marxist view that the welfare state consensus was an ideological smokescreen disguising ruling-class interest and state hegemony, and so of little intrinsic value, further undermined the normative significance of this view. Room (1979, pp. 62–6) and Reisman (1977, p. 108) were alone in recognising social integration as a central idea for the social administrative and Social Democratic tradition. More recently, there has been a renewed interest in this feature of social administration ideology (see Hindess 1987, pp. 37–9), especially among writers committed to a communitarian defence of the welfare state (e.g. Harris 1987).

The chapter discusses Social Democratic ideology from three vantage points. First, it focuses on the values in social administration comprising the consensual ethic. Secondly, it examines the ideological elements in social administration discourse that express this ethic. Thirdly, it examines proposals on the structure of the welfare state that give practical expression to this ethic.

Social administration and the consensual ideal

The consensual ethic has been a fundamental part of the value perspective of social administration throughout the twentieth century. It has provided the rational foundation for the welfare state's role in the wider political consensus of the postwar years. This can be seen if we examine briefly three rationalist tenets informing social administration: the rational bases of empirical social science, social planning and statecraft. First, following the tradition established by nineteenth-century empirical inquiry into poverty and deprivation, especially the work of Booth (1971) and Rowntree (1901), social administration has sought to study the social problems of groups in need, the elderly, disabled, mentally ill and handicapped, one-parent families, and so forth. Equipped with social science, welfare policies could be mounted on a rational footing. The connection between scientific research and 'scientific administration' (as the Webbs called it) was held as axiomatic, and acted on by Beveridge in his approach to social security reform; in his 'attempt to fix rates of insurance benefit and pension on a scientific basis with regard to subsistence needs' (Beveridge 1942, p. 15). This rationalist doctrine – however scientistic it now sounds – underpins the more explicitly normative principle of social policy that welfare services are directed to meeting human need. This view rested on the rational discourse of science as the universal basis of thought, understanding and democratic consensus (see Pinker 1971, p. 105). Secondly, from a detailed scientific scrutiny of social need, and from rationally mounted intervention, arose the belief that change ought to entail gradual movement along planned lines towards preconceived but not far-fetched goals. 'Piecemeal engineering' was preferred to grandiose notions of revolutionary change. In this context rational policy-making provided for the gradual 'permeation' of ideas and facts throughout society to secure the wider acknowledgement of social evils and of the appropriate measures for their alleviation (Mishra 1981, p. 19). Reason is the guarantee that knowledge is disseminated widely among the population. Welfare must therefore operate as an ameliorative rather than purgative practice for achieving and strengthening social harmony. Thirdly, it follows that the only institution adequate to the scope of these harmonising tasks is the state. It therefore befits the state to be concerned with the needs of all by means of the rational practices of statecraft, including the provision of welfare services. Although social administration writers have conceived the balance between the individual and state in different ways, they all agree that the state has a central role in providing welfare and security. The welfare state becomes society's rational response to its collective expectations.

The idea that the consensual ethic serves as the basis for rational policy and politics is part of an important tradition in political thought, which can be traced back to the origins of modern political theory – in particular Kant and Hegel – and today surfaces at different and apparently unrelated points. Today, the Social Democratic tradition of Fabian thought and the Marxist tradition of Critical Theory, as developed in the work of Jürgen Habermas, give rise to two versions of rationalist politics[1] – an affinity that is explored later in the book.

The establishment of the welfare state in the 1940s – specifically provision for education, health, housing and social security – provided the basis for a consensual society committed, in Beveridge's words, to 'a comprehensive policy of social progress . . . achieved by co-operation between the State and the individual' in alleviating want (1942, p. 6). The ideal of achieving social cohesion through welfare became the principal motif in social administration for the next forty years, despite changes in the balance struck between state and individual in the combination of collective and private forms of provision. In the immediate postwar years Marshall and Titmuss were the principal guides for the normative direction social administration was to take, in suggesting that the welfare state could secure for its citizens a greater sense of individual identity within a more cohesive social order. In *Citizenship and Social Class*, Marshall stressed the consensus achieved by means of the universal conferment of citizenship upon the British subject. Citizenship was defined as 'a status bestowed on those who are full members of a community' (1963, p. 87). Titmuss likewise saw consensus as achieved by the establishment of welfare institutions fostering integration and ameliorating want, thus manifesting 'society's will to survive as an organic whole' (1963, p. 39).

Though sharing the same vision of the purpose of welfare, the two writers each placed a different emphasis on the role of welfare services in securing this vision. Marshall saw social services as the last in a line of institutions which earlier had guaranteed equality before the law and political enfranchisement, and then underwrote social and economic security in a welfare state that consolidated the rights of British citizenship. Citizenship was conceived as a form of social justice and rights espoused by institutions in different areas of social life – juridical, political, social and economic. Welfare services embodied one such institution. The means of social cohesion lay at a more fundamental level in society, in the constellation of relationships between welfare, culture and legal rights, which together constituted the organic whole signified by citizenship. For example, a society that has embarked on this journey by enforcing the duty to attend compulsory education has 'begun to realise that its culture is an organic unity and its civilisation a national heritage' (1963, p. 85). Moreover, the universal rights of citizenship were not conferred by the state to revoke the rights individuals exercised in the market. They adjusted collectivist ideals of community welfare to the market ethic, 'combining in one system the two principles of social justice and market price' (*ibid.*, p. 101). We will see later how this combination was to be achieved.

By contrast, Titmuss invested state welfare with the *sole* responsibility for creating social harmony, by means of its universal provisions conferring and strengthening legal, political, economic and social rights. As such it represented the state's explicit commitment, evident in post-Beveridge reforms, to provide social cohesion and alleviate need. Contrary to Marshall, for Titmuss, the welfare state represented a society where the state has demarcated the social – its needs and cohesion – as separate from the economic, 'providing universal services outside the market on the principle of need' (Titmuss 1974, p. 31). Thus when the state intervenes in the economy, it is to secure social objectives such as the maintenance of full employment and the avoidance of poverty. Pinker sums up the contrast between these two approaches: 'Titmuss' ideal of social welfare was based on a unitary model of a good society, but, according to Marshall, the differences between these institutional elements "strengthen the structure because they are complementary rather than divisive" (1981, pp. 124–5)' (1981, p. 15); a contrast between 'unitary' and 'binary' conceptions of the welfare state.

Social conditions and social ideals

Despite these differences, Marshall and Titmuss together embraced the range of collectivist and cohesive principles embodied in the welfare reforms of the 1940s. The articulation of these normative principles entailed not only an espousal of social ideals, but an account of how these ideals operate in a society experiencing the exigencies of inequality and division. It is this account that points to a nascent theory of ideology in their work and in social administration generally. The groundwork for this theory of ideology is seen first in the relationship assumed between institutional means and normative ends, and secondly in the critical force these norms possess in indicting unacceptable conditions.

First, though essentially a normative concept, citizenship stood as the material expression of an ideal. Marshall and Titmuss saw this universal ideal as most fully embodied in welfare services. For Marshall, the purpose of welfare was not simply to remove deprivation of income, health and housing, but the material means for pursuing a higher ideal: 'What matters is that there is a general enrichment of the concrete substance of civilised life' (1963, p. 107). The physical improvement of life is but one step on the path to the greater enhancement of civilisation.[2] This conception of welfare's purpose necessarily entails the distinction between welfare as an empirical and a normative entity (see Mishra 1981, p. 22). This is a common enough distinction in sociological analysis, and implicit in the idea of policy as purposive human activity guiding means towards ends. However, this distinction raises a problem, essential to ideology, of how means and ends are conjoined as a purposive unity. Is welfare a means of securing material subsistence and, as a corollary, of achieving greater social cohesion? Or are its material objectives ancillary to its social ideals? The fact that Marshall and Titmuss both emphasised the latter normative vision of welfare brings to the fore the ideological role of ideals, as a means to justify policy in the context of existing social conditions. Hindess sums up the position whereby Marshall's 'citizenship' and Titmuss's 'social policy' 'define[s] a standard against which a society and the performance of its government can be measured' (1987, p. 44).

The dual nature of welfare also underlines the second aspect of social administration's account of ideology. As a universal ideal, the principle of collective welfare operates counterfactually, standing as a normative indictment of existing social conditions and as an ideal aspired to in practice. This relationship is both empirical and imaginary, compounding fact and value. As an empirical matter, social administration seeks to describe and explain the material conditions it deems unacceptable according to its core values, the unacceptability of inequality, human degradation, unmet need, personal suffering and public waste. As a matter of the imagination, the constellation of facts and values is, so to speak, inverted to create a sense of an imaginary social order governed by opposite ideals, by principles of human worth and respect and equitable economic distribution. These ideals are neither empty rhetoric nor groundless, because they contain positive meanings which mirror and invert the unacceptable material conditions that transgress the ideals of social administration. The constellation of facts and values is formed reflexively in the course of policy-making from the interplay between indictable social facts and hoped-for ideals. Marshall, of course, was not the first to address this dichotomy. Tawney, writing in the 1930s, developed the theme in his discussion of the 'form and reality' of government, where the two worlds of fact and value are ideologically reconciled:

> the rulers of mankind are enabled to maintain side by side two standards of social ethics, without the risk of their colliding. Keeping one set of values for use, and another for display, they combine, without conscious insincerity, the moral satisfaction of idealistic principles with the material advantages of realistic practice. (1964, p. 190)

From a critical perspective, however, the force of these normative ideals is derived counterfactually and discursively. As a universal notion, welfare as citizenship and integration acts counterfactually, providing a counterpart to the social contingencies with which welfare services contend. For Marshall, for example, this counterpart serves as a source of critique and indictment, as a standard of appraisal and an ideal to espouse: 'societies in which citizenship is a developing institution create an image of an ideal citizenship against which achievement can be measured and towards which aspirations can be directed' (1963, p. 87). A further force for critique lies in the argumentation of social administration discourse; specifically, in the deployment of the language of identity and difference. Marshall, for example, counterposes the ideals, beliefs and values of citizenship (of 'civilisation', 'universal rights' and 'harmony') with those of social class (of 'inequality' and 'conflict'). Having traced citizenship's path towards fulfilling its civilising goals, Marshall describes social class as 'a system of inequality', so that 'the impact of citizenship on social class should take the form of a conflict between opposing principles' (*ibid.*). The imagery of social class as symbols of social difference is captured in the language of pre-war social policy, for example, by terms like the 'ex-elementary school boy', 'panel patient' and 'Old Age Pensioner' (1963, pp. 106–8). However, in developing his thesis, Marshall gives an account that is not one of conflict, but of the ameliorative function of citizenship exercised over class differences. Indeed citizenship and class are today 'still compatible, so much so that citizenship has itself become, in certain respects, the architect of legitimate social inequality' (1963, p. 73). The language of citizenship is relatively over-endowed in partially nullifying the language of social class. With respect to health care – and no doubt to other services – Marshall says that, 'the extension of the service has reduced the social importance of the distinction' (*ibid.*, p. 108) between social classes. To this extent, the critical edge of the distinction between citizenship and social class is blunted, placing greater weight on the normative function of citizenship in guiding policy formation rather than indicting inequalities. As a discourse of the counterfactual, citizenship is an ideal towards which social policies can be guided in lessening class inequalities; thus transcending the paradox of citizenship in a context of inequality. In the Social Democratic conception of the welfare state, the language of difference is absorbed into the language of identity by the will of political purpose pronounced in the rhetoric of citizenship.

In Titmuss's writing stigma plays the same role as social class in Marshall's, providing a conceptual tool that conveys the idea of difference in contradistinction to the idea of integrated social identity. However, for Titmuss the relationship between identity and difference is oppositional rather than functional.[3] Whereas universal welfare promoting citizenship guarantees material improvement and enhances integration, stigma is the psychological and normative response of an individual to his or her changing circumstances on becoming different, through handicap, poverty, unemployment or social marginalisation. Stigma is the mark a person bears that brands him or her different or inferior to others because of deemed misconduct or inadequacy. In social policy it is inscribed most profoundly by the 'degradation ceremony' of the means test where the claimant's conduct is subject to constant scrutiny and regulation by officials. Thus stigma and integration are contrary moments of this ideology, providing impetus to welfare reforms. Titmuss sought to articulate the relevance of such universalist reforms for the individual, so that the dual processes of integration and stigma are understood in terms of their effect on the construction of 'personal identity'. On the one hand, it is the objective of social policy 'to build the identity of the person around some community with which he is associated' (Titmuss 1974, p. 38). On the other, the stigmatising impact of residual means-tested welfare lies in its ability 'to induce among recipients . . . a sense of personal fault, of personal failure' (Titmuss 1968, p. 134). For Titmuss stigma is antithetical to welfare.

The relationship between welfare ideals and social contingencies of need points to a further concern about the negative functions of ideology in social administration. In some cases ideology distorts welfare ideals and hampers their realisation, lessening the impact of policies on dependency. Thus the study of the relationship between ideals and contingencies must be extended from the ideals of welfare (reducing inequality, distributing resources equitably and meeting need) to the dominant ideals shaping the interests of the well-endowed and powerful. Julian Le Grand's 'strategy of equality' is an example of this extension (1982). He argues that the failure of the egalitarian ideals of welfare rests on the existence of forces impeding policy outcomes over which government has hitherto had little control. Hence, 'for any strategy of equality to succeed, it has to tackle these inequalities directly . . . to confront the ideology that lies behind them'. So, whereas the ideals of welfare represent a counterfactual standard by which to confront the conditions of inequality (e.g. 'the strategy of equality'), the 'ideology of inequality' is an argument for justifying the continuation of these conditions that might otherwise have been removed (Le Grand 1982, p. 139).

To summarise, the ideological character of social administration's discourse is read in the contradistinction between an ideal and a contingent reality, which for social administration is part of the mechanism for building social consensus through social reform. Marshall appeared especially sensitive to the counterfactual effect of social policy legislation that 'acquires more and more the character of a declaration of policy that it is hoped to put into effect some day . . . . The target is perpetually moving forward, and the State may never be able to get quite within range of it' (1963, p. 109). We will now see how the expectations behind this moving target are caught in a fundamental tension between, on the one hand, universal welfare standardised at a basic minimum – a single target that can be frozen – and, on the other, welfare tailored to the diversity of individual need – no longer one target but many. It is the tension between these images and metaphors that produces the various inflections in welfare ideology evident in the tradition of twentieth-century Social Democratic thought.

The discourse of the Social Democratic welfare state

The rise in individual expectations and aspirations experienced in the wake of the Second World War posed a dilemma, then, for a welfare state committed to providing universal social provisions for all. The makings of this dilemma were already evident in the machinery of welfare administration, which in the postwar period endeavoured to develop services geared to different individual needs alongside universal provisions. Marshall was the first postwar writer to express this dilemma in his conceptions of citizenship and the welfare state, to which we now turn.

Marshall's attempt at accommodating the divergent tendencies in the welfare state offers a discourse in the Social Democratic tradition that acquires renewed interest in the context of the ideological problems faced by the welfare state today when its consensus is dissolving. This is so for several reasons. First, Marshall's account of the integration of individual and collective principles provides a model for comparing with subsequent accounts.[4] In this light recent radical developments in social administration can be seen as part of a long tradition not so far removed from earlier postwar social administration, for example, the ideas today of welfare pluralism and the 'mixed economy of welfare' – so-called Fabian revisionism (see Beresford and Croft 1984). However, contrary to the idea of reconciling individual and collective values within the welfare state, Marxist Political Economy and Critical Theory see welfare capitalism in a state of worsening crisis. Secondly, Marshall's articulation of this model has subsequently proved problematic to writers sympathetic to Social Democracy. We can therefore trace how his ideas have been developed by these writers. Thirdly, Marshall sought to develop the administrative and not merely normative implications of this model, to understand their implications in the practical context of social policies aiming to fulfil the promises of the welfare state. We can therefore examine his normative thinking in the context of his discussion of postwar administrative structures and provisions and their subsequent development.

It is to the structural implications of the dilemma in the hands not only of Marshall but of twentieth-century Social Democratic thinkers and their Liberal allies that the chapter now turns; starting with the Webbs, then Beveridge, Marshall and Titmuss, and finally more recent writers who have sought to adapt the principles of the welfare state to the conditions of the late twentieth century.

Throughout the twentieth century, Fabian thought believed that the Social Democratic welfare state could accommodate both collective and market principles of social organisation, accepting, as Sidney Webb put it, 'certain fundamental matters of social organisation which . . . [rival political partisans] can . . . accept as indispensable to any successful carrying out of their own projects and ideas' (1911, p. 2). This accommodation was articulated in the administrative proposals for organising welfare provisions as well as in Social Democratic ideology. It was thus present in the structure and narrative of Social Democratic policy. In structural terms, the welfare state was portrayed as an 'extension ladder' built upon a universal infrastructure or 'national minimum', which sought to extend a superstructure of private, voluntary and statutory services that enhanced individual needs selectively by means of more diversified provisions. As an ideological narrative, Social Democratic thought recounts the evolution of citizenship and the extension of universal rights despite social class differences.

The Webbs' idea of the national minimum and 'extension ladder' provided the basis for a genealogy of concepts and images that informed the entire lineage of twentieth century Social Democracy. In *The Prevention of Destitution*, Sidney and Beatrice Webb spelt out in detail the implications of this binary notion of the welfare state. It involved an ' "extension ladder" placed firmly on the foundation of an enforced minimum standard of life, but carrying onward the work of the Public Authorities to far finer shades of physical, moral, and spiritual perfection' (1911, p. 252). It is this metaphor that guides Social Democratic and Fabian thought thereafter. It governs the proposals of both collectivists and welfare pluralists from the Webbs, through Beveridge, Marshall, Robson, Titmuss to Hadley and Hatch and others today. It informs the variety of welfare agencies apart from the statutory – i.e. voluntary and private – and the variety of postwar Fabian initiatives for widening the scope of social, political and educational opportunities. For the Fabians, the binary approach was the strategy for influencing relations within the welfare state between state and civil society. Amid these diverse political, economic and philosophical concerns, the national minimum and extension ladder conception of the welfare state provided a guiding metaphor, an architecture for postwar society. This conception was embodied in the wealth of concepts and imagery depicting the welfare state as an 'edifice', 'elevation' or 'structure' with 'bases', 'floors', 'foundations', 'pillars', 'ceilings', and so forth.

In his Fabian tract, *The Necessary Basis of Society*, Sidney Webb presented the national minimum as a uniform level of well-being provided by the state on or above which everyone should live, and up to which the 'destitute' should be raised. The national minimum was to be provided in several areas of social welfare. There would be a National Minimum of Health 'below which, in the interests of the community as a whole, no one is permitted to fall', of 'Sanity, below which no denizen of free citizenship is allowed to fall', of Subsistence, Leisure and Recreation, Sanitation, and Child Nurture in education and child care (Webb 1911, pp. 8–9). The maintenance of each minimum was to rely on a body of state employees, each a specialist in a particular department of welfare. Above the national minimum individual initiative in the form of voluntary welfare and individual self-help was to be encouraged.

For the Webbs, the imagery associated with the extension ladder implied that the foundation of the national minimum would continuously raise standards of civilised life, uplifting human endeavour with gravity-defying force. Voluntary agencies, for example, would promote:

> pioneer endeavours to raise ever higher and higher the standard of what human conduct can be made to be: by showing . . . how and where it is possible to raise the 'National Minimum'; in this way pushing ever upward the conception of the order, the freedom and the beauty that it is possible to secure to and for every individual in the community. (Webb and Webb 1911, p. 158)

Moreover, once established, the national minimum would enable individual enterprise and talent to flourish without interference, 'either with the pecuniary profits or with the power or the personal development of the exceptional man' (Webb 1911, p. 11). The foundation of the national minimum was to secure for both individual benefactor and beneficiary a basis upon which further standards of civilised life would be raised by voluntary effort. By mobilising the spirit of enterprise, the national minimum would 'fend off the downward way . . . divert[ing] the forces of competition along the upward way' (*ibid.*).

The notion of a national minimum provided a structural principle for delineating the welfare concerns of state and civil society, and defining the 'proper relationship' between them. As a statement of political theory, Fabian welfare saw this relationship as different from, on the one side, a market society with minimal state intervention, and, on the other, a collectivist society with a residue of private exchange and welfare. Fabianism sought to integrate public and private to provide conditions for the organic coexistence of state and civil society; a conception of the 'joint responsibility of the individual and the community, for the universal maintenance of a prescribed standard of civilised life' (Webb and Webb 1911, p. 322). The structural principle of the national minimum was the means for realising the evolutionary narrative of citizenship. This historical process entailed making the conditions for human well-being universal and raising the standards of civilised life. The national minimum in principle stood for 'the "National Minimum" of civilised life', with voluntary organisations 'constantly raising the standard of civilised conduct' (1911, p. 252).

Complementing the structural notion of the extension ladder, Fabian thought developed the evolutionary notion of universality, civilisation and citizenship. These two notions can be traced in the development of subsequent Fabian thought. The development of the extension conception of the welfare state differs only in so far as the forms of welfare beyond the basic minimum diversify and manifest new principles – and undoubtedly new tensions. The extension of different forms of welfare above the minimum provided an accretion of agencies – voluntary, private and statutory – and expressed new principles in the discourse of Fabian welfare: citizenship in a pluralist society, parity between state and private welfare, positive discrimination, social justice, participation, and so forth. Throughout this discourse, the notion of a two-tiered architecture or binary system of national minimum and extension ladder remains largely intact.

The two themes of Social Democratic welfare – the extension concept and the evolution of citizenship – were first implemented in the Beveridge reforms of the 1940s. These established a national minimum in income maintenance and health, whereby the state in principle guaranteed uniform protection from poverty and universal health care. The collective principle, however, left scope for individuals to raise standards of welfare above the state minimum: 'making provision for those higher standards is primarily the function of the individual . . . a matter of freedom of choice and voluntary insurance' (Beveridge 1942, p. 121). Beveridge added, so to speak, an extension ladder of private insurance alongside the Webbs' extension ladder of voluntary organisation, encouraging citizens to choose welfare above the minimum to complement the state's obligation to lay a minimum foundation of security for all. The welfare state rested on the same principle of co-operation between state and individual as the Webbs had formulated thirty years or so earlier: 'in establishing the national minimum, [the state] should leave room for voluntary action by each individual to provide more than the minimum for himself and his family' (*ibid.*, p. 7). In a similar though more positive vein, the Webbs had seen state social services 'tending always to increase consciousness of obligation, and to produce a more extensive fulfilment of it' (Webb and Webb 1911, p. 301). From the beginnings of the postwar era, a compact between collectivist and individualist ideals was struck, which forged a mixed economy providing the framework wherein statutory, private and voluntary welfare operated. Since this time only the balance of components has shifted, though some critics have argued that this shift has been decisive (e.g. Beresford and Croft 1984; Brenton 1985). For Beveridge, the development of voluntary insurance and voluntary services was a means for softening the stark distinction between state and market (see Cutler *et al.* 1986, p. 42).

At the close of a decade of welfare reforms associated with Beveridge, Marshall delivered his influential lecture *Citizenship and Social Class* (1963). Here he sought to articulate the philosophy underlying the welfare state, which had developed in the context of the evolution of modern industrial society. In particular, he explored the relations existing between the extension of citizenship rights conferred by a welfare state and the inequalities generated by capitalist society. These two developments reflected the contrary principles of collectivism and individualism which Marshall (1981) later saw conjoined in 'welfare-state-capitalism'.

One of Marshall's achievements was to clarify the binary nature of a welfare state based on a national minimum philosophy. In this respect, he provided a reappraisal of the Fabian welfare state that conformed closely to the Webbs' principles, while extrapolating the principle of the extension ladder beyond those prescribed by the Webbs. Complementing his analysis of the national

minimum, Marshall articulated the underlying force of social cohesion informing the development of the welfare state, the evolution of the universal rights
of citizenship.

The ideological implications of the architecture of Social Democracy are seen
most clearly in Marshall's account of the Beveridge welfare state. He sets up a
two-tiered system of a state-guaranteed minimum, supplemented by the extension of new forms of welfare. The state was 'no longer content to raise the floor
level in the basement of the social edifice, leaving the social structure as it was'
(1963, p. 100), a reference to the limited aspirations of the Beveridge model.
Rather, the state was to extend the scope of welfare in response to the growing
diversity of need; for 'what matters to the citizen is the superstructure of
legitimate expectations' (1963, p. 108). The superstructure should add to the
quantitative uniformity of the national minimum a qualitative enhancement of
well-being: 'The extension of the social services is not primarily a means of
equalising income . . . . What matters is that there is a general enrichment of the
concrete substance of civilised life, a general reduction of risk and insecurity'
(1963, p. 107). This involved the extension of benefits in *kind* to complement
benefits in cash, entailing the 'qualitative element that enters into the benefit
itself' (*ibid.*). More closely attuned to the individual circumstances of the
recipient, these qualitative benefits or services were already available in, for
example, health care and education. However, whereas the Webbs and Beveridge adhered to a scientific diagnosis of welfare needs, for Marshall the
qualitative element of the benefit – the needs it sought to meet and the rights to
confer – was essentially indefinable, almost ineffable; for 'Benefits in the form
of a service have this further characteristic that the rights of the citizen cannot
be precisely defined. The qualitative element is too great' (1963, p. 108).

In later years Marshall (1981) sought to give voice to the indefinable and
incalculable element of welfare by means of the notion of discretionary rights.
If there is a significant element that remains intractable to quantification, then
its handling must rely on discretionary powers held by administrators and
exercised on behalf of individuals in need – an endorsement of the Webbs'
(1911) faith in the judgement of trained social administrators. This element
required a particular form of administrative power to decide the justice of each
claimant's case. In turn, claimants must possess rights that their needs be met
on the basis of an assessment of their personal circumstances, without recourse
to inflexible legal stipulation. The contradiction in principle between universal
citizenship rights and administrative discretion in determining these rights did
not seem to trouble Marshall. The fact that these rights are often indeterminate,
and in practice not always universally guaranteed, shifts the onus of responsibility from legal and bureaucratic determination to the less precise, consensual
ethic of society as a source of justice. The 'notion of discretion as positive,
personal and beneficent can only be fully realized in a 'welfare society', that is
to say a society that recognises its collective responsibility to seek to achieve

welfare, and not only to relieve destitution or eradicate penury' (Marshall 1981, p. 88). The concept of 'welfare society' has since become an important rubric for the moral qualities needed in society. Thus, the dangers – ever-present within the Social Democratic welfare state – of a divisive two-tiered system of quantitative and qualitative welfare for poor and non-poor respectively was foreseen by Marshall, and others subsequently, and averted by stressing the need for an overriding consensus. But stressing such a need at times had the force of ideological conviction rather than cogent argument. Nevertheless, the tension posed between qualitative and quantitative welfare is resolved in principle by Marshall's essentially Fabian conception of the extension ladder supplementing the quantifiable national minimum. Alongside the extension ladders of voluntary effort and private insurance, Marshall added the extension ladder of qualitative welfare in kind whereby the state enhanced basic citizenship rights.

In the optimism of the 1950s, Crosland shared Marshall's vision in seeing the future of the welfare state as dependent on its ability to combine the egalitarian morality of socialism with the material prosperity of capitalism. This was all the more important, Crosland contended, during the postwar period of major restructuring of capital and the gathering pace of prosperity. The result was an interpretation of the welfare state that saw its development as combining a universal minimum in social security with the highest standard of quality in other social services – an interpretation largely in sympathy with the Webbs, Beveridge and Marshall. The Beveridge reforms were seen as meeting human need rather than relieving destitution, giving 'the most complete and explicit statement of the philosophy of the national minimum' in seeking to extend basic provisions as of right to 'those entire categories of persons . . . most vulnerable to the onset of poverty' (Crosland 1956, p. 120). In addition, 'built along side the system of social services' were health and education services based for the first time on the principle of universal prosperity, and set not only at the minimum level, 'but at the highest level which the community could afford' (*ibid.*), and ideally on a footing to compete with services in the private fee-paying sector. For Crosland, the length of the state's extension ladder should reach as high as the standards set by the private sector. Crosland stressed the need for parity between the extension ladders of both public and private sectors promoting greater equality and destigmatising public provision. Nowhere was his optimism more evident than in his belief that, 'as the gap is narrowed and facilities become genuinely comparable in quality, the mark of inferiority attaching to the public services will disappear' (*ibid.*, p. 144).

By contrast with Marshall and Crosland, however, Titmuss remained for many years firmly committed to the collectivist model of state welfare, divorced from private welfare, by which a differentiated and fragmented society could be reintegrated. For Titmuss, individual and collective principles were not open to a *rapprochement*, but subject to a basic misalliance. In *The Social Division of Welfare* he stated that the 'fundamental problem' in welfare and fiscal policies was of 'reconciling . . . the imperious demands of preferential social policies', in, for example, the privileged sectors of occupational, fiscal and private welfare, 'with . . . "a general equitable principle" of fairness' (1963, p. 49). For Titmuss, the trend in welfare was not towards accommodating individual inequalities within a universal system of citizenship rights, but, contrary to Marshall, accommodating the fact that 'The more that the uniqueness of individual needs and dependencies is recognised and relieved in an occupational society based on individual rewards the more may principles of individual equity fall into disrepute' (*ibid.*).

However, by the late 1960s Titmuss had begun to question aspects of the welfare state and examine new structures for promoting consumer choice, rights and participation (1968, pp. 67–8). Following Marshall and Crosland, he began posing the need for an element of selectivity within the broader framework of universal social services. His famous challenge to social administrators to rethink the principles of welfare questions the unitary notion of the welfare state and looks towards a binary conception denoting a universal base and selectivist superstructure. He asks:

> what particular infrastructure of universalist services is needed in order to provide
> a framework of values and opportunity bases within and around which can be
> developed socially acceptable selective services aiming to discriminate positively,
> with the minimum risk of stigma, and in favour of those whose needs are greatest?
> (Titmuss 1968, p. 135)

Within the lineage of Fabian welfare thought, Titmuss's contribution was to sharpen the principles pursued by the superstructure or extension ladder of the welfare state. For example, how should the above principle of positive discrimination developed in the 1960s be applied in area-based policies giving extra resources to schools, health and social services in deprived localities? Titmuss provided a rationale that sought to reconcile the contrary principles of universality and selectivity – in ways in keeping with the Webbs' thinking. Though this revisionism caused some contention at the time, it accorded with Fabian philosophy underlying the national minimum and extension ladder, whereby selectivity and inequality are perfectly possible *above* the national minimum.

Yet, as we have seen, it is clear that Titmuss's two-tiered model remained in significant ways different from Marshall's. Titmuss' combination of the principles of universality and selectivity is not a balanced synthesis between the different principles of collective and market welfare. Titmuss remained firmly wedded to the notion of collective welfare or 'infrastructure of universal services' over and above any individualist ethic, and maintained that there was a fundamental incompatibility between state welfare and the market.

Subsequent Social Democratic writers have developed the pluralist implications of the Webbs' extension ladder as a means for fostering the type of social cohesion that Marshall termed 'welfare society', one based as firmly in civil society as in the state. For three subsequent writers – Robson and Hadley and Hatch – welfare society gave expression to the moral and political prerequisites of the welfare state.

In the context of the dissolution of the postwar consensus, Hadley and Hatch's conception of welfare pluralism has become one of the most influential attempts to develop Titmuss's ideas about a selective superstructure of welfare. Although several critics have argued that their ideas are 'revisionist', capitalising on the short-lived revival of Social Democratic Party politics in the early 1980s (Beresford and Croft 1984; Brenton 1985), their welfare pluralism belongs to an unbroken line of binary thought extending directly back to the Webbs. The welfare pluralists' contribution has been to study the superstructure of the extension ladder in the light of the failings of the welfare state: its inability to redistribute sufficiently and justly; and its uniformity, inaccessibility and centralisation. For Hadley and Hatch, it is the birth of post-industrial society that demands new relations of welfare, especially a diversification *between* different sectors – in particular the voluntary and informal – rather than *within* the statutory sector alone, as Titmuss proposed when resting his case on an analysis of industrial society. Yet their belief in the 'overriding importance of the family' and of the voluntary sector – as 'a source of new developments, of criticism and pressure, and a medium for taking action where statutory agencies fear to tread' (1981, p. 96) – is similar to the Webbs'. The development of welfare pluralism in Fabian thought holds firm to the statutory foundations of welfare, that is to the idea of the national minimum. While advancing the philosophy of welfare pluralism, Hadley and Hatch none the less see these statutory underpinnings as securing diversity in the non-statutory sector. For example, social security as a system of cash benefits offers a base for promoting, or impeding, more personal kinds of help outside statutory welfare; for example, pensions, invalidity benefits and attendance allowances that enable dependents to receive informal care with less drain on the carers' resources (*ibid.*, p. 46). Thus, 'benefits . . . are often the precondition of care in the community' as are non-personal provisions such as housing, employment and transport (*ibid.*, pp. 91–2). This points to new forms of integration between the material foundations of welfare and the inducements for informal caring needed to promote the development of a viable mixed economy of welfare.

In these respects they endeavour to formulate a conception of the relationship between the different sectors of welfare, which, while countering the centralist tendencies of bureaucratic welfare, prescribes a binary structure based on a statutory foundation. The conception retains the Fabian notions of the national minimum and extension ladder:

> The instrument for formulating a [welfare pluralist] strategy must necessarily be the state, and the statutory sector must necessarily provide a framework through which priorities and standards can be maintained. (*ibid.*, p. 101)

Although welfare is conceived in pluralist terms, it is supported by a state infrastructure that provides a base for a mixed economy whose enterprise and innovation depend on the powers of the state, and not the market or civil society alone, to provide material support and safeguard rights.

It is Robson's contribution in the mid-1970s, in *Welfare State and Welfare Society* (1976), that gives the clearest statement of the Webbian binary principle, but which in addition infuses the welfare state with the welfare morality he felt lacking in the two-tiered system. This morality would be a force capable of both binding the increasing plurality of welfare provisions and cultural forms, and transcending the social and economic divisions between the two tiers of the welfare state. In stressing the importance of the moral component of welfare as a prerequisite for the welfare state, however, Robson, it could be said, was reversing the two-tiered structure, placing universal welfare on the moral basis of a 'welfare society' ethic, rather than seeing the universal national minimum as a precondition for moral cohesion in society.

However, against the grain of these discussions aiming at an accommodation between universal and selective principles, Townsend, himself a life-long Fabian, has consistently criticised the role Social Democrats attribute to the national minimum as a means of engineering social cohesion. Instead he sees it as inviting:

> selective, ameliorative and isolated rather than universal and reconstructional policies to relieve poverty . . . . Providing welfare can be concentrated amongst the pockets or islands of the population where it is needed all is well. The rich, the middle-income groups, the status, income and class hierarchies of society and the values and standards of many professional and voluntary associations will not be threatened. Minor adjustments alone are needed'. (1967, p. 42)

Instead of a national minimum based on the expedient principle of 'minimum rights for the many', Townsend has advocated 'distributional justice for all' founded on an objective standard of deprivation and need (1979, p. 62).

This discussion of the structure and values of the welfare state highlights some of the solutions to the problem of applying the Social Democratic ideals of social administration – especially the essential equality of human life and the democratic freedom of each individual – to the practical contingencies of human existence, such as resource scarcity and the necessity to produce sufficient to meet human needs. In general terms, the problem of applying ideals to practical reality is present in all forms of political action under whatever philosophy, producing compromises in principle and practice that give rise to policy ideologies. As we will see later, these ideologies maintain a sense of congruence in the light of the gaps emerging between principles and practice. The two-tiered solution is one response to this ideological problem. The political philosophies of the New Right and Marxism have taken different approaches, each providing their own conception of welfare. Each political approach produces its own solution to the contingencies besetting welfare and society. In the next chapter we will see how the New Right have tackled this problem of ideology.

Notes

1. The affinity that has received greater attention is the one Social Democrats have claimed between themselves and Karl Popper's philosophy of science, with its implications for an 'open' and pluralist society (see Magee 1973, p. 83).
2. Hindess (1987, p. 39) discusses the problems of defining social consensus by reference to the notion of civilisation.
3. Unlike Marshall, Titmuss remarks on the ideological power of language to ascribe deviance and difference rather than universality: 'Language is not a mere symbolic tool of communication. By describing someone as deviant we express an attitude; we morally brand him and stigmatise him with our value judgment' (1974, p. 133).
4. For recent texts that develop Marshall's concept of citizenship, see Turner (1986; 1990) and Mann (1987).

3

Welfare ideology and the New Right

During the 1970s and 1980s New Right ideology had a powerful impact on the welfare state and welfare thought. It challenged the dominant hegemony of the postwar, Social Democratic consensus. Further, it replaced Marxism as the major challenge to this hegemony by undermining expectations of an imminent crisis gathering on the horizons of late capitalist society. The Right achieved this by introducing policies that have altered the balance between forces that Marxists claimed would inexorably create conditions for crisis in the welfare state; that is, between the opposing demands for capital accumulation and state welfare. Several western governments influenced by New Right ideas have mitigated this crisis and lowered public expectations by cutting back welfare expenditure in favour of capital accumulation; a double-sided thrust informed by a particular political and ideological strategy. Further, Social Democrats and some Marxists have had their belief in an assured future for the welfare state, based on secure ethical, political and economic foundations, undermined. It is the significant role played by ideology in these political developments that has contributed in part to a renewed interest in the study of ideology, especially as an aspect of policy. In the light of these developments, one influential Marxist in social policy, Ian Gough (1979), has revised his initial expectation of a 'legitimation crisis', and criticised his approach as 'too deterministic' in not 'giving sufficient weight to the political, ideological and cultural mediations' informing Thatcherite policies (1983, p. 168).

Since the 1970s New Right thinkers and policy analysts have advanced proposals for a broad range of policies, which require government to withdraw from intervening in economic and social problems and increase the scope for market remedies. Initially, some of these proposals sought to replace the public by the private sector by introducing privatisation measures, direct charges to consumers and vouchers. In the United Kingdom privatisation has been applied in the economic sector to several large public sector monopolies. However, for public welfare this measure was limited to council house sales and competitive tendering of parts of large organisations that still retained their overall public identities. For example, in National Health Service (NHS) hospitals, laundry, catering and cleaning services have been privatised since 1983, as subsequently have local authority services such as refuse and street cleaning. In the United Kingdom the limited scope for privatising social welfare is an indication of the realities the Tory government has had to face when promoting its rightist ideology: the reality of the public's long-standing commitment to universal welfare services; the limited public support for market welfare in health care and education; and the ineffectiveness of private market solutions for the public problems of poverty and deprivation.

Yet the problems posed by these factors in limiting the scope for rightist reforms have not dampened the government's resolve in the welfare sector. The government has followed two strategies, one economic and the other political. First, it has sought to confront more realistically the institutional contingencies of public welfare, not by diluting its policies but by seeking to apply them more strategically. It is in this context that recent policies to develop an 'internal market' in health and community care, education and housing have taken shape. For these policies recognise that market principles must work with and not against the grain of institutional welfare, so that in the long term a more ambitious programme of wide-ranging reforms can be mounted. For example, by granting institutions that form part of the NHS the freedom to negotiate contracts among themselves for the supply of treatment, the government is applying a more delimited notion of the market, with its concomitants of free competition and budgetary discipline. In time, it is argued, this will change the working culture and relationships between consultants, general practitioners, managers and patients, and create new incentives and levels of efficiency. The scope for market activity can be enlarged to include private sector provisions, which the government's plans already allow in certain circumstances. In theory the internal market could become an open market, so removing the remaining institutional barriers between public and private sectors. In this way the concept of the market takes on a new shape – a 'new realism' – after its earlier more idealistic form.

As a second strategy for confronting the political realities of the welfare state, the Right has attempted to undermine Social Democratic and Socialist thought by borrowing several of their earlier criticisms of the welfare state and dressing them up as its own (see Offe 1984). For example, this gambit has expropriated radical proposals from new left manifestos of the 1960s. Arguments for 'power to the community', a 'tenants' charter', a 'citizens' charter', 'parent power' in education, and local democratic accountability have been proposed by rightist think-tanks and the Tory government to counter the left-wing policies of local councils and sympathetic welfare professionals. Using as an example the tenants' charter, Gough records that it was 'adopted from the previous Labour government's proposals, [and] was absorbed into the new ideology'' (Gough *et al.* 1984, p. 69). He quotes Michael Heseltine in 1980, when first Secretary of State for Environment, as saying that 'It represents an immediate and substantial increase in freedom for six million tenants and their families'. Such resource-fulness in repackaging old policy further underlines the important role that ideology plays in the struggle between contending interests, ideas and strategies over the future of the welfare state. These acts of pilfering on the policy front have been supported by intellectual appropriation on the theoretical front. Consequently, in the late 1970s, Offe was drawn to ask whether the Left is 'still able to offer insights and points that will not immediately be stolen by adversaries who bend them to fit their own ideology' (1984, p. 74).

This chapter examines the role of ideology in New Right thought and policy. As in the previous chapter on Social Democratic ideology, the chapter reconstructs the theory of ideology underlying rightist thought, to understand its power in replacing the alternative ideologies of Social Democracy and Socialism with one whose view of human nature and need has profoundly influenced welfare policy. The success of rightist ideology in influencing welfare debates and policy derives as much from its capacity to accommodate the needs and anxieties of sections of western society as from its ability to dismantle alternative ideologies. Its iconoclasm in turn derives from the force of the critique of ideology that the New Right holds. An understanding of this critique serves as a necessary preface to discussion in the next chapter of the various characterisations of 'Thatcherism' and its impact on the changing ideological formation of the postwar welfare state.

New Right thought and the theory of ideology

New Right thought has little to offer by way of an explicit and developed account of ideology. However, the political and economic theory of one of its dominant strands, namely the economic liberalism of Hayek, carries suppositions about human nature that underlie its understanding of ideology. In this sense, like Social Democracy, the Right possesses a nascent theory of ideology.

Market liberalism proposes that individuals are motivated more by self-interest than by ideals of collective concern (co-operation, altruism, justice, duty, etc.). Therefore, a social order that allows individuals freely to pursue their separate interests is to be preferred to one informed by universal principles applied collectively. Although universal principles exist, they operate at a level of abstraction largely unbeknown to the individual, independent of his or her concrete wants and desires. Only by permitting economic markets to operate – where individuals are free to exchange their labour, produce and services voluntarily with minimum interference – can universal ideals be achieved. By extending the market allocation of goods and services throughout society, in the public as well as private sector, in the state as well as civil society, competing interests are brought into an new order of dynamic harmony. The idea that the market is the most efficient and just system of allocation stands as a counterfactual 'standard by which all particular interests are judged' (Hayek 1976, p. 113), individual, group and organisational alike. When the interests of an individual or group dominate the market, inefficiencies and injustices result which impair the market order and damage the mechanisms whereby free exchange can operate and exchange values be appraised. By positing a distinction between the market as a meta-order which best 'comprehends nearly all of mankind' (*ibid.*), in all its diversity, and a subordinate order of incommensurable ends pursued by separate self-seeking individuals, Hayek concludes that the imposition of the ends of any one individual or collectivity on everyone else must be restricted. Otherwise this would upset the balance of the market order, for 'the market neither is nor could be governed by such a single scale of ends' (*ibid.*). Thus he proposes that a 'free society is a pluralistic society without a common hierarchy of particular ends' (1976, p. 109).

Hayek envisages the market as a spontaneous order or 'catallaxy', the study of which should be the main concern of economics. By implication, it is the pursuit of individual ends at the cost of other ends that upsets this order and produces ideology, the pursuit by one party of its ends regardless of other parties, disrupting the market order and imposing false criteria of justice, the good society, and so forth. The existence of a welfare state, which privileges the rights of the deprived over others and necessitates the provision of welfare professionals and bureaucrats to protect these rights, furthering their own dominance, leads to an unjust hierarchy of values and a false ideology of social justice, rights and needs. It is not self-interest that is itself condemned – indeed, it lies at the heart of human nature and is the impetus for the development of wealth and civilisation (1976, p. 111) – but the singular tyranny of individual or collective self-interest over the plurality of freely pursued interests, as seen in those societies such as Social Democratic welfare states that maintain a hierarchy of ends or that decide in advance which particular needs rather than others will be met.

For Hayek, the market operates independently of the wishes and preferences of the actors involved; a 'hidden hand' guides the ways of the market. It is precisely this impersonal *a priori* logic – lying beyond purposive human action – that its exponents see as the attraction of the market order. Its logic is superior to the logic of individual interests, and impartial as between different interests. The beauty of the market – its mystique – is that it assumes an ideologically free zone where human actions are guided by the price system to maximise the satisfaction of different desires without favouring any one individual. If the laws governing this zone can be discerned, humankind possesses, according to Hayek, the proper object of scientific inquiry untarnished by individual and collective politics and ideology.

However, a different interpretation can be placed on Hayek's account of the true and the ideological bases of human action, which points beyond his understanding of ideology to the ideology at the heart of New Right politics. For Hayek, the practical contingencies – the problems of economic instability, insecurity and unmet need – that disturb the actual workings of the market are not amenable to corrective intervention. Indeed, they are the inevitable costs that must be endured for the greater good of economic freedom and the avoidance of ideological interference. These contingencies are subsumed under an ideal order, the market, that defies understanding and intervention and lies beyond reason and collective human purpose. However, far from dispelling ideology, the exclusion of reason and human purpose from our understanding of the market permits irrational elements of ideology free rein and thereby inhibits the study of economic operations. The latter operations are seen as part of this ideal order where they operate according to 'the laws of the market'.[1] By contrast, Social Democracy seeks to intervene rationally in certain areas of human affairs – such as welfare – in order to enable other areas – the market – more scope (see Cutler *et al.* 1986).

Despite theoretical contradictions in Hayek's argument – which arise from combining individualism with a metaphysical, supra-individualist notion of a market order transcending conscious human designs – its political plausibility lies in the claim that the market, if given free rein, limits the persuasive power of ideology. Some critics of Thatcherism even argue that such an order eliminates politics as well, by 'promoting the exit of human concerns from politics .... a massive programme of *buying oneself out*', 'of making politics irrelevant to the pursuit of individual or collective goals and ideals' (Bauman, 1988a). If the attraction of economic liberalism lies in its ability to neutralise ideology, it has a powerful defence against any counterclaim that it is itself ideological, whether the ideologies are 'Thatcherism', 'Reaganism', or whatever.

By neutralising other forms of ideology, New Right ideology has been able to disarm several of its critics. For example, the criticism of Thatcherism as mere ideology ignored a kind of counter-strike potential inherent in its policies, derived not only from their support of economic liberalism but from their claim to offer a market order free of ideology.[2, 3] This point applies especially to interpretations of Thatcherite policy as ideological ploys for presenting need and public welfare as the proper concerns of the market and not the state. By ignoring important arguments in the Thatcherite case, these interpretations placed too much weight on a kind of cynical deception assumed to lie behind the deployment of ideology, a form of statecraft by stealth; whereas much – but by no means all – of what Thatcherism claimed had been publicly stated in one context or another as part of the background to each policy proposal. On this, Levitas (1986) has traced the ideological and intellectual roots of government policies implemented in the mid-1980s to earlier proposals of rightist think-tanks. None the less, some commentators argued that the real purpose behind welfare cuts was not only to rid the welfare state of waste and promote efficiency (its overt aim), but to squeeze more out of underfunded services in order eventually to erode quality and divert demand into the private sector, its covert aim of destabilising and running down the welfare state (e.g. Illife 1985/6; Timmins 1989). Similarly, the present policy of fragmenting parts of the corporate welfare state, such as the NHS and local authority services, and putting them out to tender is seen as preparation for wholesale privatisation. Finally, government policy to slim down parts of nationalised industries such as steel, water, gas, power, and so forth, in order to 'fatten the calves' that remain ready for market, is seen in the same light.

The strategy of using economic policy to open the public sector to the market is one that the Tory government and its supporters can claim was clearly intended all along, and that there is nothing covert, contrived or ideological in this policy. The argument is that they are simply encouraging market forces to work through the public sector and facilitate choice, which may well mean that consumers take their custom outside the state, and that productive capacity, including labour, is switched from public to private sector. This is how the market operates: supplying services competitively at the lowest cost the market will bear, and deploying resources effectively in accord with what consumers will pay. As a consequence, exchange values prevail and political values are curtailed. The mystique of the market is that it presents reality as if there were nothing under the surface, no magician pulling strings, nor ventriloquist breathing life into the dummy, only the 'hidden hand' invisibly co-ordinating the infinitude of individual projects towards realising their ends, optimising individual needs and contributing to the greatest fulfilment of all.

This suggests that the analysis of New Right ideology should not rely solely on accounts of complex ideological apparatuses or the artifice of ideologues in government, media, party research departments and think-tanks. This is not to deny the existence of devious forces behind ideology, nor the stark contrast between rhetoric and reality. However, the study of ideology needs to trace the means whereby reality – as always under the sway of dominant interests – is constructed to accord with a market ideal and denuded of human purpose, values and the horizons of prefigurative possibility (Bauman 1988a). Market thought has become a dominant ideology because it directly addresses the everyday problems of human aspirations and anxieties alive in capitalist society. New Right philosophy penetrates to the core of common-sense thinking and becomes part of the realm of unquestioned assumptions. It is as common sense, therefore, that it should first be revealed as ideology, rather than as a separate mask of distortion that can be pealed off to reveal its true nature. In general, the strength of ideology lies less in the power of its deceptive statements than in its power to reconfigure images of reality to accord with these statements. As Gamble stresses, it is not 'any single reversion to the ideal of a competitive laissez-faire economy which acts as an ideological veil for the present problems of capitalist accumulation', rather market thought 'restores a way of looking at capitalism and its problems which has been pushed aside by other conceptions and by the political intervention of the working-class movement, but which has revived because of the continuing importance of the sphere of commodity exchange in the actual workings of capitalist economies' (1979, pp. 16, 17). More specifically, the Right has sought to overturn the old common sense of Social Democracy, with its standards of collective regulation, public ownership and state benevolence, and to replace it with a new morality based on private enterprise, wealth and self-reliance.

It is because the ideology of economic liberalism sees individual propensities as infinitely open, subject only to the rigours of market discipline, that its account of human enterprise assumes a plasticity devoid of intrinsic purpose and reason, other than the narrow rationality of individual satisfaction. It is as though anything and everything is possible once the market is unleashed and its opportunities grasped. However, the meaning of this enterprise and its broader sense of human history is beyond the scope of each individual. New Right thought reverses the era of Enlightenment informing modernity that saw civilisation emerging in the purposive, rational and scientific struggle of humankind over nature. In its place it reinstates the 'natural' rule of the market to which people are subject in pursuing their individual projects, and enables them to contribute unbeknowingly to the broader development of civilisation. In this sense the Right has sought to inaugurate 'the end of history'.

Social Democracy and the New Right: their ideological scope

In an important sense this plasticity is a feature of ideologies in general. We saw in the previous chapter that Social Democracy, like the New Right, possesses a versatility in accommodating the contingencies and uncertainties faced in political and economic life, and in responding positively to developments that might undermine a more rigid system of values. However, in one respect unlike the Right, Social Democracy retains a clear idea of the scope of human nature and needs. Thus Social Democracy came increasingly during the 1950s and 1960s to acknowledge the varieties of personal need for which welfare for all tied to a national minimum could not cater. This was possible in part because Social Democratic values recognised human diversity beyond basic need, and because, since the Webbs, it has sought to match this diversity by building an extension ladder of welfare beyond the minimum. Yet this plasticity is also a feature of rightist ideology in enabling it to adapt to changing political circumstances and social needs. The New Right also has had to concede that the market cannot optimise the life chances of all, and that some casualties of economic change pose a potential threat to social order and the attainment of natural justice. Even the market order may require additional statutory supports for those unable to survive by their own efforts, and so need some 'equality of opportunity'. Hence, our discussion of these two ideologies has focused on their versatility in preserving their own ideals while accommodating various contingencies. The study of policy presentation and discourse should emphasise the pragmatic aspect of ideology in the practical context of, for example, welfare policy. It will be argued that this elasticity is more than a matter of softening ideology to suit hard-edged problems in the real world; for ideology would lose its force as a cogent value system if it modified its shape to match changing surroundings on pragmatic grounds alone. Rather – to repeat a central theme of the book – ideology succeeds best where it can effect a change in the representation of the real world to suit its system of beliefs.

This section explores how such versatility is possible without undermining the central tenets of the two ideologies. The elasticity of ideology operates in two ways: first, in terms of the encounter between an ideological system and the practical contingencies the system must accommodate; secondly, by means of the forms of social relations and individual subjectivity that ideology constructs, and which in turn support ideology.

Elasticity in ideological thought occurs first because ideology develops a grid for describing a changing world, namely a system of categories of identity and difference existing in everyday language that maps the diversity of conditions affecting the changing circumstances. Wallerstein argues that all ideologies operate with pairs of opposing propositions concerning, on the one hand the universal social features that bind all members of a society, culture or community; and on the other, the particularities that discriminate between different groups within each society, culture or community. Such concepts are not opposites but symbiotic pairs whose relations can be managed to ideological effect. In his work Wallerstein has explored 'the ways in which the present antinomies of unity and diversity, universalism and particularism, humanity and race, world and nation, person and man/woman have been manipulated' (1990, p. 39). In the same way these and other pairs such as deserving and undeserving, institution and community, and universality and selectivity are manipulated in the ideological discourses of adversaries who attempt to argue their case against a changing social and political background.

To take Social Democratic thought first, the principles of equality and difference are embedded in the structural features of the postwar welfare state, the national minimum and the extension ladder. Social Democracy can claim its commitment to a modicum of equality by virtue of the range of national minima in health, education, social security and so forth. In addition, it operates a principle of differentiation through its endorsement of voluntary, market and informal provisions that seek to provide levels of welfare above the minimum. For example, during times of postwar affluence, Social Democrats have pointed to the range of provisions created in response to the growing diversity of needs and personalised welfare requirements, as Crosland did in the 1950s. In this way, Social Democracy pursues the principle of equity, of specific services in proportion to specific needs, that builds on the principle of equality for all. In principle, for example, all children between a certain age are entitled to state schooling, but some with specific needs such as physical or mental disability receive specialised schooling.[4] In times of recession the versatility of Social Democratic ideology enables it to withstand cost limits, cuts and general retrenchment. In keeping with welfare pluralism, the extension ladder is raised while the national minimum maintained or lowered to achieve greater economies. The pragmatic adjustment of the extension ladder is able to complement the universal principle of the national minimum; an ideology uniting Fabian thinkers as diverse as Titmuss, with his constant questioning of deviations from universal welfare, and Hadley and Hatch with their active commitment to welfare pluralism. Despite the apparent statist inflexibility accredited to it by the Right, Social Democracy provides an elastic and versatile system of values, both in its earlier Beveridge model combining national minimum and 'voluntary insurance', and in its more recent advocacy of networks of mutual self-sufficiency built upon an infrastructure of state welfare.

Ruth Levitas (1986) has shown in her reading of think-tank proposals from the early 1980s that the New Right also can manipulate an elastic system of values combining liberal and conservative strands. It does this by articulating notions of equality of opportunity within the market – the neo-liberal strand with its open and undifferentiated view of human nature – with a more differentiated set of values based on hierarchical notions of patriarchy, family and property – the traditional conservative strand. It has been possible to argue for extending the privileges of private education, health care, property, share ownership and 'personal pension plans' to increasing numbers of people, and to stress the universal benefits of the market for all and not just the privileged. By extending the market, a property-owning democracy of working- and middle-class home- and share-owners is established which uses the market rather than the politics of the ballot box to achieve social policy ends. Under a Socialist or Social Democratic ideology the ideal of the social market would be a contradiction in terms; but, placed under a rightist ideology, it becomes a coherent ideal aiding the creation of a new Conservative hegemony. The wider the market extends its benefits, however unequally, the greater the image of prosperity wrought by government; a prosperity that came to be seen for a while in the mid-1980s as replacing the recessionary hardships of the 1970s and early 1980s.

In summary, the elasticity of Social Democracy and New Right ideologies stems from the way they both frame the terms of their beliefs around contrasting but complementary principles. Each ideology adapts to the practical circumstances it faces, which might demand recognition of changing social conditions and modification of political strategy and policy; recognising, for example, the injustices of specific social inequalities, or the justice of treating some groups preferentially. This accommodation is possible because ideology recognises and responds to the characteristics of identity and difference that classify the world. Both ideologies advance values based on conceptions of universal human capacities – e.g. rights and duties – around which social identity can be defined. Similarly, they both acknowledge essential differences among persons in terms of human attributes, needs and desires and the vocations and capacities to realise these proclivities. The two ideologies allow both social similarities and differences to be catered for in their various political designs. By ensuring that core values are arranged around the contrasting principles of identity and difference, these ideologies can utilise different values to justify the particular forms of intervention required as circumstance demands. Because ideology provides a coherent logic that frames a range of different values, the ideological justification for political action remains plausible. The success of Social Democracy and the New Right ideologies lies in their pragmatic grasp of reality.

Ideology, need and social relations

The elasticity of ideology is seen not only in its coherence of thought, but in the context of social and political relations. Ideology constitutes relations and experiences of need that permit specific forms of accommodation and versatility. At the centre of Social Democratic and New Right hegemonies are two kinds of social space, respectively the 'social' and the market, each constructing their own distinct forms of subjectivity and need. In the Social Democratic state, the social comprises the domain of social differences – the different groups in need, demographic categories, divisions of normality and pathology – and the state's arrangements, together with the private, for regulating these differences (Squires 1990); a domain referred to by Michel Foucault as the 'bio-political' (1979b) (see Chapter 9). The acknowledgement of the political nature of the social – e.g. the rights of citizens – places on the state responsibilities for basic types of dependency and for diversified personal needs. These responsibilities have resulted in the development of a welfare state of considerable scope in its range of provisions. The subjective dimension of citizenship is greatly enhanced by creating provisions to satisfy a broad range of needs. However regulated the management of the social, the richness of welfare provision under the Social Democratic state is unsurpassed and contrasts sharply with the narrow conception of need held by rightist states.

The different constructions placed on needs and welfare relations are seen in a comparison of founding documents of the Social Democratic welfare state – namely the Beveridge Report of 1942 and the NHS White Paper of 1944 (HMSO 1944) – with official pronouncements on the Thatcherite welfare state, such as the 1989 White Paper *Working for Patients* (HMSO 1989a).

The system of relations and needs constructed under the postwar welfare state was clearly stated in the Beveridge Report. The state was to consolidate the rights and benefits it had conferred on citizens since the 1900s, by meeting different groups in need through the provision of a comprehensive and universalist welfare state. In effect the state was establishing an ideal whereby needs and citizenship rights were defined according to personal circumstances, irrespective of means, and with little regard to state resources. (In the first decade of the welfare state, few government reports commented on the cost of resourcing social services: e.g. HMSO 1954; 1956.) Beveridge formulated a framework of need categories by which to extend the umbrella of welfare protection to a widening range of dependency states defined according to the 'Primary Causes of Need' (1942, p. 124). This would achieve a 'diagnosis of want' and result in a system of benefits and pensions 'mounted on a scientific basis with regard to subsistence needs' (1942, p. 15). A new idealised relationship between citizen and state was established. In the bleak mid-war years, Beveridge marshalled a rhetoric of expansion, national security and hope that depicted a future free of the exigencies of need. The image of a 'comprehensive policy of social progress', of 'welfare for all citizens irrespective of their means', portrayed a vision of a united and purposeful society, under the key metaphor of the state destined to lead its subjects to national salvation on 'the Way to Freedom from Want', 'the road to reconstruction'. In 1911 the Webbs had spoken of the 'indissoluble partnership between individual and the community' (Webb and Webb 1911). By 1942 Beveridge came to express the same sentiment towards a more developed framework of state welfare, involving the now familiar notion of 'co-operation between the State and the individual' (1942, p. 7). In this partnership the state would meet the citizen's needs in return for the compulsory National Insurance contributions of all in work – thereby strengthening the welfare-for-work compact. Beyond this provision of minimum universal welfare, individuals were encouraged to make additional provision for their own specific needs.

The spirit of universalism was taken further in the 1944 White Paper announcing the government's decision to establish an NHS that would ensure that 'in future every man and woman and child can rely on getting all the advice and treatment and care which they may need in matters of personal health', without reference to 'whether they can pay for them, or any other factor irrelevant to their real need'. In this way the government intended to bring 'the country's full resources to bear upon reducing ill-health and promoting good health in all its citizens' (HMSO 1944, Introduction).

Forty years later, the abandonment of the social by the Thatcher government, committed to advancing the market economy, stands in stark contrast to the aspirations of the 1940s. Social relations have become increasingly defined within the space of the market, a space in principle incompatible with the social. In the market, social and political differences that flourished in the social are reduced to economic differences, 'needs' replaced by 'demands', and 'citizens' by 'consumers'. The deployment of these diferent vocabularies is seen by contrasting the Conservative government's *Citizen's Charter* (HMSO 1991), with the notion of citizenship rights as consumer rights, and the Labour party's charter (1990) which retains a traditional social-democratic notion of citizenship. The exchange values of commodities provide a common set of equivalences quantified in strictly monetary terms.[5] The balance between what is needed and available is reduced to matters of demand and supply and regulated by price. In health care for example, subjective experiences of health and illness are fashioned out of needs pre-formed by the business strategies of the new NHS and the marketing strategies of private health, insurance and pharmaceutical industries, and gratified principally by the processes of commodification and consumerism, leaving other needs in danger of being overlooked.

The presence of these values and relations in recent policy is seen in the policies for reforming the NHS, contained in the National Health Service and Community Care Act 1990. As suggested earlier, these reforms implement principles of market welfare further than envisaged in rightist proposals of the 1970s and early 1980s. Since 1987 the proposals have become not only more far-reaching in advancing market values, but more strategic in their consideration of the institutional realities of the welfare state. This rightist 'new realism' is achieved by means of the core conceptual innovation of 'the internal market', which recasts administrative relations between different state-providers into market relations, and permits increasing transactions between the internal and external markets.

These innovations are seen clearly in the White Paper *Working for Patients* (HMSO 1989a), implemented in the early 1990s. Rather than dismantle NHS institutions and construct a market regime, the White Paper proposes keeping institutions – hospitals, general practices and administrative health authorities (central government, regional and district) – largely in place, while the relations between them are restructured along market lines; thus transforming the internal dynamics of the NHS. The proposals rely on the same personnel to staff these institutions as were established in the postwar reforms: general practitioners (GPs), consultants, hospital nurses and community nurses, with the addition of the new and strategically important 'general manager' skilled in the techniques of corporate management. However, government is reforming relations between these personnel and between the institutions along internal market lines, and changing the methods of allocating resources. As part of the policy implementation, some hospitals and community health provisions such as ambulance services have become self-governing 'NHS hospital trusts'. This new autonomous entity, similar to the public corporation, is no longer directly financed by government, but free to enter into revenue-making contracts with individual health authorities, appointed GP practices, private patients, insurance firms, private employers and other hospitals, and able to hire and fire staff, set conditions of work and produce surpluses. These relations are governed primarily by financial interest, overriding the traditional interest in providing health care for the needs of the local community without financial considerations, as spelt out in the 1944 White Paper. Similarly, GP teams appointed as self-managing fund-holders can receive fixed 'practice budgets' from Regional Health Authorities, and, with district health authorities, are free to enter into contracts – especially 'fixed price contracts' – with hospitals and hospital trusts, which will provide treatments for patients with determinable conditions. These practices can 'shop around' for the best treatment centres, selecting the packages offered on a value-for-money basis, and so outbid non-budget holding practices – in effect, introducing a preferential tier of treatment allocation into the NHS. In the same way, hospitals can compete with each other for contracts. In principle, hospitals, practices and district health authorities operate within a system of incentives that encourages maximum cost-effectiveness, efficient service delivery, and patient choice exercised by the general practitioner. In practice, new divisions are already emerging in the NHS, in what for several decades had been the jewel in the crown of the universal welfare state.

At the core of these changes lie distinct shifts in the nature of the relations between institutions and between personnel. Each relation is based on a radically redesigned set of 'incentives' imposed on the traditional responsibilities of professional staff for patient needs. The system of incentives is modelled on commercial business practices based on strict financial and contractual disciplines. As the White Paper states, today's health service is 'a complex multi-billion pound enterprise' (HMSO 1989a, p. 64), the management of all levels of the NHS should be 'reformed on business lines', and health authorities 'become more business-like in their approach to the provision of services' (*ibid.*, p. 19). NHS hospitals will be governed by new financial systems which place them 'on a more level footing with private hospitals, which have to meet the costs of capital on a normal commercial basis'. 'Capital charging', for example, 'will ensure that managers will be given clear financial signals'. Prior to these reforms, 'Hospitals and their consultants need[ed] a stronger incentive to look on GPs as people whose confidence they must gain if patients are to be referred to them', and, in turn, 'GPs themselves lack[ed] incentives to offer their patients a choice of hospital' (*ibid.*, p. 48). After the reforms, the proposed GP practice budgets will enable money 'to flow with the patient from the GP practice itself', so that 'the practices and hospital which attract the most custom will receive the most money' (*ibid.*). According to the logic of competition-led performance, the patient will be the prime beneficiary, for 'Both GPs and hospitals will have a real incentive to put patients first' (*ibid.*). The White Paper's rhetoric is concerned to embellish the new culture of competitive enterprise with the appropriate jargon of 'cash releasing cost improvements' to generate new sources of supplementary revenue (*ibid.*, p. 12); to stimulate 'Resource Management Initiatives' (*ibid.*, p. 16); 'to build up resources . . . to manage any temporary deficits' (*ibid.*, p. 19). In the light of competitive tendering in the public sector since 1983, 'Competition has not only produced substantial savings. It has also led to clear performance criteria, improved productivity, innovative ideas and techniques and better management' (*ibid.*, p. 69).

In the White Paper the concept of patient need barely figures. Needs are subverted into the efficiency criteria of prudent financial management; service effectiveness or 'value for money' is not defined in terms of the quality of care that services provide in meeting need. Needs no longer provide the grounds whereby patients exercise rights, as established in the 1944 White Paper, but a datum accorded solely financial value. In these ways the market rhetoric of *Working for Patients* is radically different from the rhetoric employed under the Social Democratic welfare state. In the early 1990s, this rhetoric has already found its way into Prime Minister John Major's *Citizen's Charter* (HMSO 1991) with its stress on the *consumer* rights of citizens.

Within the post-Thatcherite state, the restructuring of social relations has profound implications for political relations in civil society. For an extensive network of civic associations providing an element of local democratic participation in the management of the welfare state has, in some cases, been extended *and*, at the same time, constrained in its civic ethos by global criteria of management efficiency, market competition and legal contracting. For example, under the Education Reform Act 1988, many local school governing boards have been reconstituted to enable more parents to become governors controlling school management and budgets. By way of protection, section 36 of the Act states that no governor 'shall incur any personally liability for anything done in good faith'. However, in the context of the new arrangements, for which there are few legal precedents, the strength of this protection, in particular the assumption of 'good faith', could only be properly tested in court. In time it is possible that the new governors would have to arrange expensive insurance indemnities for legal actions brought against the school (e.g. in the case of accidents suffered by a child or employee). They will have to be constantly on guard for educational projects, however valuable, that might incur budget deficits. Similar problems are raised for voluntary organisations who enter into contracts with local authority social services departments to provide community care services. The effect of this type of reform in education and other areas of welfare is to extend the financial and legal values of private corporations and the corporate sphere of the welfare state – 'the new contract culture' – into local civic associations and to undermine the traditional political concerns of community representatives and volunteers (see Rustin 1989). These developments in the early 1990s complement a decade of measures reducing local democratic involvement in other civic associations, such as social security tribunals, local wage councils, community health councils and College and Polytechnic Governing Boards.

It remains to be seen, at this time (late 1991) as a general election approaches, to what extent social relations and needs will in fact be transformed by reforming the British welfare state, and to what degree these changes come to replace Social Democratic principles of national minimum protection for citizens. Shifting the public's allegiance from the ideology of state support to that of market freedom, or even bridging the divide between these two welfare ideologies, is perhaps the most significant test faced by the Tory government in implementing a radical set of policies, especially since 1987. Indeed one commentator has recently pronounced that 'The welfare state has proved to be the most intractable problem facing the Thatcher Government' (Riddell 1989, p. 127). Social Democracy achieved a degree of balance between state protection and market freedom, despite inherent problems and irresolvable tensions. Whether recent policies will have achieved a new balance can be addressed in part at least by reference to the ideological beliefs present in government policy and policy presentation.

As an example of New Right politics, the ideology of Thatcherism has been anathema not only to the values of the welfare state, but to the very conceptual language required for stating such values. The concepts of 'welfare', 'needs' and ' rights' in particular have stood in danger of being banished from the welfare state's vocabulary. In principle, Thatcherism's purpose has been to render the market more competitive by removing state and private monopolies in production and welfare, so that consumer sovereignty is strengthened and consumer needs better satisfied. Any other approach in determining need is itself an ideological project. For example, under the Social Democratic welfare state, needs are seen as ideological constructions pursued by interested groups of politicians chasing votes, welfare officials securing their jobs and aggrandising their empires, and recipients protecting dependent life-styles. The process of inventing needs leads to the privileging of new 'rights' of questionable status. Enoch Powell, for example, believed that the 'translation of a want or need into a right is one of the most widespread and dangerous of modern heresies' (quoted in George and Wilding 1976, p. 27). From this viewpoint, the extension of citizenship rights is the mass ideological deceit of the postwar years. Within a market economy, such contrivances of human interest are rendered unnecessary by the market's sensitivity to the diversity of consumer demand. The only true rights are property rights, all forms of satisfying need flow from these.

Modern market liberalism differs from earlier rightist ideologies in that it seeks to flatten the space between what it proclaims for all and what it achieves in practice. It thereby succeeds in blunting the critical edge that this oppositional space would have provided in confronting New Right ideology.[6] By contrast, traditional conservatism faced a conflict between its proclamation to achieve an organic and contented society within which everyone knows his or her place, and its achievement in maintaining the interests of a select elite (though no doubt for the good of all). This dilemma is removed for the New Right because it claims to displace conflicting selective and universal interests to a domain governed by the higher transcendent order of the market, a 'catallaxy' beyond human interest and ideology. It is the implicit assumption of this order that the richness of everyday interactions and exchange is secured in the one-dimensionality of the market. Gamble has observed that 'Since exchange relations and the market do provide a basis upon which all social relations in capitalist society can be grasped and evaluated, social market doctrine has a universal reach, constantly suggesting ways of approaching and solving practical problems' (1979, p. 22).

New Right ideology maintains a view of human nature as infinitely plastic and adaptable; in contrast to its view of the scarcity of productive resources which human nature must realistically and pliably come to terms with. In principle, every individual's needs can be satisfied in conformity with available resources, and his or her desires pursued to the furthest point of fulfilment within the rule of law. Further, each individual will comply with the strictures of gainful work provided that the price is right. This plasticity, of course, is represented by the image of the market order as a hive of individual activity, each person following his or her own ends in exchange with others, all for the greater good of society. It is this assumption of the infinite adaptability of human nature that the new theorist of capitalist ideology – such as Baudrillard (1983), Jameson (1984) and Bauman (1988b) – have focused on in their interpretation of the elasticity of capitalist values. The recommodification of human needs and desires has weakened the power of universal values to determine the shape of these needs and desires, and lessened the limits placed on market ideology by collective forms of resistance which now appear to acquiesce in the demands of capitalist society. However, such a conclusion must assume that the unfettered logic of the Right is indeed carried to its ultimate point. The extent to which this has been achieved in the welfare state, reversing the drift of postwar policy, and the degree to which a new consensus founded, is the subject of the next chapter.

Notes

1. Popper's celebrated critique of the non-amenability of Marxist, Freudian and sociology of knowledge theories to rational argument – because they attribute unconscious motives which ideologically blind their opponents to reason – extends to neo- liberal thought in this respect (e.g. Popper 1966, p. 215).
2. Of course other arguments in recent decades about the elimination of ideology – from the 'end of ideology' of the 1950s to the 'new realism' of the 1980s – have none the less contained an implicit ideological programme.
3. The influence of other strands of thought, apart from economic liberalism, e.g. conservatism, that stress the importance of the strong state and moral authoritarianism, are at odds with economic liberalism in resorting to a more traditional form of political thought which is less able to dispel ideology from politics.
4. The 1970 Education (Handicapped Children) Act and, to a greater extent, the 1981 Education Act replace those parts of the 1944 Education Act under which ineducable children, such as those with severe mental disabilities, could be withdrawn from universal educational provision and receive, if available, 'training' from local health and welfare services. In effect, the later Acts

exercise a principle of equity, which in some respects builds on and in other respects replaces the principle of equality.

5. For a discussion of exchange values, see Chapter 5 on Marxist Political Economy of Welfare.

6. The theme of 'flattening' critical discourse is developed in different analyses of modernity (Marcuse 1964; Leiss 1978) and postmodernity (Baudrillard 1983; Jameson 1984; Bauman 1988b).

4

Thatcherism, its legacy and the welfare consensus

Characterising Thatcherism

The question is sometimes put: Would there have been Thatcherism without Thatcher? One argument goes that without Mrs Thatcher as Prime Minister, Thatcherism would still have emerged as the dominant political ideology of the 1980s, but under a different name. The political and economic forces that gave rise to Thatcherism would have created a similar entity whoever was leader of the governing Conservative Party. With this insight in mind many accounts of Thatcherism produced in recent years have attended to the structural features shaping the ideological climate that swept away postwar Social Democratic ideology. Yet, as we will see, some accounts of Thatcherism acknowledge the personal qualities of Mrs Thatcher, such as her instinctive grasp of political realities that had eluded previous prime ministers. A still further line of argument plays down the idea of Thatcherism altogether, whether as ideology or person, and stresses the role of the electoral system and divided opposition, whereby about 40 per cent of voters have delivered an unassailable and sustainable majority in Parliament for over twelve years. However, the dominant approach to portraying the emergence of Thatcherism has been structural in scope. In some cases this approach has endowed the political, economic and social forces shaping the ideology of Thatcherism with a power to generate a new consensus to replace the old Social Democratic order. Thus the Labour Party and labour movement, no less than the Tories, have undergone a transformation in ideology and statecraft that amounts to a new hegemony, a new realism in policy and a New Consensus on the Welfare State.

In this chapter we will concentrate on understanding Thatcherism as the dominant motif of New Right ideology in Britain. This ideology has had a wide-ranging and profound effect, in redirecting the momentum of the Social Democratic welfare state after forty years, restructuring it, and shaping its prospects for the 1990s, long after the postwar consensus evaporated. At the same time we will suggest that the ideology of Social Democracy has proved sufficiently adaptable, as argued in Chapter 2, to be capable of reconstruction as part of a new ideological and institutional configuration to emerge in the last decade of this century.

Interest in Thatcherism has developed in two directions, focusing on its intrinsic and comparative features. One approach explores Thatcherism as a coherent ideology that brings together various and sometimes conflicting ideas into a seemingly unified political programme. A second approach studies Thatcherism in comparison with earlier ideologies, and traces narratives of continuity or discontinuity between Thatcherism and Social Democracy. Both approaches have given rise to debates that pose different accounts of the ideology of the New Right. These issues and their implications for under-standing the workings of rightist welfare ideology are explored in this chapter.

Several commentaries have provided characterisations of Thatcherism that attempt to explain the unity of the different strands comprising this ideology, economic liberalism and conservative authoritarianism. Hall (1983) and Laclau (1977) have both identified a proto-hegemony that fuses these strands into a coherent ideology, sometimes referred to as authoritarian populism. Gamble (1979) and Barry (1987), each from different political backgrounds, stress the historical lineage that unites these strands. By contrast, Levitas (1986) sees their unity as anomalous and problematic and analyses the ideological rhetoric of New Right policy that masks this heterogeneity. Jessop *et al.* (1988) also question this ideological unity, seeing its cohesion as the result of opportunities presented to the Right by structural developments that have emerged in the second half of the twentieth century. We will examine these accounts in more detail so that in the next section they can be placed in the broader context of postwar welfare history.

Hall explains the emergence of New Right ideology as the outcome of political and economic forces that have profoundly and decisively transformed the postwar Social Democratic consensus. This ideology is the result of welding together disparate ideas into a homogeneous ideology attuned to the experiences and needs of ordinary people. Thus Thatcherism 'combines the resonant themes of organic Toryism – nation, family, duty, authority, standards, traditionalism – with the aggressive themes of a revived neo-liberalism – self-interest, competitive individualism, anti-statism' (Hall 1983, p. 29). The ideology of Thatcherism is located at the present end of the long drift in British politics which Hall *et al.* in 1978 saw as a crisis of the British Social Democratic state. These developments represented a movement in British politics from consent to coercion as successive governments resorted to increasingly coercive measures of intervention to reverse long term economic decline (Gamble 1988, p. 182). This shift occurred first in a leftwards direction. In the 1960s a fresh wave of radicalism sought to build a new politics that would extend postwar achievements in social justice, equality and emancipation, in a manner that questioned traditional values derived from property, capital, patriotism and moral authority, and from the modern values of technical education and expertise. This was followed by a reaction rightwards as the state responded by orchestrating new executive, legislative, judicial and police powers to strengthen controls over money supply, immigration, industrial militancy and welfare expenditure, controls culminating in the present refashioning of sexual and moral attitudes in welfare, education and broadcasting. It was in response to what in the late 1970s was seen as the crisis of the postwar settlement that Thatcherism emerged. Hall *et al*. describes how, from the far-right periphery of libertarian think-tanks and occasional contributions to learned journals read by a few academics, senior civil servants and board directors, 'these half-formed spectres which once hovered on the edge of British politics have now been fully politicised and installed in the vanguard, as a viable basis for hegemony, by . . . the Conservatives' (1978, p. 316; see also Golding and Middleton 1982, p. 225). In this context Laclau and Mouffe argue that 'we are thus witnessing the emergence of a new hegemonic project, that of liberal-conservative discourse, which seeks to articulate the neo-liberal defence of the free market economy with the profoundly anti-egalitarian cultural and social traditionalism of conservatism' (1985, p. 175).

Hall describes two aspects of Thatcherism's ability to instil anti-collectivist ideology into popular consciousness. First, Thatcherism has liberated 'the people' from a subject status in *opposition to* the state to a position where they are seen as *working with* new political forces bent on turning back the frontiers of the state: that is, an ideology 'to construct the people into a populist political subject . . . in a great national crusade to make Britain 'Great' once more', (1983, p. 30). Secondly, Thatcherism appeals directly to the real experiences of ordinary people, in their encounters, for example, with an impersonal and arbitrary administration, or their sense of injustice at seeing welfare claimants receive benefits for not working – experiences contingent on the Social Democratic, corporatist welfare state. Such fears, aspirations and needs are openly exploited by Thatcherite rhetoric, which has acted as both prelude and accompaniment to the welfare reforms of the 1980s. Laclau and Mouffe summarise these aspects of Thatcherism as 'An antagonism [that] is thus constructed between two poles: the "people", which includes all those who defend the traditional values and freedom of enterprise; and their adversaries: the state and all the subversives (feminists, blacks, young people and "permissives" of every type)' (1985, p. 170).

Laclau and Mouffe see the resurgence of New Right thought as a hegemonic project that seeks to draw back the frontiers of democratic advance – what they describe as 'the democratisation of liberalism' (1985, p. 171) – by reconstructing the subjects of democracy. This is done by cutting what they term the chain of 'symbolic equivalences' linking the different subjects who have emerged in the evolution of democratic rights, to which the welfare state has been the main contributor in the present century. It is this chain which has conjoined with equal rights, at one end, the property owners and market participants – subjects who received these traditional liberties in the early stages of democratic evolution – and, at the other end, the subjects of the welfare state, the deprived, the poor, the undereducated, whose circumstances are seen as an affront to liberty. The latter are the social subjects whose rights Beveridge, Marshall, Titmuss and others addressed. However, presently the Right is seeking to negate these equivalences. They seek to retrench democratic rights by quashing recently gained political advances and by rendering down all rights to the single universal right to participate in the market – a primordial state of natural rights that 'construct the rights of the individual as existing before society' (1985, p. 172). The effect is to abolish the social as the domain where individuals and groups have a range of social rights which enable them to co-operate with each other and to exercise rights conferred by the state – the ultimate authority that has sought to safeguard the status of its citizens, and at the same time to extract the duties, obediences and norms that shape the social. Gamble commented in 1979 on the 'precarious attachment' of New Right thinkers to the idea of democracy, 'because during times of economic difficulty the workings of democracy are one more burden that the liberal society must carry' (1979, p. 9). Given the Right's belief that political 'democracy is dangerous and can threaten liberty', the logic of the market can only be resolutely pursued if there is a strong and active state, 'maintaining the conditions which guarantee individual liberty' over and above democratic liberty (1979, p. 10). As Laclau and Mouffe argue, it is the tradition of democratic discourse that poses an external threat to the discourse of economic liberalism by being presented as an attack on the primary rights of property.

However, the roots of the critique of democracy produced by this fusion of economic liberalism and traditional Conservatism can be traced back further. For it is not merely the internal logic of the rightist discourse that unites the two strands, but a unity that has matured through a long tradition, as writers on both left and right acknowledge. Gamble comments that the doctrine that combines the ideas of the free market and the strong conservative state 'marks the continuity of the doctrine with the tradition of political economy, not a departure from it' (1979, p. 5). Similarly, Norman Barry, sympathetic to the Right, warns against overemphasising the differences between theoretical conservatism and liberalism:

> An older tradition . . . put 'sound' money, the rule of law and public interest over sectional interest . . . this doctrine encompassed much of what is valuable in the individualist political creed. The anti-consensus intellectual movement involves, then, not just a revival of old liberal ideas but also a clearer and sharper articulation of traditional conservative doctrine'. (1987, p. 200)

The argument of Hall and others about the hegemonic status of New Right ideology has elicited three lines of criticism. First, Levitas disputes evidence of the intrinsic affinity attributed to the dominant strands in current rightist thought, and accords closer attention to the ideological resources that contrive to unite these divergent strands in policy (1986). Secondly, Riddell (1983) argues that Thatcherism, in particular, is more intuitive and pragmatic than ideological. Thirdly, the pragmatic and reactive aspects of Thatcherism are explored in a more structural vein by Jessop *et al.* (1984), who see Thatcherism as a particular accumulation strategy for regulating British capital in the increasingly international arena of capitalism.

The problematic relationship between the distinct strands of New Right thought has been stressed by Levitas in her reading of influential policy documents produced by rightist think tanks. The compatibility between economic liberal and conservative thought are explored by 'examin[ing] the kinds of society implied by the different strands – that is the utopias that can be extrapolated from them and the forms of legitimacy involved' (1986, p. 80). What emerges is a marked contrast in both rhetoric and ideology between neo-liberal and neo-conservative views of the good society. These differences are underpinned by conflicting concepts of human nature and the relations between individual and society. However, a common ground exists at the level of rhetoric. Agreeing with Gamble, she observes 'the neo-liberal position conceding to the neo-conservative as the strong state is required to preserve the 'freedom' of the market' (1986, p. 103). A similar point is made by King who sees the liberal strand as guiding the government in its formulation of policy and the conservative as dealing with the practical aftermath and setbacks of its policies (King 1987, p. 112). Like Levitas, King criticises Hall's failure to analyse the differential impact of these two traditions (*ibid.*, p. 129).

In contrast with studies of Thatcherism as ideology, Riddell has stressed the pragmatic and *ad hoc* drift, which characterises the politics of Thatcherism. He is critical of commentators such as Hall and the journal *Marxism Today* for conferring 'on Thatcherism greater coherence and consistency than it has had in practice' (1983, p. 19). This coherence is undermined, he argues, by the policy U-turns of the early 1980s, 'which were more a response to the failure of economic policies and to short-term pressures than the implementation of a carefully worked out blueprint' (*ibid.*). Riddell also refers to the gradualist strategy ('almost Fabian') of the Thatcher government of introducing a rolling programme of piecemeal legislation in various areas of policy (e.g. trade union powers, nationalisation, local government, National Health Service), which does not amount to radical change. However, he concedes that all this could add up to major changes over time – which from the hindsight of the 1990s appears more accurate. Contrary to this piecemeal account, the strategy of breaking up key institutions into identifiable parts, which are then sold off and put out to competitive tender, suggests a strategy of incremental movement towards wholesale change. This amounts to waging a widespread assault on previously unassailable institutions. The strategy fragments the targets of reform, picking off one after the other, to maximise the confusion and demoralisation of employees and welfare consumers and to minimise the visibility to the general public of what is really happening. Yet in his subsequent appraisal of 'the Thatcher Decade', Riddell still maintains that Conservative government policy derives from Mrs Thatcher's essentially pragmatic approach to politics, 'a response to events rather than the execution of a clearly prepared and argued-out blueprint' (1989, p. 11). Having been blessed with a long and unbroken period in office, Thatcher had the opportunity (between 1987 and 1990) rarely given a prime minister to pursue radical policies that 'remedy earlier setbacks and policy weaknesses' (*ibid.*, p. 5).

In contrast with more programmatic interpretations, Riddell stresses the intuitive nature of Thatcherism, which is 'essentially an instinct, a sense of moral values and an approach to leadership rather than an ideology' (1983, p. 7). This view is perhaps in danger of personalising the significance of Thatcherism in terms of the qualities that mark its subject, former Prime Minister Thatcher. Gamble would agree with Riddell's intuitivist account of Mrs Thatcher, that her 'instinctive distrust of borrowing and credit was enough' to persuade her towards the free market economy and beyond towards conservative morality (Gamble 1988, p. 48). None the less, he stresses that such instincts have played a broader role, beyond the scope of Mrs Thatcher's personal contributions, in the formation of Thatcherism, in extolling the virtues of an ideological belief system that supports the values of family, thrift, hard work, self-reliance and respectability (*ibid.*).

Ultimately, even a pragmatic approach to politics, which allows its policies to adapt to events in endeavouring to navigate through the problems befalling government, relies on a new ordering of values. It is the presentation of this ordering that is ideological when compared with the presentation of previous administrations. Thatcherism is a cultural phenomenon in a way that previous eponymous formations such as Butskellism were not. Mrs Thatcher gave high prominence to these values in her policies, in her affirmation of 'Victorian values' and disavowal of 'fuzzy' consensus and compromise. It is precisely the emphasis on style, presentation and communication that was indicative of the raised ideological profile of the Thatcher government and of its endeavour to create a new hegemony in late twentieth-century politics.

The politics of Thatcherism is placed in a more global context by Jessop *et al.* They likewise criticise the homogeneity and consistency that Hall accords Thatcherism, which they see as deriving from his 'ideologism'. An example of the latter problem is seen in Hall *et al.*'s proposition that the crisis addressed by Thatcherism was 'finally a crisis in and of ideology' (1978, p. 322), as though ideology existed *sui generis* of other aspects of the social formation (Jessop *et al.* 1984, p. 37). For Jessop *et al.*, this ideologism is seen in the central role accorded 'authoritarian populism' in explaining the success of Thatcherism. By employing this phenomenon to account for developments outside ideology, Hall mystifies the complexity of Thatcherism's support and glosses over its potentially inherent antagonisms (Jessop *et al.* 1984, p. 37). In turn, this has led to an overemphasis on the role played by the ideologues of New Right thought and policy in the political and electoral ascendancy of Thatcherism. A further problem with Hall's discourse approach is that it fails to gauge the reception of Thatcherism as it impacted on the minds and actions of people: 'it does not tell us about discursive consumption. Ideologies must not only be transmitted; they must also be received, understood and acted upon' (Jessop *et al.* 1988, p. 45).

As an alternative to Hall's account, Jessop *et al.* outline the economic, political and institutional reconfiguration that gave birth to Thatcherism: the new regime of accumulation that seeks to make Britain more competitive within the world market, more flexible in its use of labour and other means of production, and more enterprising in a deregulated home economy. This approach provides a global framework within which the pragmatic elements of Thatcherite politics are cast. In sum, it leads to a critique of Hall's overdetermination of ideology on several fronts, of which three can be mentioned. First, Jessop *et al.* are wary of the way ideological consistency glosses the contradictions that Thatcherism seeks to mask. They warn that in the analysis of Thatcherism 'style should not be confused with substance' (1984, p. 43). In a critique that could apply equally to Laclau and Mouffe, they comment that the characterisation of Thatcherism as a new chain of equivalences 'tends to reify these linkages and ignore their changing emphases and conflicts' (*ibid.*). Secondly, the overdetermined consistency of the postwar consensus likewise glosses the conflicts and dissensions that have also shaped this period. Finally, placing the unity of working-class conservatism under the rubric of authoritarian populism misrepresents the disparate nature of working-class culture, confounding deferential ('as you say, sir') with instrumental ('loadsamoney') Toryism. Contrary to Hall, Jessop *et al.* suggest that the organic link between working-class and Tory pragmatism reveals an historical continuity that goes back well beyond authoritarian populism (1984, p. 42).

By exploring the broader conjunctions directing the postwar period, Jessop *et al.* point to the underlying material reasons for the emergence of Thatcherism, in particular to the forces producing a 'dual crisis' of parliamentarianism and a 'two nations' Britain. In the crisis affecting British parliamentarianism, the growing autonomy of the state elite had become increasingly divorced from representative parliament in the management of Keynesian policies. At the same time the corporatist experiments of this elite proved ineffective. Such crises created a form of autonomy in the state apparatus which Thatcher exploited by appealing to people over the heads of the opposition in Parliament and in her own party and class (1984, p. 46). In their account of the two nations, Jessop *et al.* stress Thatcher's attempt (more successful than Social Democracy's) to impose policies that discipline rather than integrate the growing underclass, and to project a social vision of a society divided in its approbation of the productive and in its condemnation of the unproductive. The two nations analysis of Thatcherism tries 'to offer an account to complement and integrate the economic and political-ideological dimensions' (1988, p. 119). In conclusion, Jessop *et al.* attempt to codify more systematically the global framework that shaped the emergence of Thatcherism. Against homogeneous conceptions, they argue that 'Thatcherism must be seen more as an alliance of disparate forces around a self-contradictory programme' (1984, p. 38).

In developing an institutional-structural account of Thatcherism, Jessop *et al.* underline what precisely distinguishes Thatcherism from earlier ideologies. Compared with the benign paternalism of Butskellism and the modern techno-logism of MacWilsonism (both portending the 'end of ideology'), Thatcherism has exploited the ideological domain of politics, despite the disavowal of ideology proclaimed by economic liberalism (in its 'new realist' version of the 'end of ideology'). This is seen in the hiring of Saatchi and Saatchi PLC and other sources of marketing skill to promote its ideological message, in the popularising of various strands of New Right thought and tradition, and in its stress on the moral purposes of policy.

Whatever view is taken on the coherence of Thatcherism, an ideological coherence it must have, or appear to have. Hall's – and others' – work has endeavoured to account for this effect of ideology. King has commented that Hall's thesis on authoritarian populism 'is accurately grounded in the tension between liberal and conservative thought which are presented by this [Thatcher] Government' (1987, p. 134). What distinguishes different accounts is the degree of coherence they accord Thatcherism. We will see that different assessments of its strength imply different accounts of the historic role played by Thatcherism in postwar Britain.

Continuities and discontinuities: the postwar consensus

What emerges from comparing these characterisations of Thatcherism is an awareness of how different views of postwar history figure in them, in particular the view of the postwar consensus and its subsequent dissolution. Different conceptions of Thatcherism rely on different accounts of history. We will concentrate on those narratives that see the development of Thatcherism as a response to the settlement established in the immediate postwar years of the welfare state.[1] Different accounts of early postwar history will be seen to shape recent accounts of Thatcherism.

Although these accounts cannot be subsumed under a neat typology depicting the different relations between Thatcherite ideology and early postwar events, they do provide markings for different readings of the postwar terrain. Generally speaking, accounts that see the postwar period as governed by a strong consensus binding different governments of the left and right – e.g. Cutler *et al.*'s 'liberal-collectivist *a priori*' (1986) – portray a less distinct ideology embracing the politics of both the welfare state and its Thatcherite restructuring. On the other hand, portrayals of a weak Social Democratic consensus emphasise the strong ideological identity of Thatcherism (Hall 1983; Gough 1983; Gough *et al.* 1984). These differences in conception come down to an important point of debate about the supposed rupture dividing postwar history. Hall *et al.*, and several other writers, provide the dominant account that sees Thatcherism as a proto-hegemony representing a fundamental break in postwar politics, caused by the growing crisis in capitalist society as it has decisively shifted from consent to coercion. By contrast, Jessop *et al.* and others portray a process of gradual long term change driven by successive capital accumulation problems. In this scenario Thatcherism is accorded a less distinctive ideological identity, one whose main purpose is to disguise inherent economic and political contradictions than to form a new hegemony. The connection between the influence of the postwar consensus and Thatcherism leads to a final contrast between, on the one hand, a view of Thatcherism as a degeneration of the settlement (e.g. Cutler *et al.* 1986), and, on the other, as the genesis of a new hegemony (Hall 1983; Laclau and Mouffe 1985), and a new consensus in which a revisionist left is seen to converge with the right (Ginsburg 1979; Gough 1983; Brenton 1985). The notion of convergence implies an element of continuity between Labour and Tory governments since the 1970s, but of discontinuity between the 1940s Settlement and 1980s Thatcherism.

In emphasising the long wave in political and ideological formation, these accounts are liable to obscure developments between the founding moment of consensus and the final moment of dissolution. Further, they are in danger of overlooking significant differences between successive Labour and Tory governments, and even of interpreting the formative moment of the postwar settlement in terms of its present configuration. Metaphorically, this suggests that the seeds of dissolution that broke out in the 1970s and 1980s were already lying dormant in the 1940s and 1950s. Some writers, however, have wished to distance their accounts from the sense of inevitability they claim characterises this unfolding of the broad sweep of events culminating in Thatcherism – which Jessop *et al.*, with reference to Hall's work, call a 'celebration of Thatcherism'. In light of these different accounts, it is important to clarify the nature of the ideological changes affecting developments in social policy under recent Labour and Tory governments.

A further consequence of narrating so broadly the sweep of history leading to Thatcherism has been a tendency to blur the distinctive features of earlier Social Democratic governments and to disparage their welfare achievements. This is seen in the thematisation, first, of the founding moments of the postwar consensus and, second, of its subsequent turning to dissensus. The second theme is discussed in the next section. On the first theme, Hall *et al.*'s version of events sees the foundations as being laid in the 'critical interlude' immediately after the war when several formative events occurred: the restructuring of international economic and political relations and the stabilisation of welfare capitalism, all contributing to unparalleled productive growth; the stabilisation of parliamentary democracy and the interventionist state; and the freezing of East-West relations into the Cold War – three developments that contributed towards the 'reconstruction of ruling-class hegemony in Britain' (1978, p. 227). In this light the formation of the welfare state under the 1945–51 Labour Government represented less 'the high water mark of social democracy' and more 'the end of everything that had matured during the extraordinary conditions of a popular war' (1978, pp. 227–8), given the pressures of continuing working class austerity and Cold War hegemony, and the expectation of affluence and full employment. Thus the Labour government is characterised as sacrificing its welfare principles: 'ideologically and politically the "Left" was already in retreat' (1978, p. 228). The welfare state consensus was thus confined within the strictures of reorganised capitalism which were hostile to welfare principles and which brought Labour to heel.

The narrative of retreating from the principles of the welfare state is deployed further by Golding and Middleton in *Images of Welfare* (1982; see also Ginsburg 1979, p. 8 *et passim*). They narrate the abandonment of the Social Democratic principles enshrined in the Beveridge welfare state of the 1940s; a narrative that draws successive Labour and Tory governments into a protracted sequence of withdrawals, and so sees them as both bound from an early stage by the same identity as part of the 'settlement' (1982, p. 206). They recount the distance Social Democratic achievements have departed under the weight of capitalist economic change from Beveridge's aims – 'The Retreat from Utopia' (*ibid.*) – coupled with the Labour Party's growing impotence since the 1940s – 'The Message with no Messenger' (1982, p. 213). Golding and Middleton portray the capitulation and collapse of Social Democracy as paving the way for the New Right and the politics of Thatcherism. They argue that 'the so-called "welfare consensus" has never taken deep root, and was therefore relatively easy to dislodge by the return of an incisive neo-liberal rhetoric in the wake of the significant material shifts in working-class experience in the mid-1970s (supervised at crucial stages by a Labour government . . .)' (1982, p. 229).

A contrasting view of the impact of Beveridge is given by Cutler *et al.*, who stress the politically and economically positive, though ultimately flawed, advance – rather than retreat – that Beveridge's plan achieved in conjoining Social Democratic collectivism with capitalism. They argue that Beveridge's proposals for social insurance:

> transform the 'social' relations between the individual and the state . . . social
> insurance has a negative value because its characteristics limit the possibility of

dependence and a positive value because they maximise the possibility of independence. (1986, p. 13)

Beveridge's contract between state and individual placed considerable emphasis on the responsibilities of the individual citizen. Yet his collectivism saw the state's role as providing not only a national minimum insurance scheme, but a set of corollary conditions, such as full employment, national health care and rehabilitation and universal child allowance, as the prerequisites for social welfare (1986, p. 17). The balance between positive and negative effects of policy, characteristic of the postwar settlement between capital and labour, survived with varying degrees of modification up to the 1980s. Cutler *et al.* examine key policy texts that show how 'the liberal-collectivist *a priori*' embodied in the complex apparatus of the welfare state – in particular in National Insurance, pensions and employment policy – underwrote certain incentives and disciplines involving voluntary action, private investment and statutory compliance.[2] This *a priori* constituted an ideology informing the institutional structures, behavioural patterns and discourses of the welfare state, along the lines adumbrated in Chapter 2.

In conclusion, there are two narratives. The first recounts a weak consensus established in the 1940s, which already contained the seeds of anti-collectivism and which subsequently gave rise to the New Right, the antithesis of Social Democracy. The second narrates a stronger consensus – containing, to be sure, inherent tensions and unrealistic ideals – that would last through to the 1980s, until finally transformed by the Thatcher government. The former narrative portrays the emergence of Thatcherism as a strong ideology, which replaced the inherently weak Social Democratic consensus, and that represents today a new consensus formed as the Left has capitulated to the Right. However, the problem with this account of the abandonment of Social Democracy is that it conveys the false notion that its founding ideals were more akin to full-blooded and uncompromising socialism than the Fabian forebears envisaged. Jessop *et al.* comment on this 'genetic fallacy' in Hall's account, which argues that 'because Labour presided over the establishment of the welfare state and the commitment to full employment, these must have been socialist in political and ideological character' (1984, p. 39). In fairness, however, Hall *et al.* acknowledge the weakness of Labour's presidency of the postwar welfare state from the start.

As an alternative view, we attempted to show in Chapter 2 the extent to which the Social Democratic – rather than socialist – ideology embodied in the Fabian and social administration tradition of early postwar policy sought throughout the twentieth century co-operation between collectivism and market capitalism in building the welfare state. This elastic feature of Social Democratic ideology, its enduring ability for pragmatic accommodation, is a point overlooked in accounts that see the convergence between Left and Right as a development occurring much later in the 1970s and 1980s.

In this way Social Democracy used its versatile ideological and institutional resources throughout the postwar years to provide a pragmatic basis for compromise with capitalist interests within a corporatist state of government, business and unions without compromising its basic principles. For its ideological tenets already respected a degree of market freedom and private property rights within the mixed economy of welfare (especially the private and voluntary sectors of the 'extension ladder', discussed in Chapter 2), and saw welfare services as performing an enabling role on behalf of the wider economy. This degree of accommodation demonstrates the power of Social Democratic ideals to respond to political and economic contingencies within a capitalist society.

Continuities and discontinuities: restructuring the consensus

The continuities characterising the formative postwar years of the settlement underwent a transformation in subsequent decades, especially in social policy, as several accounts have shown. As we have seen, these accounts refer to political and ideological factors marking the directions followed by the Social Democratic Labour government of the 1970s and the Thatcher government of the 1980s. Thus the narrative of Labour's retreat provides a setting for accounts of a subsequent and more recent ideological convergence between Left and Right.[3] Hall again sets the scene by describing Labour's ideological slide to the right in economic and social policies:

> As Labour lost parliamentary strength, so it drifted deep into the ideological territory of the right . . . . It was Labour, not the Conservatives, which applied the surgical cut to the welfare state [in the mid-1970s]. And there was Healey's not wholly unexpected conversion to orthodox monetarism and fiscal restraint . . .
> (1983, p. 20)

In social policy, mainstream and Marxist accounts of policy developments in the 1980s stress four kinds of convergence: the Thatcher government's continued reduction in welfare spending introduced by the previous Labour administration (the 'cuts'); the convergence of attitudes towards the mixed economy of welfare, in particular the scope for greater involvement by family, voluntary and commercial sectors ('welfare pluralism'); the emergence of a shared ideology justifying cuts on the grounds of economic realism ('the new realism'); and the growing awareness amongst Left and Right that underlying different social issues lies a core problem, so far unresolved by social policy, of the 'underclass' that remains isolated from wider society. In these accounts, each instance of convergence signifies different governments' coming to terms with the wider political economy of late capitalism. Far from maintaining the settlement between labour and capital, these developments have occurred because of the weakness of labour and the restoration of capital's dominance. The welfare state is seen as an ideological smoke screen laid by the Right, and insufficiently exposed by the Left, that disguised the Right's deeply held reservations in the early postwar period about the welfare state. These reservations erupted in the 1970s into outright hostility, resulting in the Thatcherite restructuring of welfare. The postwar consensus was – to repeat a favoured metaphor – fertile ground for planting seeds, which, in a changing climate of competitiveness, individualism and materialism, grew into the residual welfare state long nurtured by the Right (e.g. Gough 1979, pp. 135–6; Hall 1983, pp. 26–9; Golding and Middleton 1982, p. 224). We will discuss each of these four lines of convergence.

A major concern of Marxist and mainstream social policy analyses of the collapse of the settlement has been the contraction in social spending – in *relative* terms – since the mid-1970s following decades of assured expansion. This trend is described in a narrative of continuity as different governments, Labour and Tory in turn, enact 'the cuts'. For example, Brenton, a mainstream analyst, comments that 'Both parties since the late Seventies endeavoured to cut expenditure on the social services, and it is arguable that the 1979 Thatcher Government only fulfilled in some of its policies the intentions already mapped out by its Labour predecessors' (1985, p. 134). From a Marxist perspective, Gough decisively points to the destructive intent of the Labour government, and recalls the reduced levels of social expenditure during the 1974–9 Labour government and the first four years of the 1979 Tory government, following the relatively high increase in spending in the first half of the 1970s: 'There can be no doubt that the welfare state was under attack and that the attack began with the Wilson–Callaghan administration in 1975' (1983, p. 152).

A second aspect of convergence between centre-Left and Right, reflecting in part the growing impact of public expenditure cuts, is the search for alternative resources to the state's that will form part of a new complex of welfare pluralism. Both Labour and Conservative governments and politicians have become interested in shifting the balance in the mixed economy away from a predominance of statutory provision towards a mix of informal, voluntary and commercial provisions. In the late 1970s, Ginsburg was commenting that 'at both national and local levels of government, it is often difficult to distinguish the *welfare* policies of the two major political parties' (1979, p. 10). A decade later, Lee and Raban refer more specifically to how 'the Conservative government is promoting, and right-wing elements in the Labour Party are accommodating themselves to, forms of welfare provided commercially, voluntarily and informally' (1988, p. 153). Brenton refers to speeches by leading Labour and Tory ministers in 1978 and 1980 (1985, pp. 136 and 160) which suggest an untapped potential of human resources available in the voluntary sector at a time when spending on statutory personal social services is contracting. This points to 'an element of convergence between Labour and Conservative parties, in their support for the voluntary sector' (1985, p. 133) – though Brenton identifies differences between Left and Right on specific issues of welfare pluralism. Several commentators see the Labour government's investigation in 1977 into social security abuse, its introduction of new anti-abuse measures and nil-cost reforms in 1978, and the party's subsequent endorsement of council house sales, as attempts to control the statutory sector and expand the commercial sector. Documenting Fabian and academic contributions to welfare pluralism, Beresford and Croft reveal 'a new more right-wing Fabianism'. This convergence is set in historical terms underscoring a Fabian revisionism 'now rooted more to the right', providing a narrative of deflection stemming from the Left's 'long-standing ambivalence and uncertainty about welfare . . . [which has] been compounded by the emergence of welfare pluralism' (1984, p. 35), and suggesting a source of weakness in Social Democratic will that led to its recent concessions to Thatcherism.[4] By the end of the 1980s, the Thatcher government began wide ranging reforms of the NHS and community care that demonstrated its commitment to welfare pluralist policies. The reforms separate the independent *provision* of services in the voluntary and private sectors from the *purchase* of these services by the statutory local authority social services and health districts (see HMSO 1988; 1989a; 1989b). The response of a future Labour government to these reforms would be a major test of how far it shared this commitment, and so of the extent to which it embraced a new welfare consensus.

Accompanying developments in welfare cuts and policies, a third line of convergence is discerned concerning the new realist ideology of welfare pluralism. Brenton underscores the growing interest in welfare pluralism expressed by both Left and Right, providing for the former a way of facilitating popular participatory democracy, and for the latter a return to private enterprise and competition. Despite these differences, both rationales are motivated by a growing concern with the economic realities of social policy. Brenton observes that in the context of economic recession these two perspectives share, 'in terms of ideology, a great deal of common ground and both feed, in effect if not by intention, the anti-welfare sentiment that is fostered by a sense of scarcity and crisis in recession' (1985, p. 176; see also pp. 212–13). Beresford and Croft focus specifically on the function that Fabian revisionism (e.g. of Hadley and Hatch 1981) has performed in welfare pluralism and observe that this 'radical' ideology 'has concealed its status quo policies . . . having a regressive influence on left welfare policies and thinking' (1984, p. 35). The continuity seen in the ideology of welfare pluralism is also evident in the new realism of the Left and Right that now informs juvenile justice, education, employment training and so forth.

Finally, leading analysts on the Social Democratic Left and the Right have come to see the problems of deprivation addressed by social policy in terms of the shared problematic of the underclass. In both the United States and United Kingdom commentators increasingly refer to a common residuum among different groups of the poor who are immune to economic prosperity and entrapped in a culture of dependency. Despite differences in interpretation and emphasis, these commentators contend that the underclass is formed by two processes: the loss of moral qualities, which results in differentiating some groups of the poor from society at large; and the emergence of structural problems in the welfare state itself. On the Right, Charles Murray (1990) defines its membership as consisting in predominately unmarried mothers, teenage criminals and workshy youth – the principal groups he identifies among the American underclass (Murray 1984). The formation of these groups divorces young fathers from their family responsibilities and contributes to the overwhelming fragmentation of lower-class community life. In turn, in recent years the British (and American) welfare state has been sending out the wrong signals, by way of a benefits and council housing system which has become more generous than a few decades ago in its treatment of young single mothers, and a penal system that has become less effective and harsh. For the Left, Frank Field acknowledges the emergence of an underclass in Britain consisting in lone mothers, the long-term unemployed and, additionally, the elderly. However, he differs from Murray in his interpretation of the structural problems of the welfare state. Its failure lies not in its enticing signals, but in its persistent, increasing and tightening grip on the poor caused by the variety of poverty traps it imposes on specific groups as a consequence of means-testing. Once subject to these conditions the moral attitudes of the poor change. Though their interpretations of causality differ, Murray and Field agree that a vicious circle of structural problems and moral decline takes hold. However, despite the area of agreement on the question of the underclass, some on the Left reject this view of poverty because of its blaming-the-victim ideology (e.g. Oppenheim 1990).

Even when some commentators see ideological differences rather than convergences between the two governments, they agree with the aforementioned commentators that the different patterns of ideology reflect the same underlying trends towards crisis in welfare policy. Gough, for example, underscores the 'distinct ideological reversal championed by the Thatcher Government' (1983, p. 152), to justify its privatisation of welfare, its widening divisions between deserving and undeserving, and its intensifying work disciplines and incentives; that is, its restructuring of the welfare state (*ibid.*, p. 153). However, in contrast with these '*qualitative*' or ideological differences, he stresses the '*quantitative*' continuities in the expenditure trends and pluralist policies pursued by Labour and Tory governments alike. 'The distinct ideological reversal' lies in the different justifications for policies deployed by the Tories, that bring to fulfilment economic and political forces already active in the mid-1970s when Labour was in office. Whether Marxist and mainstream – and rightist – analysts see ideological continuities or discontinuities between Social Democratic Left and Right, all agree that the significance of ideology lies at the deeper level of the growing crisis in the political economy of the welfare state.

The impression given by these accounts of cuts, policies and ideology is one of continuity between governments ostensibly committed to different political philosophies, an impression of an emerging identity that somehow blurs traditional political differences. Underlying these narratives is the ironic question: why are two governments that normally represent opposing political interests in reality behaving in the same way? The thematic tension and ironic commentary underlying these narratives foretell an explanation that will resolve the apparent contradiction. Irony arises because these narratives assumes two distinct planes of appearance and underlying reality; the former seen by all, and the latter only by the writer. By revealing the latter plane, the writer is able to offer an ironic commentary on the former which resolves the apparent contradiction whereby two different political programmes are converging in their welfare policies. This form of analysis is most explicit in Brenton's critique of welfare pluralists who:

> make the mistake, common among social policy writers, of focusing myopically on the formal structures of the welfare state only, ignoring the *real determinants* of poverty and inequality in the wider economic and political system. If their institutional diagnosis is faulty, it follows that their alternative institutional remedies will fall seriously short of solving the *real problem*. Given their superficiality, and given the relative naivety of welfare pluralists in failing to perceive both their own origins and their popularity as stemming not merely from 'the crisis of the welfare state' but also from the ideological swing towards the Right, their arguments cannot be viewed as separate and independent from those put forward by the New Right. (1985, p. 214, emphasis added)

What is problematic about these narratives of convergence is that they erase important differences between Labour and Conservative governments over the past two decades, let alone during the earlier postwar years. One consequence is that this erasure contradicts the central proposition developed by Hall and others of Social Democracy and Thatcherism as two distinct ideologies that represent the polarities of a fundamental hegemonic shift occurring during the second half of the century. For the convergence thesis argues that by the 1970s these two ideologies were moving closer together and were no longer distinct. However, it can be argued that it is as important to keep in sight the differences that distinguish the Social Democratic Labour governments of the 1970s from their successor Tory governments as it is in the long run Thatcherite Toryism from its Social Democratic predecessor.

In contrast to Hall and others, Jessop *et al.* have criticised the idea that Thatcherism represents an historical rupture. Jessop *et al.* insist on qualifying 'any argument that there has been a radical break between a social democratic era and the present Thatcherite ascendancy' because of significant areas of continuity in policy and because 'crucial ruptures . . . were actually initiated during the so-called Social Democratic consensus: abandonment of full employment, public expenditure cuts and privileging the fight against inflation' (1984, p. 40). However, there is a problem here in that the continuities and anticipations implied by Jessop *et al.* blur the specificity they argue distinguishes the New Right programme of the 1980s. Providing a more forthright denial of both this specificity and the crisis tendencies underlying recent social policies, Taylor-Gooby asserts that 'In the major areas of state policy, it is the continuities in policy rather than the departures of new administrations that provide dominant themes' (1985, p. 61). Social policies of Labour and Conservative governments betray more continuity than crisis narratives suggest. In this light, the turning-point in expenditure trends in the mid-1970s constitutes no more than 'a fresh stabilisation of expenditure' (*ibid.*), stemming increases rather than imposing cuts. This long-term narrative provides a more staid appraisal of the development of the postwar welfare state that renders ideological shifts of less importance, and substantially modifies the crisis characterisations of Marxist writers. However, the impression that the long line of postwar policy reforms are all of a piece, as one government succeeds another, is a conclusion rejected in both Hall's and Jessop's accounts.

A further continuous reading of postwar history is given by Cutler *et al.*, who see the long-term continuity in state policy as confirmation of a strongly wrought ideology around the 'liberal collectivist *a priori*' (codified in the writings of Keynes and Beveridge) which broadly embraces the welfare state between the 1940s and 1980s. This *a priori* represents the strongest and most comprehensive version of the ideological hegemony of Social Democratic welfare based on a utopian belief in the best of both capitalist and collectivist worlds. For Cutler *et al.*, policy in the 1980s is still seen as informed by the liberal collectivist problematic. As an example, Sir Norman Fowler's Green Paper proposals, *Reform of Social Security* (HMSO 1985), for abolishing the state earnings-related pension scheme, are 'cast entirely in a liberal collectivist form which would have been familiar to Beveridge' (1986, p. 150). On the face of it this would seem an eccentric claim given the opposition the Green Paper has aroused 'in retreating ever further from Beveridge's aim of a benefits system "for all citizens without distinction of rich and poor" '(Bennett 1987, p. 128).

We can examine Cutler *et al.*'s claim by studying the text of the Green Paper. Fowler's rhetoric clearly, and perhaps deliberately, echoes Beveridge. The repeated notion of 'a partnership between the individual and the state' parallels Beveridge's 'co-operation between the State and individual'. It is embodied in arrangements for a state national minimum with private insurance enhancements on top, so that social security 'should respect the ability of the individual to make his own choices and to take responsibility for his own life. But at the same time it must recognise the responsibility of government to establish an underlying basis of provision on which we as individuals can build and on which we can rely at times of need' (HMSO 1985, p. 1; cf. Beveridge 1942, p. 12 *et passim*). The message is that social security should be put back on the sound basis Beveridge had laid forty years earlier, but which subsequently has been abandoned because, as the Green Paper declares at the beginning, 'To be blunt the British social security system has lost its way' (HMSO 1985, p. 1). Social security thus

> grew out of Beveridge's clear concepts but has developed into a leviathan almost with a life of its own. The proposals in this Green Paper will bring the social security system firmly back under control. Social security will be based on twin pillars of provision – individual and state – with stronger emphasis on individual provision than hitherto. (HMSO 1985, p. 45)

Thus, while the ideology of combining in one structure state minimum and private enhancement was, in Cutler *et al.*'s verdict, 'classic, the novelty was that the "reform" proposed in the Green Paper offered very little' to, for example, the next generation of pensioners. In their second term in office, more than the first (and the third), the Thatcher government chose for ideological reasons to adopt a conciliatory stance in their handling of several areas of postwar policy.[5]

However, following the line of continuity that inscribes welfare state capitalism, Cutler *et al.* see liberal collectivism as now entering its degenerate stage and playing 'its last and least heroic role' in supporting the case for welfare-diminishing cuts (1986, p. 150). In this respect they acknowledge something substantially different between the first and last moments of liberal collectivism: 'Just as Keynes could hardly be enrolled as a dogmatic free trader of the modern type, so Beveridge can hardly be enlisted as the prototype of this kind of liberal capitalism'; thus 'in the case of liberal capitalist ideology, the first time round it was a progressive justification and the second time a reactionary excuse' (1986, p. 152). However, this recognition of differences between the beginning and end of the settlement leaves Cutler *et al.*, given their use of the all-embracing tendency of 'liberal collectivism', without a distinctive characterisation of the ideology – Thatcherism or whatever – marking its ending and auguring a new era, a characterisation of the kind offered by Hall and others. For, recounting the opening remarks to this chapter – Would there have been Thatcherism without Mrs Thatcher? – even if we cannot agree the name to give Thatcherism, we must at least grant it an identity.

One of the concerns of the last two chapters has been to stress the pragmatic and ideological features that characterise Labour and Conservative politics. On the one hand, the 1974–9 Labour Government was marked by its essentially pragmatic – though ham-fisted – use of economic and social policies, which reluctantly and selectively departed from Keynesian and Beveridgean dogma *in order* to broaden the repertoire of intervention while preserving the material and ideological bases of the Social Democratic welfare state. King notes the continuing Keynesian commitment to maintain full employment and implement reflationary policies that went alongside a more monetarist control of public expenditure (King 1987, p. 69). On the other hand, Thatcherism represents a wholehearted ideological commitment to new policy devices that narrow the range of strategies and are committed to achieving a new economic and ideological order. In response to these contrasts, one line of argument states that the Labour Party's embrace of new realism in its policies – supposedly to distance itself from more ideological leanings on its left – demonstrates the degree of ideological shift towards the new realism of Thatcherism. However, another line of argument can be made – though empirical support for it would have to await a future Labour government – that what matters is the use to which Labour's new realism is put in developing policies whose objectives remain quite distinct from those of the Right. The Fabian approach to the welfare pluralism discussed in Chapter 2 suggests that Social Democratic ideology is still a powerful enough strand by which to distinguish Labour Party welfare policy from that of Thatcherism (see Clarke *et al.* 1987, p. 130). There remains an essential difference between the approaches to welfare – to the welfare pluralism – of Right and Left.

Notes

1. For a discussion of accounts of the early formation of the postwar settlement in the welfare state, see Deacon (1984).
2. For a definition of the term 'liberal-collectivism', which comes close to my account of Social Democracy, see Williams and Williams (1987, ch. 1).
3. See Taylor-Gooby's adumbration of accounts describing continuities in different areas of policy during the 1970s (1981, pp. 19–20).
4. It is interesting to surmise what this critique of Fabian welfare pluralism would make of the analysis in *Marxism Today*, the theoretical journal of the former Communist Party of Great Britain, of post-Fordism applied to industrial organisation, state governance and welfare services, in which for the latter welfare pluralist policies are advocated (see Hall and Jacques 1989; e.g. *Marxism Today*, October 1988; May 1991).
5. This was seen in, e.g., Mrs Thatcher's assurance in 1983 and again in 1985 that 'the NHS is safe only with us' (*The Times*, 15 October 1983; 13 October 1985), and in her stress on the continuity between the 1944 Employment White Paper (HMSO 1944) and the policy of her own government (*The Times*, 13 October 1985).

PART 2

Marxist theories of ideology and the welfare state

Unlike Fabian and New Right approaches, the Marxist tradition offers a developed theory of ideology, indeed several theoretical perspectives, as the three chapters in Part II and the first in Part III indicate. This theory derives from the scope of Marxism, its claim to understand the breadth of human production – cultural and political as well as economic – and the diversity of human activity. Within this compass, state, welfare, ideology and need are set in the context of production and explained in terms of the struggles shaping social and economic life. For Marxism, the dynamics of change arise as the forces of production come into conflict with existing social relations of production, and so give rise to new forms of social and economic organisation. The dynamics of production provide the focus for understanding the development of human history, and the varieties of social and economic organisation or social formation, that have evolved. In particular, it provides a basis for understanding twentieth-century capitalist societies and their systems of welfare capitalism. This said, any account of Marxism must recognise the emergence of critical voices among latter-day Marxists, who believe that recent social, political and economic developments have, if not repudiated all Marxist tenets, cast grave doubts on their very scope and comprehensibility.

The starting point for Marxist studies of modern capitalist society and ideology is Marx's focus on the dynamics of the mode of production arising from the conjunction of specific forces and relations of production. By 'forces of production', Marx is referring to the organisation of the resources – labour, raw material, machinery, land – that form the technology or means of production, by which workers can harness raw material to produce finished products for capitalist markets. By 'relations of production', he means the relations formed between two classes, the owners of the means of production who extract surplus value and profit, and the working classes whose labour power is applied to the means of production, but who are paid no more than for the bare necessities. The complex formed from the forces and relations of production, the specific forms they take in capitalist society, is the mode of production. For Marx the mode of production provides the characteristic form of society, its social formation.[1] Ideology is one of the main components of the social formation, along with the economy, polity and law.

Because of the significance of the forces of production, and the key role of labour therein, Marx is drawn to elucidate a theory of social need that acknowledges the historical processes shaping human labour. It is this historicity that marks a break in modern thought about social need. For the historicity of need requires an understanding on two counts: first, of the infrastructural conditions satisfying need and sustaining labour's capacity to produce; and, secondly, of the ideological constructions of need, including the shared perceptions and social aspirations influenced by prevailing conventions. Marx identifies these concerns in the following way:

> [the individual's] means of subsistence must therefore be sufficient to maintain him in his normal state as a working individual. His natural needs, such as food, clothing, fuel and housing vary according to the climatic and other physical peculiarities of his country. On the other hand, the number and extent of his so-called necessary requirements, as also the manner in which they are satisfied, are themselves products of history, and depend therefore to a great extent on the level of civilisation attained by a country; in particular they depend on the conditions in which, and consequently on the habits and expectations with which, the class of free workers has been formed. (Marx 1976, p. 275)

Thus, Marxism has generally sought to understand the nature of need as it is constituted at a particular historical moment in the development of economic, social and ideological forces; Marx's 'civilisation of a country' above, and 'the historical and moral element' (*ibid.*) that determines labour power.

This notion of need is substantially different from social administration's. Against the idea of a universal and minimum basic need that defines the requirements of all persons – implicit in the notion of the national minimum – Marx proposes an historically relative definition denoting what is needed by people and capable of being satisfied by productive forces within society at a specific time. However, Marx also introduces a critical concept of need. Agnes Heller has commented that Marx's notion of need is not only historically relative but universal in a critical and prefigurative sense. For needs that are in fact determined by a particular mode of economic exploitation could be radically different, understood without ideological distortion, and met universally under a mode of production where there was no exploitation – Marx's 'society of associated producers'. She suggests that 'In order to be able to analyse the economic categories of capitalism as categories of alienated needs . . . it is necessary to create the positive category of a "system of non-alienated needs"' (Heller 1976, p. 27). Marx's idea of the historicity of need sought to demonstrate critically the contradictory forces shaping society and producing fundamentally unjust forms of economic exploitation and social deprivation, which could be transformed through the creation of socialist society. The critical purpose of Marx's notion of need was more developed than social administration's, whose purpose was more practical than critical in promulgating policies and interventions that would ameliorate the deprivations its investigations uncovered. It is precisely because Marxism offers a critical theory of historically defined need, that the following chapters dealing with Marxist approaches to welfare ideology will discuss need more explicitly than the previous chapters.

Part II examines two main streams of Marxist theory: Political Economy of Welfare and Critical Theory. A third stream, Structural Marxism, is the subject of the first chapter of Part III on discourse theory and welfare ideology. In each stream, two aspects of needs shaped by their historicity are stressed. First, need is studied in the context of the development of state and civil society. Secondly, needs are understood as ideologically constituted, in that need functions as one of the principal vehicles for transmitting ideology and shaping individual values in advanced capitalist society. In such a society the relationship between state and civil society – where the boundaries are drawn and on what terms – is governed by the economy's needs for productive human labour, and by the social needs of individuals, families and communities. Economic and social needs come into conflict with each other and give rise to contradictions that are of central importance in the different streams of Marxism in understanding the crisis tendencies affecting capitalism. Each type of need cannot be met entirely by either the industrial economy or the family/community and must rely on the services of a third component, the state. The economy relies on the state to provide the reproduction of the labour power of workers who are born, grow up and mature into adults in civil society; and civil society relies on the state to supply a range of basic and non-basic needs it cannot meet itself. In each case, the state must ensure that economic and social needs are met.

The ideological construction of need – the second aspect of Marxist studies of need – arises in the context of tensions between the needs of capital and the needs of people as the state deploys ideology in managing these tensions. The economy's needs demand that the state secure an adequate supply of labour with the requisite levels of knowledge and skill. Yet the state must also secure a variety of welfare services to meet the social needs of the members of society when its informal and market provisions are insufficient. Drawing on a finite stock of resources, the state must balance the demands of the economy and those of the people. Part of the strategy for maintaining equilibrium will involve not only responding to competing needs, but also influencing the formation of needs and containing their expression. This involves the ideological construction of economic and social needs in accordance with the needs of industrial capitalism. For example, in the economy, state education and training, in principle, can anticipate industry's needs for types of labour that are equipped with specific kinds of knowledge and skill such as information technology. 'The needs of industry' are presented in a specific ideological light. For instance, today's needs for information technology, information storage, retrieval and packaging determine the shape and content of the entire productive process including research and development, product design, marketing and sales. Likewise, in the social sphere, the state's concern for the welfare of society can lead to codifying needs in a more systematic way, so that each need is constructed in accordance with the standard administrative categories that welfare provisions are designed to meet. The social security reforms implemented in 1988 have furthered a process begun in the late 1970s in categorising social need, with more targeting and selectivity to designate 'premium' groups, in an attempt to remove the apparent anomalies and injustices in the discretionary provision of income maintenance and to contain rising costs (see Deacon and Bradshaw 1983). The implementation of computerisation into social security administration facilitates this trend (e.g. see HMSO 1985, p. 43).

In broader terms, James O'Connor has referred to an ideology of 'national individualism' in the United States that redefines social needs in accordance with the individualistic assumptions of the labour market. As a result, an ideological compromise is reached between working-class and capitalist notions of justice, whereby 'the modern liberal theory of citizenship' provides an individualistic slant to social needs, service delivery and transfer payments. He suggests that 'Social policy was thus oriented to . . . integrating individuals not into corporatist groups (. . . which many European countries have attempted to apply), but rather into social functions defined in individualistic and nationalistic ways' (O'Connor 1984, p. 217). O'Connor lists such processes as the professional ascription of individual pathologies to social ills, the designing of physical and social habitats along privatised lines in housing estates, urban renewal, recreation programmes and individualised social-service administration and delivery. Consequently, US citizens came to construe 'their needs as social entitlements within the problematic of the nation's destiny as the "world's first democracy"' (*ibid.*).

These developments in the ideological construction of need arise from the impact of wider structural changes on public policy. In the late 1970s and early 1980s, economic recession and the shift towards a right-wing ideology altered the balance between economy and civil society. The Conservative government in the 1980s endeavoured to strengthen the linkage between state and industry in the provision of labour, by providing, for example, personnel training programmes, new City Technology Colleges financed by industry and run by central rather than local government, and a national curriculum to guarantee basic levels of numeracy, reading and writing for school-leavers (see Glennerster 1987). At the same time, the government has sought to reduce its responsibilities for civil society by reformulating needs and duties as the private provenance of the family and community, expecting civil society to provide more provision from its own informal, voluntary and private welfare resources – an expectation that a long line of official reports in the 1980s has shown, culminating in the White Paper, *Caring for People* (HMSO 1989b).

Although Marxist accounts of welfare share these perspectives on the state's management of ideology, crisis and the state–civil society nexus, they none the less differ in other respects in their accounts of need, ideology and advanced capitalist welfare state. These differences produce various interpretations and critiques and revise understandings of modern capitalist society and its imminent crises. Several issues, therefore, are examined in the next three chapters: for example, the validity for welfare studies of the distinctions between basic and non-basic needs, use-, exchange- and surplus-value, and civil society and the state. In Marxism, one way of seeing the distinction between basic and non-basic needs is to describe the latter as ideologically rather than materially produced, a view seen unproblematically in Political Economy, but problematically by Habermas and Offe within Critical Theory. How ideology is seen in this and other cases depends on the view of the relationship between reality and ideology held by each writer.

Recently, and somewhat more vexing for orthodox Marxists, a post-Marxist perspective has emerged that must be considered in the context of ideology and the welfare state. This perspective argues that history has reached a stage of postmodernity when knowledge is no longer based on the sure foundations of reasoning that supported modern capitalist society (see Lyotard 1984). Rather, knowledge must content itself with more limited foundations and pragmatic assumptions, more localised and short-lived in their application. This lack of certainty affects political institutions and state legitimacy, eroding mass support and undermining prevailing rationales for government policy and provision (see Hall and Jacques 1989). Postmodernity is characterised by a plurality of rationalities that provide little basis for secure political and moral judgement and firm governance. By contrast, Marxist *orthodoxy* is based on a belief in the secure, often scientific, foundations of critical social analysis. Its achievements have been threefold: to reveal the illusory nature of the value categories of classical political economy and modern economics; to provide a theory of 'exchange value' generated within and between different value forms of modern capitalism (money, labour, wage, commodity, etc.); and to identify the expropriation of use values in a society subject to ideological distortion. Such critical analyses illuminate the way to human emancipation and overcome the power of ideology.

However, recent writers have suggested that advanced capitalism operates in a less organised way, less subject to dominant orders of reason and ideology, and governed by the different logic (or logics) of 'disorganised capitalism' (Lash and Urry 1987). Disorganised capitalism is one facet of a large body of literature emerging in the 1980s on the restructuring of production in advanced capitalism and commonly referred to by the figure of post-Fordism. This figure captures the important shift from Fordist production, from mass production technology, large-scale industrial organisation, state bureaucracy, mass communication, standardised needs, the centralised welfare state and Keynesian demand management, developments which since the mid-century have taken place in the industrial world. Today post-Fordist production, especially in the context of economic crises, represents an important mode of restructuring, characterised by an increasingly flexible use of plant, time and labour ('flexible specialisation'), a greater diversity of products, receptivity to individual needs and preferences ('customisation') and decentralised organisation. For example, accounts of post-Fordist production refer to the flexibility of reprogrammable machine tools enabling firms to switch with ease from one production run to another in response to changing consumer tastes, and to new information technology that computerises stock control and greatly speeds up retailing through-put (see R. Murray 1989; Hoggett 1990). However, although these technological advances promote decentralised forms of organisation and management, they also enable greater degrees of strategic control by the centre, that is the contradictory processes of 'centralisation of command and decentralisation of production'.

There are clearly dangers in stereotyping the opposing moments of Fordism and post-Fordism. However, there are advantages in following through the logic of each form of economic structure to its associated forms of political and social structure. For example, by comparing the post-Fordist form with the predominantly Fordist forms of welfare which have become an encumbrance in the context of modern social and political structures, it is possible to highlight the nature of some of the problems facing welfare today, namely the bureaucracy, standardised needs and lack of choice facing the welfare client. In this respect Hadley and Hatch's (1981) work on welfare pluralism can be seen as one of the earlier post-Fordist analyses of the welfare state. The present restructuring of welfare along the lines of devolved budgeting and decision-making, competitive tendering to independent providers, more rigorous cost-limits, and the imposition by central government of a business culture of efficiency and contract-compliance can be seen as a New Right version of post-Fordist strategy. However, it is questionable whether these strategies are indicative of necessary treatments, or symptoms of the ills besetting the welfare state. For the broad changes restructuring production during successive periods of recession are having far-reaching effects on the divisions within labour, creating on the one hand a core of highly paid and skilled workers and on the other a periphery of poorer, deskilled and unemployed workers, and by extension a growing underclass dependent on welfare. The increased demands for welfare provisions have themselves given rise to a greater centralised control of expenditure and a growing concern about the impoverishment of service quality. The restructured welfare state of the late 1980s has not only been on balance unsuccessful in narrowing these divisions, its policies of 'targeting' and residualisation – as suggested in the following chapter – have further exacerbated them.

Moreover, the nature of post-Fordism as a new hegemony raises the spectre of a dominant ideology of economic prosperity, such as Thatcherism portrayed in the 1980s, which obscures widespread deprivation among social minorities. If the postmodern culture that accords with post-Fordism is characterised by a loss of universal values, then this ideological change can be sustained with little resistance. However, this vision assumes that the social costs of restructuring can be confined to particular social classes and areas. In fact this proposition is refuted by the impact of the recession since 1989 hitting financial, legal and service sectors in London and the South-East as well as the more traditional manufacturing sectors of the North.

These developments associated with restructuring raise questions about the nature of welfare and ideology within disorganised capitalism, which are addressed in the work of Offe within Critical Theory and Laclau and Mouffe (1985) within Structural Marxism and discussed in Chapters 7 and 8 respectively. In addition, new insights into the logic of advanced capitalism shed light on the changing relationship between state and civil society (Keane 1988).

Note

1. Though there is considerable dispute about the nature of the relationship between the forces and relations of production, see e.g. Hindess (1987, p. 102) and, from a Marxist economics perspective, Catephores (1989, ch. 1). For a discussion of Marxist theories of welfare see Mishra (1981).

5

Ideology, political economy and the welfare state

Marxist Political Economy sees productive activity as the engine of social life, determining all forms of social relations and practices. In the course of history men and women have applied their strength and technological ingenuity to the forces of nature in order to harness its resources to meet basic needs and secure human survival. The very exigency of survival connotes the primary importance attached to the material aspect of human life. In this sense, all forms of social and political life are determined by economic activity. It is this stress on the formative role of the economic – present in the writings of O'Connor, Gough, Ginsburg and others – in explaining the relations formed between economic, social and political processes that distinguishes Political Economy from other Marxist approaches concerned more with culture or ideology. According to this perspective, both welfare services and ideology, for example, reflect the dominant mode of production in modern capitalism. The needs of the capitalist economy for a trained and disciplined workforce – for the reproduction of labour power – give rise to a consciousness in society that stresses work and enterprise and instils conformist attitudes and appropriate technological skills. The welfare state complements and reinforces these beliefs in a multitude of ways. It provides services that socialise and educate children in correct attitudes, that support families in socialising their children, provide health and social security services to cure or prevent disease, and that relieve or avert deprivation caused by disruption of work through unemployment, sickness, childbirth and retirement. Welfare is an important vehicle for disseminating ideology as the forms of consciousness and behaviour appropriate to capitalism.

This perspective, then, in the words of Gough 'treats the welfare state as a constituent feature of modern capitalist societies' (1979, p. 2), that is, as a necessary part of the social formation that provides material services involving care and control, and fulfils ideological functions for the economy. The capitalist mode of production – the exploitation of the means of production, including labour, for profit – determines relations between the social classes of labour and capital, the workers and the owners of production. This exploitative relationship is in turn reflected in welfare policies that support *and* discipline the unemployed and other casualties of capitalism and discipline those still in work. Gough describes the formative role of capitalism whereby 'The mode of production – the way one class extracts surplus labour from another – ultimately determines the nature of the entire social structure' (1979, p. 19).

However, the determining role of the economy in the analysis of the Political Economy of Welfare is not conceived in simplistic monocausal terms. Welfare applies disciplinary practices to workers and non-workers. Yet it also provides welfare services, organised on a more altruistic basis, in the form of provisions for the non-working as well as the working population. Although these can be justified as fulfilling capital's needs, welfare provides obvious benefits to its recipients as well; indeed benefits that the labour movement has struggled hard and sacrificed much to gain. This poses a contradiction at the heart of the capitalist welfare state: that the needs of capital, when disturbed by changes in the balance of class forces, causes capital to underwrite welfare at a price that eventually threatens to undermine capitalism. Labour extracts from welfare considerable benefits over and above what individual workers could possibly afford themselves. Ultimately, under capitalism any balance between the benefits to capital and labour breaks down. This tendency forms what is referred to as the 'contradictory' or 'dual character' of the welfare state (Gough 1979, p. 175; Ginsburg 1979, p. 19). This contradiction is glossed over by social administration writers such as Marshall, in a 'grand narrative' about the evolution of the capitalist welfare state, which confers universal rights of citizenship through the growth of social services. Such an account, with its emphasis on rights and needs, provides a definition of the purpose of welfare policy that Marxism sees as an ideological myth; one that is exploded by the exploitative nature of capitalist society underpinning the welfare state.

For Marxism, welfare provision is seen mainly as a means to achieve the further accumulation of capital. The purpose of capitalist production is to further accumulation, by ploughing back into production the surplus value accrued over the combined value of various components: labour (e.g. wages), other forms of capital (e.g. fuel and machinery), and raw material. The value produced surplus of these costs constitutes profit. This is surplus value above the cost of reproducing not just workers, but workers with the capacity to work, that is, reproducing labour *power*. The production of surplus value signifies in large part the exploitation of human labour – of a different order from the exploitation of inert capital – stemming from the specifically social nature of capitalist production. For economic production is essentially a social enterprise that transforms inert raw materials into products for human consumption, and involves individuals in different social relations; relations of collaboration between members of the same social class, and relations of exploitation, of the working class by the class owning the means of production. Seeking merely to satisfy the working class's basic needs for biological survival and efficient functioning, to maintain labour's productivity for capital, the capitalist system proves insensitive to the complex human needs of working people. This leaves a large gap in meeting labour's needs that must be filled by the state to secure the reproduction of a healthy and educated workforce.

We can see further the contradictory nature of capitalist production if we examine the process of producing value and in particular the transformation of use value into exchange value.[1] This is a process which creates certain values and needs while obscuring others, such as the needs for human welfare, a process that is subject to historical change. In principle, goods are produced because they have use – as tools, food, pleasure, etc. – and give value to those who consume them, i.e. their use value. However, the expansionary thrust of capitalist accumulation requires an extensive network of markets for exchanging a multitude of goods, and an independent medium of exchange in the form of money to facilitate this process. Markets work on the principle of exchange; goods are bought and sold for their exchange- value, a value different from their use- value, and not directly related to the consumer's need for them. Again, capitalism proves insensitive to human needs, preferring to shape needs to the prerequisites of commodity production rather than consumers, by a process of commodifying needs into marketable goods sold at their exchange value. We will see later that the commodification of needs has implications for the operation of ideology in capitalist society, as understood by writers in both Political Economy and Critical Theory.

Capitalist production is driven by an internal dynamic to further accumulation in competitive markets that have a tendency to pursue individual rather than social ends, and to reduce all human and non-human resources to the common denominator of exchange- value. The emergence of the state from the eighteenth century onwards can be seen as a response by the ruling class to the essential anarchy and asocial character of markets, and as an attempt to impose a degree of order on capitalist production. Government began to play a key role in organising the national market, and promoting the nation's interests within an increasingly international, competitive market. In addition, government must pursue a more far-sighted design, which takes responsibility for the needs of capital for requisite quantities of labour, and the needs of labour, employed and unemployed, for a modicum of welfare. In this respect Gough defines the welfare state as 'the use of state power to modify the reproduction of labour power and to maintain the non-working population in capitalist societies' (1979, pp. 44–5).[2] This represents the dual or contradictory rationale of the capitalist state – capital's need to accumulate further capital and the state's need for legitimation and popular support – which points to the inescapable dilemma that the state faces in attempting to manage the tensions between capital and labour (O'Connor 1973, ch. 1). On the one hand, the state supports capital accumulation, and, on the other, it seeks to provide for the needs of its citizens. In appearing to balance these conflicting class interests, the state takes on an *ideological* semblance of class neutrality, committed to the interests of all rather than those of a single class. In the light of this universalism, the welfare state appears concerned to meet the social needs of all in progressively better ways. However, inevitably the law of capital accumulation tilts the state's impartiality in the direction of the interests of capital. In this sense, the contradictory character of the welfare state is made plain.

O'Connor has applied this account of crisis to the fiscal problems experienced by United States city administrations since the 1960s and 1970s (1973). In major cities 'fiscal crisis' and even bankruptcy loomed large as administrations faced the growing need to support public services from a limited tax base. City Hall feared that high taxation would undermine electoral support and encourage private corporations to desert to new locations where the tax base was lower and labour cheaper. Christine Cousins provides an empirical study of the fiscal crisis in the British welfare state (1987, pp. 127–30).

Political Economy of Welfare sees the ideological tasks of the state in the way it manages the deployment and reproduction of labour and the construction of need. For example, in ensuring a ready supply of labour for capital, the welfare state manages the 'reserve army' of labour – e.g. immigrants, married women and the low paid – by sustaining its barest needs when the economy contracts and is surplus to requirements, and by encouraging it into the labour market when the economy expands. The reserve army is also a source of cheap alternative labour when employers wish to resist wage demands (Gough 1979, pp. 25–6; Ginsburg 1979, p. 24). Throughout the cycles of economic activity, the welfare state is seen to deploy social security and social work personnel in policing and disciplining the reserve army.

The ideological function of welfare is seen in several examples of the way welfare manages the construction of need and the reserve army, by drawing new groups under the umbrella of dependency and by withdrawing cover from existing groups. As an example of the former, the 'school-leaver' was traditionally a transitional category between states of dependency and independence. Today the category has come to connote a first staging-post in the dependency career of the chronically unemployed as they transfer from school to unemployment via youth training schemes. This construction of dependency is supported by several policy changes affecting youth training and social security. Principle among these are the introduction of new regulations requiring young adults under twenty-six to periodically change residence as a condition for receiving board and lodging payments; and the introduction in 1988 of Income Support (the new social assistance provision in Britain replacing Supplementary Benefit) which among other things extends the lower rate of benefit for young adults from its previous limit of eighteen to under twenty-five, extending the marginal status of the young and enforcing their dependency on parents, who reacquire the Poor Law status of 'liable relative' (see Chapman and Cook 1988; Finch 1989). Similarly, 'students' represent a career variation for school-leavers who, though better qualified than the above, might previously have elected to enter the labour market directly, but now defer entrance and the possibility of unemployment in favour of prolonging study; a study or training for jobs whose status under the impact of credentialism now requires higher qualifications, contributing to an increase in graduate unemployment. As an example of movement *out* of dependency, traditionally dependent groups, such as lone mothers, increasingly are being encouraged to leave welfare dependency and enter the labour market, sometimes as cheaper and more flexible workers to replace older redundant workers. The proposals in the 1990 White Paper, *Children Come First*, are designed to reduce the dependency of lone mothers on Income Support by instituting new arrangements to enforce child maintenance payments by fathers (*Guardian* 30 October 1990).

Walker (1982) has mapped the changing territory of dependency in his account of the social construction of need, for example, as growing numbers of the elderly become increasingly dependent under postwar government policies. When the economy contracts or is restructured along more capitalistic lines, relatively expensive labour is shed by providing older, long-serving and postretirement workers with pre-retirement inducements, redundancy payments and pensions – all to some degree underwritten by the state – as occurred increasingly during the 1960s and 1970s. More recently, the government has attempted to offload its 'burden' of responsibility for the retired elderly. In 1985, it sought initially to scrap the state earnings related pension scheme (SERPS). Subsequently, after public pressure, the government decided to retain SERPS, but at a reduced value which would substantially reduce its cost in the next century (see Cutler *et al.* 1986; HMSO 1985).

The theory of crisis

O'Connor and Gough's work on the fiscal crises of modern capitalism has provoked an important reappraisal of the welfare state in capitalist society, one that in a number of respects overturns Social Democracy's appraisal. Whereas Marshall in the late 1940s saw the postwar future optimistically, based on a *rapprochement* between relations of equality founded on citizenship rights and relations of inequality derived from the differential rewards of capitalist production – citizenship as 'the architect of legitimate inequality' – today Political Economy sees a fundamental incompatibility between the two relations. However, in one important respect a continuity between some Social Democratic writers, notably Marshall and Titmuss, and the Political Economy of Welfare persists.[3] This lies in the concerns they both share about the social relations formed in welfare state capitalism. In raising the possibility of a future *rapprochement* under welfare capitalism, Marshall explicitly prefigured the possibility of legitimation problems if the state were unable to redeem its welfare promises (e.g. 1963, p. 127); though he expressed an overriding confidence in the long-term prospects of the welfare state. True to the social administration tradition, Marshall's analysis rests on an idealistic optimism in the evolution of the cultural norms of the welfare state – expressed by writers like Robson by the idea of 'welfare society'. It remained for Marxist Political Economy to demonstrate the underlying economic tensions that were to undermine an optimistic faith in the fulfilment of state welfare's civilising mission. In Chapter 6 on Marxist Critical Theory, this optimism, dismissed as ideological by Political Economy, is re-examined as a way of resurrecting the possibility offered by the welfare state of mobilising a universal interest in social solidarity, so reviving the vision of Fabianism discarded by Marxist Political Economy.

The Political Economy of Welfare has made an important contribution to understanding some of the political consequences of the contradictions of the welfare state; especially the state's desire to socialise some of the costs and benefits of accumulation, while preserving surplus value for private accumulation. An inherent part of the accumulation process is the tendency for the costs of accumulation to rise, especially investment in flexible hi-tech capital and in an educated, fit and secure workforce. Some of these costs can be met only by the state. In the long run, the state intervenes to control these costs by regularising the uncertainties of competitive markets. This in turn leads to increasingly monopolistic forms of production in the private sector and corporate forms of provision in the public sector, both of which develop their own means for evading state control. At the core of these critical tendencies is a problem that Marx stressed and O'Connor more recently underscored, stemming from 'the fact that production is social whereas the means of production are owned privately' (1973, p. 40). The accumulation crisis arises from the problematic relations formed between the economic means of production and the social relations of production, a conflict between the accumulation and legitimation functions of the state. This entails a fundamental conflict between the state's function in maintaining or creating the conditions for profitable capital accumulation, and the more universal function in maintaining or creating the conditions for social harmony (O'Connor 1973, p. 6). With the growth of large private monopoly and public service sectors, increasingly severe social and fiscal crises are generated.

These crises have provoked various economic and political responses on behalf of the welfare state. Gough has explored the economic strategies of the 1970s for managing the welfare state (1979, p. 132). By the 1980s, in the wake of the widening gap between expenditure and revenue, the Thatcher government responded by restructuring welfare to control the level of expenditure. However, the inexorable tendency to crisis has persisted. For the reduction in welfare services interferes with the reproduction of labour power and the maintenance of social integration, and threatens the fabric of social relations under capitalism. This in turn places new demands on the state for social control measures, for law and order and selective social security benefits, which ensnare the poor in the poverty trap and weaken incentives to work. The political economy approach underlines a crisis over needs. In Gough's words: 'In a period of prolonged recession . . . the "need" to restore profitability directly conflicts with the quite different "need" to improve living standards and levels of social consumption' (1979, p. 151; see also Ginsburg 1979, p. 7).

Gough portrays two options for managing relations between the state and private sectors and their different needs – corporatism and the New Right. Each option highlights different ideological strategies. During the 1970s, corporatism involved a stronger tripartite unity between state, industry and the trade unions – then three increasingly monopolistic sectors – to control wage and price levels, supervise investment and employment policy, and underwrite welfare provisions. This strategy raised the ideological spectacle of a united society engaged in furthering postwar welfare aims, including the promotion of social justice, while at the same time holding down wage demands (e.g. the 1970s' 'social contract') and extending work discipline, both with union support. The imagery of consensus and fairness associated with these developments provided ample justification for such controls and sacrifice. For Gough, corporate welfarism involves financing welfare expenditure by containing total labour costs (the value of labour power) rather than by taxing profits (surplus-value) (1979, p. 149). With the coming to power of a right-wing Conservative government in 1979, this strategy was replaced by Thatcherism. By contrast, during the recession of the 1970s and 1980s Sweden stood as an example of continuity in corporatism, seeking to 'consolidate' rather than to dismantle its welfare state (Olsonn 1987).

The alternative strategy of the New Right endeavours to restructure the welfare state, by making its social services more efficient, by privatising public services, such as council housing, health and personal social services, and by gearing services like social security and education to the needs of labour reproduction (Gough *et al.* 1984, pp. 44–75). In the face of increasing needs resulting from demographic and economic change and cuts in government funding, some local authorities are extending the privatisation of personal social services (see *Guardian* 16 November 1987). The Department of Social Security is likewise contracting out specific services such as computerised benefit payments, cleaning and security guards to private agencies (see *Guardian* 16 February 1988).

Gough's argument is that both strategies, corporatism and New Right, are doomed to fail because of the inexorable and contradictory demands that accumulation places on the welfare state. However, this account overlooks ideological aspects of the welfare state that have thwarted the economic and class forces that Gough's perspective highlights. First, corporatist strategies which employ political decision-making to influence market activity and view human labour as instrumental to its productive targets, adopt a strategy of 'dictatorship over needs' – to use a phrase applied to Soviet societies (Feher 1978). Here welfare state institutions and practices fix concepts of need in public consciousness that exclude alternative concepts and possibilities. The ideological construction of need is discussed more fully in Chapter 10.

Secondly, ideological aspects of rightist policy are seen in the Tory government's ability to manipulate need, through reducing public expectations, by shifting responsibilities from central to local government for dependents discharged from long-stay hospital into the community, and by redefining need as non-need. Regarding 'care in the community', in 1981 the Secretary of State for Social Services, Patrick Jenkin, addressed the chairpersons and members of District Health Authorities and stressed their local responsibility in planning for needs within parameters set by central government. He expressed his wish 'to give [them] as much freedom as possible to decide how to achieve . . . policies and priorities in [their] localities'. However, he stressed the importance of central financial control by adding that 'a National Health Service must have regard to *national* policies and priorities' (HMSO 1981, Preface). A further strategy, the ideological one of removing needs from the public domain – a radical move after decades of government commitment to identifying public need – is also evident in the way the document sought to involve 'the whole community' in the support of the elderly (and other dependants). The consequence is that need, let alone resources, are redefined: 'Public authorities will not command the resources to deal with it alone. Nor could official help meet all those needs which go beyond the provision of material benefits' (1981, p. 32). Here, the process of redefining needs entails distinguishing between material and immaterial needs without defining what constitutes the latter domain, and displacing specific needs, such as those of the elderly, from one domain to the other, while at the same time assuming that new resources for 'needs which go beyond the . . . material' will emerge at no extra cost to government.

However, these ideological strategies for managing need are limited by the fact that there remains in need a subjective content quite distinct from its objective, institutional and state-imposed form. Though pliable, needs remain a property of individuals and groups who operate outside as well as within formal state structures and institutions. This realisation by groups whose needs remain unmet has given rise to new social movements organised around interests of gender, ethnicity or state-clientage that play an increasingly important part in the political economy of the welfare state and occupy a new space in the interstices of state and civil society in becoming adversaries of state bureaucracy (see O'Connor 1984, p. 220). Ginsburg and others (1979, p. 10; also Golding and Middleton 1982) have observed that the closing of political space in the 1970s and early 1980s occasioned the decline of the Labour Party as a creative force in welfare policy, and the emergence of pressure groups that recreate this space along different lines, more pluralistic than unitary, and located in civil society rather than the state. However, such developments have also contributed towards 'hasten[ing] the restructuring of the state apparatus, designed to resist these demands with bureaucratisation and closer control of the welfare professions' (Gough 1979, p. 10). This was seen in the 1980s as the government replaced discretionary elements of social security benefits, with which welfare rights groups could negotiate, by legalistic provisions with reduced rights of local appeal, which severely limited scope for local welfare rights action and increasingly necessitated High Court litigation.

Marxist Political Economy: an appraisal

The Political Economy of Welfare accords a determining role to the economy in the formation of ideology (Gough 1979, p. 10). Changes in the mode and relations of production – i.e. between the employed and unemployed, and between different age, gender and ethnic groups and the state – give rise to a new 'consciousness' or framework of ideas, which explains, rationalises and justifies these changes. In this, Political Economy is an advance on other analyses of social policy in removing the ideological misconceptions that welfare policies are primarily motivated by benevolence, and that economic contingencies demand a more 'realistic' approach, which subordinates welfare to the imperatives of industrial growth.

However, there are serious limitations in Political Economy's approach. The assumption of determining economic processes obscures the formative influence of ideology on society and welfare. The Thatcher decade, for example, has averted a legitimation crisis by lowering public expectations of state welfare and offloaded some of the state's responsibilities onto the mixed economy of welfare. These changes have altered the long-standing balance between state and society, by, for example, relieving capital of some of the tax burden of rising welfare costs, and by stimulating new markets for social needs. These reforms are only possible if public expectations – the rising expectations underwritten by the state since the 1940s and constituting its principal claim to political legitimacy – are lowered at little cost in popular support and replaced by an enterprise culture where expectations are tied 'realistically' to market opportunity. At the centre of these changes lies a new ideology, which seeks to transform people's consciousness, their expectations and responsibilities, their rights and duties as citizens. These ideological changes modify the growing alliance between state and monopoly capital, which O'Connor foresaw in the early 1970s. Such alliances have indeed continued throughout the past two decades, but have not resulted in the state bearing the costs of growing diswelfares and dependency. Capitalism has shown an ability to adapt to new demands, to restructure its organisation and shed surplus labour, and to move into social markets now free from public monopoly. Both the economic domain of capitalist relations of production and the ideological domain of social aspirations and welfare practices have proven more malleable than theories of legitimation crisis envisaged.

These limitations in Political Economy's account of ideology stem from theoretical tunnel-vision, namely a tendency to see ideology and welfare in late capitalism in functionalist terms. O'Connor, for example, depicts the ideological role of welfare policies as 'fulfilling the state's "legitimation" function", a function portrayed as obscuring the real function of welfare in diverting attention from the state's bias towards the interests of capital; thus 'the state must involve itself in the accumulation process, but it must either mystify its policies by calling them something they are not, or try to conceal them' (1973, p. 6). The postwar consensus between capital and labour was thereby an ideological phenomenon that O'Connor explains by reference to a functionalist notion of unspecified deep 'fears' of crisis which capital and labour share. The motivations, needs and so forth that the welfare state satisfies and the fears and anxieties it dispels are seen as the functional correlates of the state's legitimation function.[4]

A further problem lies in the way Political Economy portrays welfare as performing widely differing roles. For this suggests that welfare has no identity of its own to distinguish it from other institutions. An example of this blank ascription is O'Connor's coupling of war and welfare in the 'Warfare-Welfare State' where 'the structural determinants of both military spending and welfare outlets are broadly the same and the two kinds of spending can be interpreted as different aspects of the same general phenomenon' (1973, p. 150). Without a positive conception, welfare stands as a *tabula rasa*, a neutral entity, upon which the state inscribes the functions required of it in support of capital. Such functionalist accounts rely on attributing to welfare (and other activities) an absence of significance, which only the capitalist state can fill with meaningful tasks. This reasoning can lead analysts to describe welfare practices and agencies in obscurantist terms as possessing inherently positive *and* negative qualities. These antinomies are projected onto the 'contradictions of the welfare state', where, 'Because of the dual and contradictory nature of the capitalist state, nearly every state agency and every expenditure has this two-fold character' (O'Connor 1973, p. 7; see also Gough 1979, p. 11).[5]

However, more recently, O'Connor has modified his account of these contradictions by incorporating a Marxist theory of the subject into his analysis of Political Economy (see Chapter 8). Contradictions emanate from political and economic processes which simultaneously objectify and subjectify the individual. On the one hand, capitalist political institutions of parliament and government have constructed the citizen as a passive voter: 'the object of political and technocratic administration, the lonely and colonised state client', a political subject least threatening to economic interests. On the other hand, these institutions have 'also reproduced the active "participant" form of political life and in this way politically subjectivised the individual' (1984, p. 198). However, this theory of the subject remains functionalist and disallows subject-initiated action, as our discussion of Althusser in Chapter 8 suggests.

At the root of the Political Economy of Welfare lies a problem that betrays the extent to which capitalist ideology and its categories inform the functionalism in this strand of Marxism. The blanket ascriptions of functionalist reasoning – e.g. O'Connor's 'warfare and welfare' – blind critical analysis to the different ways in which key social distinctions operate in the analysis of different societies. This is seen in the Marxist distinction between productive and non-productive labour, and its application to state administration. For Marx, the latter is essentially unproductive in absorbing rather than creating surplus value. Political Economy writers such as Gough retain much of this distinction. However, the distinction between productive and non-productive labour carries one set of normative meanings in capitalist society – e.g. between the deserving and undeserving – and a different set in non-capitalist societies (see Keane and Owens 1986). Gough's analysis of productive and unproductive forms of welfare recognises this, but at certain points slips into an essentialism that loses sight of the cultural variety characterising this distinction, a slip with ideological implications. For example, Gough tells us that '*all* societies contain groups that are unable to work for their living . . . children, the elderly, the sick'. Therefore, 'it follows that *all* societies must develop mechanisms for transferring part of the social product from the direct producers to these groups'. Essentialism creeps in when he states that this is done by instituting 'two basic activities of the welfare state', which 'correspond to two basic activities in *all* human societies: the reproduction of the working population and the maintenance of the non-working population. The welfare state is the institutional response in advanced capitalist society to these two requirements of *all* human societies' (1979, pp. 47–8, my emphasis throughout). Gough and others recognise that the boundaries between the productive and unproductive are not fixed and are determined by the prevailing mode of production; which under capitalism sharply differentiates production from non-production. Moreover, Gough insists that 'No moral evaluations of any kind are implied in using the concepts of productive and unproductive labour' (1979, p. 105). However, for Gough, the universal category distinction between production and non-production, work and non-work, and consequently between worker and non-worker, is an essential distinction that characterises the differentiation of labour in all societies. For O'Connor and Gough such work is classified as 'an expense' because, following Marx's definition of unproductive labour, it produces no surplus value because it is exchanged for revenue rather than capital (Gough 1972). What capitalist ideology achieves is the promotion of production and the relegation of all other activities, such as welfare service, to a domain where 'production' is absent. For

Political Economy, to accept the *distinction* between capitalist production and its other as a fundamental *opposition* between production and non-production and to apply this to all societies is to partake in this ideological construction.

All societies engage in labour as a universal lifeform, but they conceive of labour's constituent activities in widely different ways and attribute different values to them. Production, physical effort, tending, nurturing, caring, artistic creativity, and the exercise of wisdom and authority are each different forms of labour with specific outcomes and use values. Each constituent can be combined with others to constitute organic forms of labour that differ from one society to another. In capitalist production, the private firm, for example, will combine productive workers producing commodities and services for sale with unproductive workers producing services, such as management, training and research, who none the less make an indispensable contribution to the firm's surplus value. In the capitalist state, welfare services take on functions that private firms cannot undertake themselves. Under the above rubric these services are seen as an expense or at best as indirectly productive. Because these productions take place *outside* the market they are viewed as unproductive or not directly productive. However, the distinction between the production of commodity producing firms and the activities of service firms are not so designated because they take place *inside* the market. The metaphorical distinction between inside and outside that characterises the relationship between state and market further underpins the value distinction between production and non-production.

Once the opposition between work and non-work has taken hold, the ideological connotations abound. Welfare plays a circulatory role within capital accumulation – it diverts, transfers, distributes, allocates, but does not produce. At best it is indirectly productive. An account of welfare and state functions that began as a critique of capitalism now takes on some of the value assumptions of capitalism. There remains an important need for an account of the production of welfare, and of the labour process involved therein, that explores its productive role.[6] In the following chapters, especially Chapters 6 and 7 on Critical Theory and Chapter 9 on Foucault, we will see how far this is achieved, by what different means, and with what consequences.

Notes

1. Marx's classic exposition of the transformation of use value is found in Marx (1976, Vol. I, ch. 2). Ginsburg summarises these arguments in the context of welfare state capitalism (1979, ch. 2). See also Catephores (1989).
2. In Chapter 7 we will see that a similar analysis was provided by Offe at about the same time, from within the tradition of Critical Theory (1984, p. 69).
3. A similar conclusion is reached in Lee and Raban (1988).
4. By contrast, Levitas comments that such fears of social chaos do not simply arise because the circumstances justify them, but had themselves to be ideologically constructed by, in part, the New Right (1986, p. 16).

5. However, political economic analysis has highlighted the contrasting functions welfare performs at *different* moments in capitalist development. For example, the dual functions of care and control, social investment and expense, etc., have been shown to operate with a greater emphasis on care and welfare expansion during times of economic growth, and on control during recession (Gough 1979).

6. Gough seems to acknowledge this problem in his analysis of the gains and losses to capital and to labour caused by state expenditure. The implication is that there has been a tendency to assess the state in terms of its role in the realisation of existing output rather than its contribution to the production of output (1979, p. 122 and Appendix B).

6

Critical Theory and welfare ideology

In contrast to Marxist Political Economy, Critical Theory has paid greater attention to the normative features of human existence by giving serious regard to questions concerning the pursuit of universal human ideals – such as truth, freedom and justice – and the social and economic conditions that foster or impede their advancement. Indeed, Critical Theory has throughout its history maintained that the crisis conditions of advanced capitalism undermine the possibility of making truth claims about human existence and achieving a good and free society (see Held 1979). Moreover, the ideology of capitalism advances alternative claims about goodness and freedom. Consequently, the validity of the welfare state in capitalist society has become a central concern for Critical Theory in seeking to unmask the ideological distortions that the welfare apparatus performs for capitalism, and to advance its own arguments for human emancipation. In these endeavours, questions of human welfare have become central.

This chapter discusses recent writings in Critical Theory on ideology and the welfare state, and examines the notion of ideology critique, as both a critique and positive contribution to the development of human emancipation and well-being. Specifically, the chapter discusses Jürgen Habermas's understanding of ideology as a form of distorted communication that can be resisted only by means of advancing what he calls 'universal validity claims'. Such resistance has created a renewed interest in the role of new social movements in the promotion of human welfare.[1] Habermas' contribution has been to set such philosophical considerations about welfare and ideology within a comprehensive political economy that explicates the crisis tendencies of late capitalist society. Claus Offe has furthered this understanding by examining several features of 'disorganised capitalism'. Taken together, their analyses provide a thorough reappraisal of the Marxist theory of value realisation, and contribute towards defining a new rationality for welfare.

The social critique of Critical Theory has a double focus. First, in common with Marxism generally, it seeks to expose the discrepancy between the ideals of bourgeois society and the reality of its institutional practices. For example, the welfare state in principle confers universal citizenship rights on all; whereas in practice some enjoy these rights to a greater extent than others. In Chapter 2 we saw how the provision of a national minimum attempted to reconcile the discrepancy between universal objectives and individual preferences, but at the cost of underwriting inequalities in the exercise of citizenship rights. Secondly – and this is distinctive to Critical Theory – there emerges from examining bourgeois values in social institutions and practices, a sense of emancipatory human values that expose the illusions of bourgeois ideals; that, further, reveal forms of social organisation allowing universal human values expression by permitting society to determine democratically and with full critical voice its own direction; and that, finally, show the grounds for determining these emancipatory social values. A dialectical relationship can be discerned between the two lines of critique: between a critique of existing social institutions that belies the validity claimed for their dominant values, and the critical search for a basis for values and practices that further human betterment and emancipation. Hence, the critical thrust of Critical Theory; though some have disputed its claim to be truly critical.[2]

Of modern critical theorists, Habermas has followed these two lines of inquiry in an enlightening series of sociological and philosophical studies. Implicit in these is the idea that truth is intrinsic to all forms of rational inquiry and social practice that give unfettered expression to human dialogue; that ideally, as long as open debate and unimpeded discourse prevail in human interaction, what Habermas (1970) terms an 'ideal speech situation' will operate. Such an ideal is, of course, far from realised in everyday discourse. But Habermas contends that it is an assumption underlying, if not achieved in, all instances of rational debate.

By contrast, Habermas discusses a different situation associated with power and ideology where two parties are engaged in communication based on shared misunderstanding or false consensus. Here the participants conduct a pseudo-communication, which 'produces a system of reciprocal misunderstandings'. Habermas calls this 'systematically distorted communication' (1976b, p. 348). Two instances are cited: pathologically deformed communication typical of mental disorder; and ideological communication where two parties systematically misunderstand each other because one party enforces its interests over the other. In both instances language is distorted and cannot be remedied by recourse to a set of rules, which translates incomprehensible or misunderstood speech into normal speech. For, in both cases no such rules exist, and (except in the most bizarre mental disorders) both parties are participants in the same distorted language. Understanding only occurs when a third party (also participating in the same language) – e.g. the psychoanalyst or critical theorist – can reconstruct the origins of distorted communication, that is, the primal scene experienced in childhood or the causes of exploitation and alienation occurring in society. In each case a discrepancy exists between a statement and what the statement refers to, which results from a systematic distortion whose roots lie in some basic event or crisis in the underlying structure. As an example, a critique of Thatcherism cannot rely on dismissing its ideas as mere ideology, for in that case one could retort that the critique itself is ideologically founded. Rather, in the light of ideology critique, a systematic discrepancy must be shown between the ideals and practices of Thatcherism; that is, between the language used in its claims and the reality this language refers to, a reality that appears the more discrepant because of the underlying crisis producing Thatcherism. Thus, it can be argued that within the context of the 1988 social security reforms, the implementation of benefit cuts for large sectors of the poor, together with substantial tax cuts for the rich, expresses a systematic discrepancy between the espoused aims of Thatcherism – to achieve greater market freedom and opportunity for all – and evidence of widening inequalities of opportunity and deteriorating circumstances for the poorest (see Townsend 1991). In this context, many commentators have responded with disbelief to the government's claims for its policies since 1987.

Habermas has subsequently explored, in *Legitimation Crisis* (1976a), *A Theory of Communicative Action* (1984; 1987) and associated essays, the crisis tendencies underlying advanced capitalist society that give rise to ideological distortion and to counter-tendencies that seek truthful justifications for state policy. Thus, on the one hand, he examines the limitations affecting meaning and truth caused by the impact of economic and political crises on the cultural and normative spheres of human life. On the other hand, he examines the role of social movements whose demands of the state to justify its actions place in question the claims of public policy and challenge state legitimacy. The critical force of these actions is to rekindle rational debate in the public domain. What Habermas calls truth or validity claims can be raised and redeemed or refuted, so correcting distorted communication. In the course of this long and complex project, the ideology of the welfare state has become of increasing importance.

Habermas's theory, though influenced in part by O'Connor's notion of legitimation crisis, differs from Political Economy's in its attempt to give a more comprehensive account of the processes generating, deferring and transforming crisis. The Political Economy approach sees a legitimation crisis arising from tensions between the accumulation demands of capital and the mounting expectations of the people. This account gives an unmediated form of determination that implies the inevitability of crisis and obscures the potential for its ideological management. By contrast, Habermas's account describes a process in which the emergence of crisis in one part of society is displaced onto another and thereby transformed. It permits an analysis of crisis management and containment as well as generation, and accords an explicit role to the mediations of ideology in the welfare state.

The crisis of the welfare state

Habermas divides advanced capitalist society into three systems and functions – the economic, the political-administrative and the socio-cultural – corresponding to the conventional demarcation of economy, polity and society. Each system is identified in terms of the types of crisis tendency that occur when these functions break down. For example, in the economic system the production of insufficient value leads to an *economic crisis*. In the political-administrative system, the lack of rationally cogent decision-making leads to a *rationality crisis*, followed by a *legitimation crisis* when the public withdraws its support because the state no longer meets its needs. Finally, in the socio-cultural system, the production of meaningful values and symbols that strengthen social cohesion is threatened by the demise of traditional and bourgeois sources of meaning – such as reside in the family, work and Protestant ethics – and by the weakening of identification between individual and state, giving rise to a *motivation crisis*. Crises occur because demands placed on one system outstrip the limited resources – economic, rationality, legitimation and personal motivation – upon which it must rely, causing either the system to break down or crisis to be displaced into another system. However, this shift only places new demands on a different system so that new crisis tendencies eventually emerge. Habermas places importance on the inherent resource limitations which, when they are subject to overload, predispose each system to crisis.[3] We will examine each of these system crises in turn. While there are several accounts that apply Habermas's theory to social policy (Mishra 1984; George and Wilding 1984; Johnson 1987), they focus on its implications for the wider political economy rather than the ideological aspects of welfare. The present discussion attempts to place more stress on ideological aspects of legitimation and motivation crises in the welfare state.

First, following O'Connor, Habermas contends that in the economic system, the competitive nature of capitalist enterprise disregards resource scarcity, and inhibits a rational approach to achieving economic objectives. Producers must conform to the principles of the market and forego the possibility of co-operating in the planned production and allocation of scarce resources. As a result human needs and welfare become subservient to the exigencies of market demand and supply. Marxists have often commented that 'the legitimacy of market institutions is difficult to secure because the market is essentially amoral, directionless, and to some extent arbitrary in the way in which it distributes income and wealth, rewarding luck and status as much as skill and effort' (Gamble 1979, p. 18). The value of economic production has no rational relationship to social needs. The needs of some are met, while those of others are left deprived.

The achievement of growth in surplus value to sustain accumulation therefore requires the state to regulate markets, plan long-term economic objectives, and distribute value in a more economically efficient way. *Economic crisis* is thereby averted and its management transferred to the political-administrative system. Here the state is expected to make rational decisions in the interests of capitalist production and distribute surplus to the public in the form of welfare provisions. Thus, the administrative-political system contains the means, unavailable to the economic, to influence and 'steer' the direction of the economy through crises, tempering swings and moving towards a fairer distribution of values. An important means of steering the economy is provided by the welfare apparatus. First, it directly intervenes in economic production to enhance personal welfare through investment in material infrastructures, such as transport, housing and health care and in prioritised production sectors (i.e. 'social capital', to use one of O'Connor's three categories: 1973, pp. 6–7) and by seeking to sustain full employment and enhance labour power by means of education, training and job and retirement security (i.e. 'social investment': *ibid.*). Sweden, for example, maintained the fabric of its welfare state in order to counter the recession of the 1970s. It continued its long-term commitment to full employment – part of a wider commitment to citizenship rights – by investing in training and retraining, job protection, continuing education and equal opportunities policies (King 1987, p. 186; Olsonn 1987). Secondly, welfare provisions relieve the costs and diswelfares that fall heavily on the poor (i.e. 'social expenses': O'Connor 1973). Thirdly, it supplies 'market replacing' commodities (Habermas 1976a, p. 55), which possess use value more directed to the needs of recipients than market commodities purchased and exchanged according to their exchange value (1976a, p. 66). By contrast, it has long been recognised that countries with mainly private health care systems, such as the United States, tend to overtreat fee-paying and insured patients. Quam (1989) cites evidence showing wide variations in treatment patterns, for example in coronary bypass, carotid vendartectomy and knee and hip replacements between different areas of the United States which have no noticeably different levels of morbidity. The evidence also suggests inappropriate applications of such costly treatments in a considerable proportion of cases.

However, lack of market information and technology undermines rational economic planning and poses the possibility of *rationality crisis*. In general terms, the mounting costs of socialised production fall increasingly on the government. For example, it shoulders the costs of infrastructure investment, research and development, social consumption and welfare expenses, and the costs of environmental pollution originating in the private sector. The instrumental and individualist rationality of capitalist production comes to be replaced by a universal rationality concerned with social welfare and the quality of life. To these ends the state must provide welfare provisions that underwrite citizenship rights and extend social justice. However, the impossibility of government underwriting both accumulation and universal welfare undermines public support and threatens to create a further crisis in the political domain, a *legitimation* deficit. This can be partially remedied either by recourse to coercion or by deploying the ideology, rather than the substance, of the welfare state with its connotations of universal social justice to maintain a semblance of legitimacy.

The economic crisis is then, according to Habermas, *replaced* by a political crisis involving mounting inflation and a permanent crisis in public finances (1976a, p. 61). However, though a legitimation crisis takes the form of manifest conflict between state and populace, this hides a more latent contradiction between the private capitalist beneficiaries of state policy and labour which bears disproportionately the burden of increased productivity and deteriorating work and living conditions. Thus, Habermas argues that, 'In the final analysis, *the class structure* is the source of legitimation deficits' (*ibid.*, p. 73).

The final displacement occurs when crisis tendencies within the state shift to the socio-cultural system. It is this development that most distinguishes Habermas's account of crisis from others. Although postwar societies have averted rationality and legitimation crises by providing public services and capital investment financed from relatively high levels of public expenditure, ultimately there are economic, rationality and legitimation limits to such adjustments. These limits are complemented by limits posed in the social-cultural realm set by an individual's personal and social identity.

The formation of individual identity relies on the input of material provisions that contribute to shaping personal needs. In turn, the formation of identity sustains patterns of motivation that contribute cultural inputs to the legitimation system. However, late capitalism and the rise of state intervention undermines individual identity in two ways, leading to *motivation crisis*. First, motivation is weakened when the individual develops expectations fired by accumulation that the state can no longer fulfil. Secondly, personal values are declining in importance with the erosion of an individualist bourgeois tradition that offered only limited scope for individual participation in democratic civil institutions, and that limited personal achievement to family and vocational activities – 'the syndrome of civil and familial-vocational privatism' (Habermas 1976a, p. 75). In turn this tradition has suffered further from the impact of the rationalisation processes accompanying modernity, and from the erosion of important elements of bourgeois culture.

In response to the alienation associated with the demise of traditional values, new social movements have emerged that raise afresh normative demands of the state distinct from the demands of the Right. The women, peace and green movements, for example, differ from earlier movements such as the labour movement in pressing for policy changes that cannot be met solely by re-allocating resources from one section of the population to another, but demand fundamentally that government rethink its policies according to more universal criteria of justice (Habermas 1987, pp. 392–3). These movements play an important role in demanding rational justification for state policy. The consequence of failing either to provide these justifications or to produce a fairer distribution of value is that insufficient personal motivation is available to maintain state legitimation.

Welfare, morality and universality

We can see more clearly the implications of legitimation crises for welfare services; namely that the state's growing interest in welfare matters, such as education, health and personal care, interferes with areas traditionally outside the state, the preserve of family, community and professions (Habermas 1976a, pp. 71–2). This interference weakens traditional authority, leads to the politicisation of new areas of policy, and redefines the boundaries between state and civil society. Not only is justification demanded of the state for intruding into the civil sphere, but also the state demands that civil society justify its ability to protect the sanctity of family, community and civil life. These values are placed in question as the state seeks to extend its influence in education, health and parenting. For example, in recent years the state's interest in childcare has grown markedly with the consequence that parental rights have been weakened by the enhanced powers of social workers, health workers and the police to intervene in family life. Parents have grown increasingly concerned about the ease with which social workers can take children away and place them in care, especially in the wake of inquiries into child protection practices in Cleveland, Rochdale and the Orkneys. The new 1989 Children Act restores some rights to parents, for example by enabling them to appeal after 72 hours following the removal of their child. But at the same time the standards of legal proof, of actual or *likely* harm to the child, that social workers must meet in order to intervene have been lowered to those of civil law, so easing the process of intervention.

These shifting alliances between state and society have unsettled established norms. The legitimation crisis is made particularly severe by the erosion of traditional values and bourgeois morality, which in pre-modern times had universal significance and esteem, but whose disappearance today contributes to the dissolution of the cultural base of society. Welfare has come to be seen as an attempt to rebuild collective forms of solidarity and resurrect social and moral cohesion out of the material and cultural morass of modern industrial society; a theme that Fabian social administration also has advanced this century in its quest for universal welfare services.

From the contrasting perspective of the Right, however, the moral questions posed by the legitimation crisis have a different salience. The failure of bourgeois ideology to sustain order in late capitalist society is seen as a reason to encourage the welfare state to revalorise traditional areas of moral life in family, community, and gender relations, in a way that stresses selective rather than universal values. During the late 1980s, the Thatcher government entered this moral territory, having crossed and reformed the economic and political terrain. This was seen most strikingly in the former Secretary of State, John Moore's proposition that the welfare state saps the will to work of the poor *en masse*, deliberately 'corrupting the human spirit', and engendering a 'dependency culture' (*Guardian* 2 October 1987). Recently, the government has turned its attention to the role it ascribes to social security in subsidising family break-up and contributing to the increase in single parent families since the early 1960s. Lord Harris, for example, detects a link between welfare and permissiveness when he suggests that 'the dramatic increase in unmarried mothers owes a good deal to the special payments and subsidised housing priority won by the pressure group for the biological curiosity of 'single-parent' families' (1988, p. 23). In addition to advocating increased selectivity in social policy, some on the moral right now argue for an overlay of moral or spiritual guidance:

> we must work towards a system that, first, confines 'free' resources to deserving victims of adversity; and, second, accompanies cash with counselling and pastoral care which ministers to each individual's disability or deficiency. Since care is best lavished by those with love for their handicapped neighbour, it is better provided *wherever possible* in the local community and by voluntary action which, like mercy, blesses giver and receiver. (Harris 1988, p. 26; cf. Murray 1984)

In its critique of 'welfare dependency', the Right stresses the importance of recoupling social work help to the relief-giving functions of social security – reviving memories of the Poor Law – in an attempt to get professional social workers to co-operate with the new Social Fund in judging which claimants are most deserving (see Laurance 1988).

However, Habermas (1985/6) contends that the use of the welfare state to revalorise morality in this way risks inciting a critical discourse based on moral universalism rather than selective and strategic considerations. Attempts to restructure social services in ways that diminish social rights, dilute provision and displace responsibility from government to family and community are in danger of provoking renewed criticism of the government's legitimacy. Ultimately, for Habermas, core issues of cultural and moral value – such as those about the future direction of the welfare state – must stand the test of universal validity, open to the judgement of all people willing and able to engage in rational debate. At the crux of the crisis tendencies of advanced capitalism are questions of truth sustained or refuted in rational discourse.

Welfare, truth and discourse

Habermas's theoretical interest in the nature of debates about justice and the legitimation of the welfare state in late capitalism took a 'linguistic turn' in the mid-1970s. Understanding legitimation and ideology involved attending to philosophical questions about truth claims as much as political-economic questions about the nature of capitalist society. To understand his position on the universality of truth statements, we must now introduce Habermas's theory of communicative action, albeit in a summary manner that will unavoidably gloss its rich and complex character.

As crisis tendencies are displaced, the issue of legitimacy becomes one of sustaining the grounds of truth between individuals at one level, and between citizens and government at another. In addressing issues of truth and normative legitimacy, Habermas has developed a theory that reconstructs the bases of communicative action at whatever level. By this he is referring to the way that understanding is reached between speaker and hearer, in the semantic sense of what is said (i.e. the speaker's content), and in the pragmatic sense of the expectation each holds of the other. Thus the hearer expects that what is said and communicated accord with what is done or the state of affairs described by the speaker (see 1979, ch. 1; also Roderick 1986; and White 1988). This is a communicative or pragmatic model of understanding. Thus individuals 'speech acts' as well as their 'propositional content' are oriented to understanding (cf. Searle 1969). When an individual makes a statement – about, for example, the objective world, interpersonal relations or subjective feelings – she is committing herself to the supposition that the proposition of her statement can be verified for the other speaker if required. In making sense of her speech and action, the hearer assumes a congruence between the content of her statement and the facts, relations or feelings she refers to by her speech act. In Habermas's terms speech acts, or what he prefers to call communicative actions, involve truth or validity claims that can be rationally redeemed if necessary. The consequence of communicative action is that social actors are governed by the 'binding force' or mutual expectation of a communicative ethic by which they can co-ordinate their actions and achieve a level of social cohesion (e.g. 1979, p. 63).

Habermas identifies three types of 'validity claim' whose truth involves specific types of rational argumentation: *truth* claims that refer to objective reality and require cognitive forms of reasoning such as scientific argument; *normative* claims about the rightness of social relations and institutions that require normative reasoning as in moral or political argument; *sincerity* claims about the truthfulness of someone's subjective feelings that require reasoning about the authenticity found in expressive forms of communication such as subjective statements or works of art (1979, pp. 63–4). In each speech act, one validity claims is explicitly thematised while the others are implicitly assumed

(1984, p. 121). Because of linguistic competence, individuals are not only able to make validity claims, and to reconstruct each type for the purpose of understanding, but to interrelate the three 'worlds' that each validity claim refers to. The speaker is empowered through the medium of language with a comprehensive range of rational faculties to enter the objective, interpersonal and subjective worlds he or she inhabits (1979, p. 67; 1984, p. 100).

In welfare discourse the three types of claim provide the following examples of rational propositions, each with its own forms of valid argumentation that must be open to testing if the hearer so demands. First, welfare policy relies on claims about the objective conditions of individuals, groups and society; about, for example, the states of need of dependants or the resources and administration required to meet need. Secondly, welfare policies contain normative claims about the justice of welfare arrangements – in many ways the principal type of statement in policy discourse: which groups ought to receive welfare; whether welfare should be universally or selectively available. Finally, welfare discourse contains claims – the least researched in welfare literature – about the authenticity of individual expressions of need and offers of help; claims between, for example, clients and welfare workers concerning the sincerity of each other's expressions of hardship and willingness to help. It is precisely the last two types of claims about welfare provision that Marxists have dismissed as ideological in the context of capitalist society. But according to Habermas, the grounds for repudiating or redeeming them require close attention to the specific type of speech act made in the claim, which crude ideological critique tends to overlook.

Communication in each area is built on the assumption, Habermas claims, that the truth of what is communicated is verified intersubjectively between speakers, and by extension that truth claims are universally applicable. It follows that Habermas is proposing a procedural theory of truth that assumes reasoning is grounded in a process of fair and rational dialogue unfettered by compulsion of any kind. Hence his references to the ideal speech situation and by contrast to the ideology entailed in systematically distorted communication.

Essentially, Habermas wishes to provide an account of rationality that is based on foundations secured in a universal form of understanding (e.g. 1984, p. 137). Thus he claims his theory serves as a more adequate account of rationality than those based on strategic rationality, which see social action as driven by a dominant class, interest group or power elite. The rationale for such action is located in a self-determining group whose legitimacy is an expression of its self-interest. Though this appeal to strategic rationality grasps the essence of self-determination, it cannot embrace a universally founded theory of rationality that explains different forms of determination, economic, political and social. Without this there can be no other basis for explaining and appraising the existence of such groups beyond their strategic interests.

In this vein Habermas is able to argue that normative claims must be advanced on the basis that they are universal rather than sectarian. What constitutes a universal claim, of course, cannot be taken for granted, but would need to be advanced through argumentation between the different parties involved (some of whom will wish either to protect sectarian interests, or to preserve false interests held in ignorance or because the party is prey to ideological distortion). Habermas contends that an awareness of universal interests will emerge if the debate between parties is conducted solely on the basis of rational argument founded on communicative rather than strategic reasoning. An explanation of real needs becomes central to the task of establishing arguments for interests advanced according to universal validity criteria. For 'norms regulate the legitimate chances for the satisfaction of needs' (translated and quoted in White 1988, p. 69). The interpretation of needs that inform normative claims must be subject to critical assessment as well as debated fairly (*ibid.*, p. 71). The implication for welfare discourse and ethics of Habermas's communicative theory are central, as we will see later.

It follows that a morality based on principles of truth allows only universal norms, that is, 'norms without exception, without privileges, and without limitations on the domain of validity' (Habermas 1976a, p. 88). Here, Habermas is arguing for a communicative ethics that 'guarantees the generality of ad-missible norms and the autonomy of acting subjects solely through the discursive redeemability of the validity claims with which norms appear' (*ibid.*, p. 89). The suggestion is that the ideological forces in advanced capitalism, which seek to bolster up state legitimacy – technocratic mastery, instrumen-tality, impartiality and welfare benevolence – are themselves in principle open to validity testing. However, in reality, such testing is limited when governments lack legitimacy and personal motivation is low. Only those forces that advance universal truth and reason can transcend these restrictions and adequately confront ideology. Ultimately, the source of crisis and the means of its tran-scendence stem from the germ of rational debate that critical forces can nurture in the public domain, prompted by the universal concerns of human reasoning and the desire to uncover ideological distortion.

This implies that validity claims based on moral selectivity (e.g. restricting welfare entitlement to the 'deserving') cannot be sustained when exposed to a communicative ethic. The question remains as to whether welfare policy can promote a universal morality as an ethical counterpart to the universal provision of welfare. Does 'welfare for all' rest on, and in turn support, the ethical claim that 'one ought to do to others as one would be done by'? Habermas's position is, as Roderick argues, that 'universalism must be possible both at the level of the common good and universal access to participate in communication', that universal welfare is embedded in a communicative ethics (1986, p. 88). A connection can be imputed between universal principles of morality and welfare services available to all without let or hindrance or regard for differences in income, class, race and gender.[4] This suggests that universal forms of welfare are conducive to a climate of democracy that encourages greater participation in political discourse about social ends, raising to a higher level of possibility – without fully actualising – Habermas's 'ideal speech situation'. This in turn removes the ideological entrapment of 'systematically distorted communication'. A further connection can be seen here between the welfare principles of the Fabians and the normative principles of recent Critical Theory.

The welfare state and the colonisation of the lifeworld

Habermas has made important contributions to understanding the ideological distortions and crises affecting welfare capitalism, and the social forces that counter these tendencies by demanding of government universal justification for its public policy.

However, Habermas's speculation in *Legitimation Crisis* of emerging crises has not proven – two decades later – entirely correct. Rather, structural and ideological forces have developed to contain and even dissipate critical tensions. In this light, a broad range of writers has argued that Habermas's expectations – and Marxists' generally – have been thwarted by the emergence of a new ideological consensus on the welfare state held by both Left and Right. As we saw in Chapter 4, for example, Hall and others see this consensus as a proto-hegemony of ideological proportions. Further, Papadakis and Taylor-Gooby (1987) argue that a new consensus in the academic discipline of social policy has taken theoretical shape amongst thinkers on the Left and Right concerned about economic growth and 'unproductive' welfare, political overload and government legitimation, the failure of welfare states to redistribute, and continuing paternalism in the welfare state. Riddell more generally records the views of Mrs Thatcher's political colleagues on the emergence of 'a new common ground', which has laid the foundations for a new political, moral and intellectual order (1989, p. 208).

Habermas, for his part, has qualified his assertions about legitimation crises by exploring further the ideological nature of late welfare-state capitalism. In developing his earlier work, Habermas has explored concerns he anticipated earlier – especially the effects of crisis on formal democracy and bourgeois values, and the tensions between strategic and communicative rationality – and has identified a broader range of crises and pathologies. Welfare ideology is at the forefront of his recent thesis on 'the colonisation of the lifeworld' (1987). A further concern for Habermas is to address these issues in the context of several major themes of central interest to twentieth-century sociology: Weber's concern with the growing disenchantment in the modern world, which results from scientific and bureaucratic rationalisation; Marxism's concern with the commodification of social life; and Critical Theory's concern with the subtle forms of domination and loss of freedom, which the eighteenth century Enlightenment inflicted unwittingly on modern social life (see Roderick 1986, ch. 2). In exploring these themes, Habermas is considering the extent to which economic and political systems have come to dominate communicative reasoning and social solidarity, and the extent to which welfare policies that sustain everyday life now fall increasingly under the sway of new forms of legal domination.

While sharing these critical concerns – though conceding more positively the gains of modernity – Habermas has been drawn to examine the gradual intrusion of economic and administrative systems into the social 'lifeworld'. The lifeworld involves the everyday assumptions which individuals implicitly share in their lives together and which provide the background to action and communication of all kinds (1987, p. 119). As the assumptive basis of social life, the lifeworld remains implicit and pre-critical. Yet its presence is a necessary condition for shared social action, being essential to the presuppositions upon which factual, normative and sincerity claims rest. Habermas contrasts the lifeworld with 'social systems' which operate as self-regulating forms of social organisation geared to fulfilling specific social functions, and employing explicitly stated norms to achieve strategic ends (1987, p. 151). The social systems of economy and state are particularly important in using their respective 'media' of money and power to steer social action towards achieving the wider system's goals. Habermas is contrasting two spheres, the lifeworld based on communicative action, and the system based on instrumental and strategic action.

With the advancement of modernity, the system imperatives of economy and state make increasing demands on the lifeworld, aided by the media of money and power on which individuals become increasingly dependent in their everyday lives. Specialised forms of institutionally-based knowledge originating in these two systems come to replace traditional forms of knowledge, emptying the lifeworld of its implicit and shared understandings. However, for Habermas, this 'colonisation of the lifeworld' is not a simple process whereby the social system replaces the lifeworld, but a process in which the lifeworld has already acquired modern structures of consciousness for tackling cognitive, normative and sincerity claims (e.g. 1987, p. 318). The scope of system-influences on the lifeworld has become so extensive that the differentiated and enhanced forms of rationality are formalised, detached from the lifeworld, and appropriated by economic and state systems in a way that is functional to their maintenance.

For Habermas, these developments contribute towards a fragmentation of everyday consciousness that has rendered impotent the dominant and unifying political ideologies of modernity: socialism, social democracy, conservatism and fascism. In the nineteenth and twentieth centuries, these ideologies provided world-views that shaped everyday experience in the lifeworld, encompassed broader perspectives of the economic, social and political systems, and integrated lifeworld and system. With the advancement of modernity, however, such ideologies no longer have the power to grip the popular imagination – a reflection earlier formulated in Daniel Bell's 'end of ideology' thesis (1962). Instead economic and administrative systems have imposed their own 'expert' rationalities of law, planning and technology, that prove alien to the lifeworld and prevent the emergence of political ideologies that offer global solutions and a sense of solidarity. New forms of reification emerge linked to expert rationality which estrange individuals from their lifeworld. These are, Habermas argues, 'the structural equivalents for ideology formation' available in the modern world (1987, p. 355). Individuals experience themselves as 'things' in a world of objects that lack intrinsic meaning and have been commodified and administered through the media of money and power. What counts as success is the effective exploitation of other 'objects'. These processes of reification accompany the differentiation of modern thought into the separate spheres of science, morality and art, establishing specialised areas of expertise that have become detached from the everyday experience of the lifeworld. Thus 'in place of (ideological) "false consciousness" we today have a "fragmented consciousness" that blocks enlightenment by the mechanism of reification' (*ibid.*). Habermas is suggesting that the capacity of ideology to provide holistic worldviews, to synthesise different viewpoints and experiences, is undermined by the pervasive rationalities of modern capitalism, namely the three forms of social abstraction associated with commodified labour, bureaucratic administration and the formal rule of democracy.

The welfare state has played a significant role in the reification of these three areas, in ways that show how far Habermas has developed his theory of capitalist crises and the welfare state since the early 1970s. For Habermas, the welfare state serves as the source of compensation for the exigencies befalling social life and labour (accidents, sickness, unemployment, retirement and old age, poverty, homelessness). Thus it provides a system of public support that cushions the impact on labour of the capitalist economic system. Together with modern forms of collective bargaining, welfare compensation permits a degree of distribution of surplus value in the form of use values, and helps to extend citizenship rights to the least powerful. However, this support is gained at the cost of a high degree of abstraction. For in reality, benefits are fixed in relation to prevailing levels of monetary and exchange value and so drawn into the abstract commodity form. The rights of citizens to participate in the democratic polity rarely translate into universal entitlements, but rather are formalised into selective, often means-tested, and highly regulated conditions of entitlement. Consequently, securing these rights requires a formal system of bureaucratic administration, law and surveillance to monitor clients' circumstances, their changing needs, incomes and domestic conditions in relation to fixed conditions of entitlement. This reification of client needs and rights violates shared experience and communication in the lifeworld.

For Habermas the welfare state is the main institutional form which the state takes in late capitalism and provides one of the main avenues for colonising the lifeworld (1987, p. 361). The crisis nature of welfare capitalism stems from conflict within the welfare state between its compensatory functions, geared to the distribution of use values to satisfy human needs that are vital to the lifeworld, and its reification functions that promote forms of system domination and abstraction inimical to the lifeworld.

For Habermas, the core element in the rationalisation of the lifeworld is the process of 'juridification' or the legalisation of social life: the increasing tendency, complementing the media of power and money, for law to regulate aspects of everyday life, especially those subject to welfare state bureaucracy (1987, p. 357). Citizens of the welfare state are governed by state rationality, and by a process of 'compulsory abstraction' or reification pervading social life. Law has become the principal means of exercising control and steering the welfare state apparatus, complementing the 'steering media' of money and power. The welfare state is the latest stage in the development of the paradoxical forces of juridification: extending universal democratic rights, on the one hand, and pervading legal forms of rationalisation and control, on the other. This process has been under way since the formation in the eighteenth century of the constitutional state, with the authority to confer civil rights and protect citizens from the arbitrary use of sovereign power. It reaches its present stage with the formation of the modern democratic welfare state which derives its legitimation from its capacity to address citizens needs. The welfare state continues the process of 'freedom guaranteeing juridification' (1987, p. 361) by restricting the demands of the economic system on social life, by for example redressing the unequally distributed benefits and diswelfares of production in the lifeworld. Habermas describes the welfare state as the 'institutionalisation in legal form of a social power relation anchored in class structure', and instances the limitations placed upon working hours, the freedom to organise unions and bargain for wages, job security, social security, etc. Each is an instance of juridification in the sphere of social labour that was previously subject to the unrestricted powers of the private owners of production.[5]

We can now see more clearly the fundamental ambiguity affecting the welfare state, of bestowing freedom while also retracting freedom (1987, p. 361). This ambiguity stems from the characteristics of juridification. On the one hand, it is required positively to guarantee freedom, in the form of compensation for deprivations and restrictions suffered in the lifeworld. On the other, juridification necessitates less positively a formal apparatus that administers, monitors and exacts individual conformity to general norms. While in principle aiming to protect the viability of the lifeworld, the legal system of welfare in practice violates its values and concrete forms of life, its free-forming communications and life-projects. These effects are felt beyond the influence of democratic politics. Together 'juridification and bureaucratisation [act] as the limits to welfare policy'. The dilemma of juridification:

consists in the fact that, while the welfare-state guarantees are intended to serve the goal of social integration, they nevertheless promote the disintegration of life-relations when these are separated, through legalised social intervention, from the consensual mechanisms that coordinate action and are transferred over to media such as power and money. (1987, p. 364)

The crisis of the welfare state becomes a crisis of social integration itself. For example, welfare provisions for geriatric care have 'burdensome consequences for the self-image ... for ... relations with spouse, friends, neighbours, and ... for the readiness of solidaric communities to provide subsidiary assistance' (1987, p. 362). In Chapter 9 we will see how Foucault develops a similar account of welfare in his portrayal of the disciplinary technologies for 'normalising' individuals.

In addition to these inherent contradictions, the welfare state is besieged from Left and Right by influential critics fearful of its possible side-effects and critical of its failures. Against the belief that a welfare state would humanise the sufferings of social labour, both critiques wish to prioritise production, and the system needs of instrumental and formal rationality, over the lifeworld (Habermas 1986). On the Left, pro-welfare and mainly Social Democratic elements wish to replace socialist belief in a freely labouring society with a new realism that more effectively welds the welfare state to modernised capitalism. On the Right, neo-conservatives seek to remove the public burden of welfare from capital's shoulders so that unfettered and restructured capitalism can strive for new levels of accumulation. With the loss of the utopian vision of the welfare state, Habermas argues that both critiques fall prey to a 'new obscurity', an incapacity to see a future characterised by 'a collectively better and less endangered way of life'. The future of modernity thus appears 'exhausted of utopian energies' (1986).

Welfare and the renewal of social solidarity

Yet, for Habermas and Offe (Offe 1982) the welfare state remains an important part of advanced capitalism, one that it cannot afford to relinquish. More significantly, it has the potential to revive a new utopianism, no longer connected to the vision of emancipated social labour, but tied to the desire to re-establish solidarity and consensus. It is this ideal of consensus which relies on the lifeworld for its formation, and which the welfare state has the resources and authority to advance. Thus, Habermas argues for a new balance in the exchange between the media of money, power and welfare solidarity that would redress the exploitation and reification that the economic and administrative systems inflict on the lifeworld (1986, p. 14). This requires that 'the socially integrating force of solidarity would have to be in a position to assert itself against ... money and administrative power' (*ibid.*). The welfare state, however, as noted above, is caught in a dilemma in giving and retracting freedom, so that its potential for solidarity is weakened by its susceptibility to economic and political forces. However, the administrative-legal institution of the welfare state has one redeeming feature, compared with other examples of juridification. In seeking to underwrite the broad range of social needs, the welfare state must be seen as legitimate in the eyes of its citizens.

The need for normative justification is an institutional feature of the modern juridical welfare state. However, the democratic basis of the welfare state vies with its procedural, legal rationality that contributes to the new forms of reification discussed earlier. As a consequence of the process of juridification, a growing body of procedures and practices emerges, and law acquires an autonomous form that furnishes its own legal norms and forms of justification which do not have to make reference to the range of needs and values in society. However, ultimately welfare interventions and sanctions, such as those involved in education and family policy, receive their legitimacy from a democracy whose vitality can stem only from the lifeworld itself. In this sense their existence depends on their relevance for the lifeworld, a relevance that translates into questions about the normative justifications for welfare policies. It is the conflict between these two forms of legal sanction – procedural and institutional – and their different sources of authority – legal positivism and democratic legitimation – that forms the basis of the crisis and dilemmas faced by the welfare state, and which today generates most acutely the confrontation between the norms of system rationalisation and lifeworld communicative reason (Habermas 1987, p. 365).

A significant case for the welfare state was a High Court decision in 1990 affecting the legitimacy of the Conservative government's Social Fund. Under the provision of the 1986 Social Security Act, the Department of Social Security is empowered to give Social Fund loans to claimants according to their needs (replacing a previous provision that gave 'exceptional needs' *grants*). However, the High Court declared that the government was acting unlawfully in denying discretionary loans to deserving cases on the grounds that the Social Fund had, or was about to, run out of money. Directions from the government about budgeting constraints had the effect of nullifying need criteria in determining the exercise of discretion (*The Times*, 22 February 1990). This decision can be described as giving voice to the communicative rationality required of social needs in a welfare state over the strategic rationality of budgetary discipline. Though the communicative rationality associated with human need is by no means guaranteed – indeed subsequently the government has amended the law to restore financial control – it stands as a major principle for testing normative claims in a welfare state.

For Habermas, the dilemmas of the welfare state cannot be resolved by government attempts to impose new legal, bureaucratic and economic disciplines that violate the lifeworld. Moreover, the lifeworld has itself generated new forms of resistance and dissidence to these intrusions. These arise in the form of new social movements which share a concern to revive the autonomy of particular lifeworld cultures – havens for cultural and ethnic autonomy, women's liberation, environmental conservation and world peace – threatened by economic and state powers. Such movements are characterised by their 'self-limiting' rejection of total revolutions (e.g. of the Marxist variety), their defence of autonomous forms of life, and their advancement of new collective identities (see White 1988, pp. 123–4). The struggles of these movements centre on the preservation and enhancement of their distinct domains of life; for 'only the dissidents consider it essential to strengthen the autonomy of a lifeworld that is being threatened in its vital foundations and its communicative infrastructure' (Habermas 1986, p. 13) by the process of colonisation. On the basis of their communicative morality, they can demand normative justification of administrative and economic policies, provisions and practices. The welfare state offers a terrain where these movements can struggle to generalise their specific interests and enhance communicative values and universal norms. But 'the answers could be turned to the offensive only if the project of the social welfare state were not simply carried on or abandoned, but rather continued to a higher level of reflection' (*ibid.*, p. 14). By this Habermas is pointing to 'the difficult task' of making possible within the public domain a democratic generalisation of different interest positions and a universal justification of social norms. This would call for innovative 'combinations of power and intelligent self-limitation', qualities that the state planning apparatus is no longer capable of exercising.[6]

Habermas's theory of ideology: an assessment

In keeping with the tradition of Critical Theory, Habermas' theory of ideology performs a critical function that seeks to disclose the distortions produced by ideology within capitalist society. As we have seen, this tradition, expressed most clearly in the work of Horkheimer (e.g. 1972), sought to reveal the discrepancy between the ideals and actions of key social institutions. However, Habermas sees this form of 'immanent' critique as insecurely founded, liable to lapse into relativism because it takes its bearings from the ideals internal to the institutions being criticised (cf. Roderick 1986, p. 43). To avoid this slippage from reality to relativism, Critical Theory needs a stronger foundation from which to mount critical judgements. Habermas adopts a more philosophical foundation for ideology critique, one that affirms an ideal speech situation which, as we saw at the beginning of the chapter, demands a rational discourse free of all forms of domination as a precondition for establishing truth claims about reality. In this discourse 'the "force" of the argument is the only permissible compulsion' and 'the cooperative search for truth the only permissible motive' (1978, p. 363). As we also suggested earlier, such universal grounds for truth apply not only to cognitive and scientific truth claims, but to normative and sincerity claims as well. A universally valid argument for a particular social arrangement, executed in conformity to the standards of ideal speech, would also be an argument for a universally just arrangement. It is on the basis of such universal reasoning that Habermas mounts his critique of ideological distortion.

While this is a powerful and subtle argument for ideology critique, there are several problems. First, Habermas's presupposition of an ideal speech situation as the consensual basis upon which truth claims are made places a considerable burden on the procedural aspect of verification: establishing truth is a matter of *agreeing* about truth. Similarly, systematically distorted speech refers to a denial of the means for reaching agreement. In either case, a procedural position on truth – has the claim been arrived at consensually? – need not address the substantive features of a claim – what is it that the claim asserts is true? For, whatever the procedures followed to verify a claim, they must always refer to a specific claim (involving 'propositional content') about something, the object or set of circumstances referred to. There is a danger of a vacuous or even untruthful content invading consensual propositions that advance claims about the world whose substance is itself not addressed. This vacuity problematises rather than advances the earlier notion of ideology critique as revealing discrepancy between a substantive institutional reality and its ideals. In Habermas's revision, the absence of substantive verification of claims about reality cannot guarantee freedom from ideology. We are asked – at least in Habermas's earlier work (e.g. 1978) – to accept that the procedures of communicative action are sufficient to establish truth claims; that the very act of communication implies a desire for consensus – an invisible force drawing communicants to the altar of truth. This theory of truth indeed has an element of the mystery of faith about it. For, despite a belief in the validity of democratic judgement, what is to stop a consensus forming around an ideology which has little or no basis in truth?

In responding to this criticism, Habermas has formalised his position by identifying two distinct realms of truth claims: its objectively correct referential meaning (where a statement corresponds to the facts or conditions referred to in the claim) and 'discursive verification', the means for coming to an agreement on the status of the truth claim. Habermas acknowledges both realms, but insists that there cannot be objective meaning about real facts or just arrangements unless there is first discursive verification, which 'reflects the intersubjective validity, on the basis of which something may be predicated of objects of experience' (1978, p. 361).

An approach to ideology founded on a theory of truth, as Habermas provides, may give rise also to an overly negative view of ideology as the denial of truth, which overlooks several positive features of ideology. The problem in understanding ideology is that it exists in complex discourses containing distortions *and* truths. For example, the structure of a social institution such as welfare may contribute to a division of policy into separate discourses. This happens in public policy where theoretical, normative and practical discourses are held by academics, politicians and practitioners, and where the views in one discourse come to influence others. What is judged ideological distortion in a theoretical or normative discourse may be extended to a practical discourse in a way that obscures beneficial developments at the operational level of policy. For example, the media are sometimes held to manipulate public opinion to gain support for government pro-market policies, such as the sale of council houses. The fact that policy is supported by ideological manipulation, and therefore domination, may lead to a view of the policy as systematically distorted. However, the value of pro-market policies may lie in an entirely different direction, affecting the practical outcomes of policy, such as the impact on consumers in advancing their individual autonomy. Theoretical and normative discourses may be slow to recognise these beneficial effects of policy.

However, this criticism of Habermas's negative view of ideology assumes that there can be different and unconnected policy-discourses that ideology has, as it were, hermetically sealed off from one another. Although this may be the case, different truth claims must ultimately refer to the same objects, outcomes, circumstances or reality, and cannot be judged sufficiently by the adequacy of the propositional content they each separately contain. In this respect, Habermas would hold that all discourses maintain some relationship to each other by virtue of the relationship each – including lies – has to truth. The problem from this view is one of overcoming the artificial separation of policy, and other discourses, into theoretical, normative and practical spheres – a concern at the centre of Habermas's project.

As a further example of the drawbacks of his negative view of ideology, Habermas appears to maintain by his notion of 'systematically distorted communication' an absolute view of ideology as distortion that leaves no room for the prefigurative function of ideology in intimating a normative state that more genuinely reflects social justice, such as a welfare state where need is better satisfied. Of course, prefigurative thought can lead to a utopian perspective which blinkers the subject's view of the reality of present sources of oppression. Evidently, there is a delicate balance between ideology's distortional and prefigurative moments. Habermas's recognition of the counterfactual turn implied by critical thought can be taken as a recognition of prefiguration; though he does not incorporate this in his account of ideology as distortion. Earlier Critical Theory, developed by Adorno, Bloch and Marx, maintained a more multivalent view of the functions of ideology. Despite the complex structure that Habermas ascribes to systematically distorted communications (see J. B. Thompson 1982), he retains a univalent view of its function as distorting truth. This stems from a conception of knowledge that, though recognising its different forms and corresponding validity criteria (cognitive, normative and sincerity), is concerned solely with its truth or falsity. In this respect a richer characterisation of ideology will be suggested in the discussion of Althusser and Lacan in Chapters 8 and 10 respectively.

A further problem lies is Habermas's theory of reification. His account of reification as functionally equivalent to ideology, as fragmenting rather than unifying individual consciousness, does not explain how individuals none the less appear by and large to retain their identity in modern everyday life. For if powerful expert cultures that are increasingly insulated from everyday life have the effect, as Habermas contends, of 'cultural impoverishment', of denying ordinary people access to cognitive and normative understanding, how is it that forms of personal identity are sustained none the less, if not by forms of ideology that effectively unify an individual's self-image in everyday interaction?

White makes a further point about ideological fragmentation. If everyday consciousness has lost its synthesising power, the effect is to undermine the power of Critical Theory's critique of ideology, for 'traditional ideology critique loses its foothold, since it depended on beginning from the *positive* ideals projected within ideology' (1988, p. 117). This problem has led Habermas to develop a critique of cultural impoverishment and fragmentation, for which the communicative model provides a critical foothold that exposes the perverse effects of systematically distorted communication in generating new and subtle forms of reification in the modern world.

Legitimation and the modern welfare state

Critical Theory's account of the welfare state in crisis is structured around several contradictions that alter the balance between state and market and between state and civil society. These contradictions point to a basic opposition between personal needs and the needs of the collective state that lie at the roots of legitimation and rationality crises. In a democracy, the extension of the state into new areas inevitably politicises the public realm by requiring the state to justify its policy. Conversely, the state's refusal to furnish reasons for policy will inhibit the formation of communicative action, cutting off relations between the lifeworld and the state through the imposition of alienating systems of domination. Hence, in the public realm the limits to state legitimation are determined by what Habermas terms the 'communicative organisation' of political action. What is accepted as normatively valid in the public realm must have its basis in the 'lifeworld' of shared understandings forged in the everyday dealings between people, and must be acknowledged in the public realm by the state if it is to retain legitimacy (1987). In *Legitimation Crisis*, written in the early 1970s, Habermas could argue hopefully that:

> As long as we have to do with a form of socialisation that binds inner nature in a communicative organisation of behaviour, it is inconceivable that there should be legitimation of any action . . . that, even approximately, guarantees an acceptance of decisions without reasons. (1976, p. 43)

This 'inconceivable' possibility could only arise 'if the procuring of legitimation were detached from a communicative structure of action' (*ibid.*). Habermas's recent work shows the extent to which he is now prepared to countenance the possibility that the grounds of legitimation have been cut adrift from the lifeworld. This possibility raises important questions about recent policies to restructure welfare. The strategies of welfare privatisation, 'devolved budgeting' in social work, probation work, general practice, the Social Fund and higher education, and the general development of a mixed economy of care, hold out the opportunity of achieving just this possibility. For in the face of demands for justification, the state could resort to a strategy of 'depoliticising the public realm'. Yet against this possibility, we should also consider the alternative, that such moves might inevitably heighten the public's awareness of universal needs that go unmet, and of demands for welfare rights unheeded.

A major test for Habermas's speculations, concerning the force of democratic argument in the redemption of normative claims, can be seen in several examples (discussed in Chapter 3) of current policy to restructure welfare that are ostensibly concerned with facilitating consumer choice, devolving decision-making and improving efficiency. For example, the 1988 Education Reform Act delegates the management of school budgets from local education authorities to reconstituted school governing committees, giving more power to parents to influence the education their children receive. Further, some local schools can elect to be independent of local authorities and receive central government finance directly. A similar 'opt out' arrangement is available under the 1988 Housing Act to council housing estates enabling tenants to 'pick-a-landlord', such as a property company, independent housing association or co-operative instead of the local authority. Similarly, the practice budget arrangements under NHS reforms enacted in 1990 enable general practitioners to purchase hospital treatments and exercise choice on their patients' behalf; coupled with the requirement in the new general practitioner contracts for group practices to make information about the practice publicly available, and so facilitate patient choice. In these examples, the exercise of democracy, the dissemination of information, and the devolution of budgeting and decision-making should ostensibly generate a greater concern in citizens about service quality and rights to welfare. Yet an important objective underlying the government's strategy is to devolve *responsibility* for – as well as control over – welfare provision from central and local government to local agencies as close as possible to the recipients themselves. This restructures not only the locus of supply but also of demand for welfare. Entitlement is no longer the right to state welfare where the state is the universal benefactor, but the right to local welfare where the community or agency is the benefactor and in some cases the beneficiary as well.

In Habermas's terms, under the Conservative government, the redemption of normative claims about welfare no longer lie with the state, but with local and increasingly private agencies, displacing the burden of legitimation to more local communities directly responsible for welfare consumers. Whatever the intention behind recent government policy – whether to increase consumer choice and service efficiency *or* more comprehensively to restructure the welfare state along pro-market and cost-efficient lines – the government is relieved of its responsibilities for failures in welfare quality and delivery. It is possible that a government inspired by these New Right ideas has found the answer to the legitimation problem. In this light some commentators have argued against Habermas's faith in communicative understanding, observing how vulnerable democratic decision-making is to strategic manipulation (e.g. Lukes 1982). Certainly, these possibilities must raise doubts about whether in the real world of politics the abstract rules of communicative understanding have any place. However, a more favourable response to Habermas's project would point to the stimulus democracy presents – however manipulated its arrangements – in that movements of opinion have arisen to challenge these reforms. In undermining communicative order, the denial of universal democratic rights already in place, as much as the denial of universal welfare rights, may act as a spur for political action to regain lost ground and further strengthen the democratic welfare state. There is interesting evidence of support for the welfare state. During the 1980s when Thatcherism was dominant, public support for welfare, recorded annually between 1983 and 1989, has increased to a point where commentators talk of a 'growing consensus' that embraces all income groups (*Guardian* 14 November 1990, p. 21; see Jowell *et al.* 1990; also Taylor-Gooby 1985).

The importance given to the question of need is in part dependent on the emergence of a new political consensus. The provision of administrative welfare poses expectations in the public realm where few existed before, and thereby problematises questions of need. For these issues of welfare policy are public and not exclusively private concerns (Habermas 1976, p. 71). The development of public welfare – welfare in the public domain – means that truth claims concerning needs and the best ways of satisfying them must rely on discursive redemption. Welfare and the assuagement of need become central concerns of a communicative ethic. In this way, Habermas's thought can be seen as a development of the ideas of postwar thinkers on the communitarian basis of the welfare state; such as Titmuss, with his notion of universal welfare strengthening the bonds of social cohesion, and Marshall, with his concept of citizenship as the evolution of civil, political and welfare rights of all. In addition to this, Habermas alludes to a further ideal, the transcendental community of the ideal speech situation whose presupposition is necessary in order to understand the conditions for redeeming truth claims in the normative and political spheres. While its realisation in a fallible world of less than perfect men and women may be far from achievable, it stands as an important and necessary ideal for a community in which universal will-formation is oriented to reason, democracy and social cohesion.

Notes

1. For a discussion of the role of social movements within the context of the contradictions of modern capitalism, see Castells (1977, ch. 14); Habermas (1987, pp. 391–6); Laclau and Mouffe (1985, p. 159); Lash and Urry (1987, ch. 7).
2. See, e.g., Fraser's 'What's Critical About Critical Theory?' (1985) and McCarney's 'What Makes Critical Theory Critical?' (1986).
3. In several respects, similar ground is covered by State Overload theorists on the political right who use a crisis theory of the state to argue for reducing government functions (see Birch 1984).
4. Townsend, for example, has described this phase of welfare development as 'distributional justice for all' (1979, p. 62; see also Doyal and Gough 1984).
5. Unlike Political Economy and feminist theories of welfare, Habermas does not appear to spell out the differences between the welfare protection and compensation due social labour and that due non-working groups. The assumption is that the latter is contingent on the former, either as former workers (the retired), future workers (children, trainees and students), unemployed workers, and domestic workers supporting productive workers.
6. Habermas treads close to neo-conservatives who make similar calls for self-restraint. Bell, for example, argues that the basis of consensus in advanced industrial society must rest on a 'public philosophy' that provides moral criteria for determining the balance between growth and social consumption (1976, p. 236).

7

Disorganised capitalism and the problems of need and welfare

Some of the implications of Habermas's account of welfare and need have received a more thoroughgoing sociological treatment in the work of several writers on disorganised capitalism, of whom Claus Offe is central. These writers also attend to the contradictions of advanced capitalism and accord a critical position to welfare within this framework of disorganisation. Like Habermas, they divide capitalist society into three systems – economic, political-administrative, normative – each governed respectively by the organisational processes of exchange, coercion and normative compliance (see Etzioni 1961). According to Offe, for example, the stability of capitalist society is unsettled by two processes undermining economic exchange and accumulation. First, capitalism becomes increasingly dependent on the coercive interventions of the state, which, if not tamed, impose norms antithetical to exchange and the free market. Secondly, capitalist organisations attempt to repel these untamable non-market processes, treating them as exogenous 'foreign elements'. For the capitalist state, the problem is how to harness this trinity of irreconcilable but necessary processes so that coercion and normative compliance complement rather than undermine market exchange (Offe 1984, p. 39).

For Habermas and Offe in particular, the inherent limits to accumulation arise from the confrontation between the unremitting logics of accumulation and legitimation, which together produce the inescapable crisis tendencies of late capitalism. It is this confrontation that undermines attempts at harmonising economic, political and normative systems. The conflict is seen especially in the disorganisation of late capitalism. Several writers have suggested recently that late capitalism is characterised by a process of disorganisation that causes fragmentation and diversification in the productive, political and cultural spheres. These processes contrast with the concentration and convergence that characterised the previous more organised stage of capitalism (see Lash and Urry 1987). In turn these processes unsettle the normative and cultural foundations of modern society and are seen by some to usher in a new age of postmodernity (see Lyotard 1984).

The movement from organised to disorganised capitalism underlies several processes contributing to the nature of ideology and crisis in the welfare state, which are discussed in the work of Offe and others. This chapter examines each in turn, namely: the commodification and decommodification of needs; market utilisation and state subsidisation of labour power in the production of value; the loss of needs criteria of value under disorganised capitalism; and the growth of the service sector, distinct from the productive, with its contrasting communicative rationality. Although each of these problems raises questions of intrinsic interest, they bear on the broader questions of ideological distortion in capitalist society, and the possibility of redeeming undistorted truth and directing collective action towards social welfare.

Commodification and value realisation

A significant feature of the disorganisation of late capitalism is the contradictory processes that arise as more and more resources are allocated to meeting social needs. For Offe, these processes transform need into either individual demands for commodities supplied in the market – i.e. commodification – or collective welfare provisions allocated by state bureaucracy, by a process of decommodification.[1] For example, in the market housing needs are met through exchanges between consumers and suppliers that commodify needs. Conversely, housing needs are met by the state according to administrative processes that decommodify need. These processes reflect the historical development in the commodity form – from commodification through decommodification to recommodification – that inscribes the long term movement from organised to disorganised capitalism. When workers could successfully exchange their labour value as a commodity and acquire sufficient market goods for their subsistence, there was no need for state intervention and accumulation continued undeterred. However, when workers cannot exist by means of commodity exchange alone – when there is a 'paralysis of the commodity form' (Offe 1984, p. 122) – the state begins to decommodify some of these goods by subsidising them, thereby generating the wider process of welfare formation. However, both processes are subject to the same logic directed towards enabling units of labour to *function as commodities* within the market – a process recently requiring 'administrative recommodification' as various western governments in the 1980s sought to privatise state provisions (*ibid.*, p. 124). In an analysis of the labour process in the health service, Christine Cousins provides an account of management strategies to recommodify parts of the NHS during the 1980s, when government policy was directed towards opening up public services to market forces (1987, pp. 136, 177).

Developments in the commodity form began in the nineteenth century with the destructive impact of manufacturing and urbanisation on the working population. Increasing rates of illness and mortality reduced the lifespan and productivity of workers and gave rise to demands for decommodified forms of welfare and improved work conditions. The implementation of these reforms not only improved living conditions, but contributed to raising the level of labour productivity (see Fraser 1973). While the contrary tendencies of commodification and decommodification are worked through, Offe argues that powerful state apparatuses, professional dominance and heightened public expectations, prove obstacles to eventual recommodification – major themes shaping the political agenda for the 1990s.

Directing the cycle of commodification and decommodification is the state's desire to organise labour more effectively for the labour market. Offe charac-·terises the organisation of labour power in late capitalism as the tendency for capitalist relations between employers and workers to absorb ever smaller portions of labour time, thus pointing to 'the relative decline in the organising potential of the wage-labour-capital relationship *vis-à-vis* total social labour power' (Offe 1984, p. 42). However, in principle the capitalist accumulation process requires the full employment of labour power to maximise value production. Indeed, in the early and mid-periods, capitalism had to convert non-wage agricultural labour into wage-labour subject to the discipline of industrial production. This period, represented by the growth of capital formation, required an increasing absorption of labour power until a point of maximum utilisation was reached, the high point of organised capitalism. Thereafter, in late, less organised capitalism, the declining rates of profit and capitalisation of production reversed the process of absorption and led to the shedding of labour power. Hence, with the support of government, capital has had to further the accumulation process by continuing to resort to practices influenced by principles other than exchange, especially coercive disciple and normative compliance, to facilitate the conversion of wage-labour. For example, employers have introduced new methods of work organisation to raise productivity, such as 'scientific management', and the state has extended welfare provisions underwritten by the work ethic, such as contributory insurance and means-tested social assistance. Offe's work recognises the significance of the complementary roles played by work disciplines and welfare inducements in the transformation of labour power.[2]

In this respect, Offe identifies the key function of social policy as 'a state strategy incorporating labour power into the wage-labour relation' (1984, p. 98); a perspective that complements Gough's view of the welfare state as in part 'the use of state power to modify the reproduction of labour power' (1979, pp. 44–5). Consequently, 'The owner of labour power first becomes a wage labourer as a citizen of the state' (Offe 1984, p. 99). This suggests that the state's interest in personal welfare is a direct function of its interest in labour reproduction and indirectly in commodity production, and that overall social policy contributes to the constitution of the working class. This perspective therefore places the notion of citizenship rights within the framework of conflicting labour-capital relations – relations viewed with a contrasting equanimity by Marshall (1963) in his earlier portrayal of the evolution of citizenship.

This account of the functions of social policy is radically different from the conventional view held by social administrators; that social policy enhances welfare by satisfying need. It also differs in some respects from the orthodox Marxist view that welfare controls the dependent population. Rather, social policy is deployed by the state to manage the wage-labour relationship. It meets need and it controls the population, only in so far as these requirements accord with the dictates of this relationship. Offe's notion of social policy as the incorporation of labour power into the wage-labour relationship suggests that the traditional definition of the purpose of social policy as meeting human need is misguided. For example, the argument of both social administration and Political Economy that social policy has followed in the wake of, and has corresponded to, the mounting diswelfares caused by industrialisation, and the growing organisational strength and demands of the labour movement, requires a demonstration of why the system of political institutions is sufficiently aware and responsive to working class demands. More specifically it requires a demonstration of why the response is proportional to these demands rather than over or underdetermined by them. In this light, Offe concludes 'that policy development cannot be fully explained by needs' (1984, p. 102). Need cannot count as the single *raison d'etre* of social policy, as is often claimed. Rather this view constitutes an ideological construction of the subject and purpose of social policy. A better explanation of welfare formation, Offe contends, would argue that the ruling class only concedes welfare reforms when such compromises entail the coincidence of interests of ruling and working classes alike (*ibid.*, p. 103).

The loss of need criteria under disorganised capitalism

The critique of the idea that state welfare meets needs has implications for the more theoretical concerns of Critical Theory. In questioning the needs function of welfare, Critical Theory has cast further doubt on the presupposition in Marxism and mainstream social administration that need has an objective and independent status as a social variable. Marx, for example, adopted as his standard of need the needs of labour to secure its own reproduction. As we saw in Chapter 5, though acutely aware of the historical and cultural factors constructing need, Marx assumed that once formed, need defined use and surplus value alike. But in advanced capitalist societies, the political system develops forms of welfare that provide collective means more directly geared to meeting need and producing use values than is possible in the productive system alone. This means that ideological processes are active in the political system and therefore implicated in the formation, identification and satisfaction of need – making problematic the assumption that need is an independent variable in late capitalist society.

Modern theorists have developed these insights into the problematic status of need as a standard of human value. Before discussing Habermas and Offe's treatment of these insights, we will refer to two theorists – William Leiss and Frederic Jameson – who themselves use these insights to provide a critical understanding of modern capitalism, but who do so on the basis of a radical critique that at times appears to lose the foothold needed to mount an alternative understanding of need and welfare – a task that Habermas and Offe remain firmly committed to. Both writers focus on the submission – increasingly total, they argue – of the human faculty of rational and critical judgement to the cultural system of modern capitalism, rendering the individual incapable of independent judgement in identifying his or her needs, wants and desires. This loss is depicted in terms of the rapid changes affecting social time and space. For Leiss, this concerns the unnerving pace of modern market operations, and for Jameson, the total diffusion of social space by a modern culture marked by its ephemerality and instability. Jameson refers to 'a prodigious expansion of culture throughout the social realm, to the point at which everything in our social life – from economic value and state power and practice to the very structure of the psyche itself – can be said to have become cultural in some original and untheorised sense' (1984, p. 87). The result is a loss of critical distance, the impossibility of locating 'an Archimedean point' from which to critically dissect capitalism. More specifically, Leiss sees capitalist values dominating the process of market valuations in which each consumer gauges the degree to which commodities satisfy his or her needs. Thus, 'the perception of the usefulness of things related to needs such as food and clothing is . . . conditioned by cultural or symbolic mediations' (1978, p. 87). In 'high intensity market settings' the satisfaction of need is characterised by confusion as commodities become 'progressively more unstable, temporary collections of objective and imputed (symbolic) characteristics – that is, highly complex material-symbolic entities. The disintegration of the characteristics of objects stands in reciprocal relation to the fragmentation of needs' (*ibid.*, p. 92).

Given the loss of critical judgement, Leiss and Jameson both argue for the dialectical reasoning of Marxist Critical Theory to re-establish judgement in postmodern society, and to harness those progressive features of capitalism that have the capacity to remove the alienation individuals experience in relation to their real needs (Leiss 1978, pp. 111–12; Jameson 1984, p. 88). Such thinking moves beyond an orthodox Marxism that posits the notion of need as an independent and absolute standard for measuring use value, welfare and the reproduction of labour. Needs, Leiss argues, are not the intrinsic property of objective things like commodities. For needing arises in relations between consumers who need and objects needed, and must be understood in terms of the duality of the material and symbolic correlates shaping these relations. This duality 'does not allow us to postulate the existence of direct (i.e. unmediated) needs at any stage in . . . human development' (Leiss 1978, p. 88). However, it is not clear from this critique how we are to see need in a more positive light. Leiss proposes the use of Critical Theory to understand true needs by utilising a 'negative theory of need' as a way of arriving at true need (*ibid.*, p. 111), but does not elaborate on this project. By contrast, Critical Theory's contribution to understanding need is further advanced by Habermas and Offe, in their critical rethinking of the process of value realisation in the capitalist welfare state.

This new direction in the theory of need is seen in the way they recast a central component of Marx's theory of value realisation – the labour process. We saw in Chapter 5 that O'Connor and Gough accept the Marxist distinction between productive and non-productive labour and that they apply the notions of indirectly and non-productive labour to different sectors of welfare activity. Offe and Habermas raise doubts about whether such hard-and-fast categories apply to the labour process in advanced capitalism, with its large political-administrative system influencing economic exchange. Indeed they note the presence of a service sector in the economy guided by normative rather than exchange principles, and the significance of what is termed 'reflexive labour' within this sector. This focus has considerable pertinence for their characterisation of welfare and the value of welfare production, and particularly for the question of the 'productivity' of the administrative sector, the 'elasticity' of economic value, and consequently the question itself of welfare ideology.

The productive and service sectors: instrumental and reflexive reasoning

The emergence of a large service sector in late capitalism arises from the growing need for contributions to the productive process from independent agencies that are indispensable to this process. The provision of services such as health and welfare, education and training, information and advertising entails specialist skills whose cost and development it would be uneconomic for individual producers to bear as in-house activities. A large number of producers can, however, buy in services from independent, specialist agencies. The stock of knowledge and technology acquired by each agency means that the service sector can contribute towards commodity production without being owned by a single producer; for example, by restoring unfit workers to health, by making available research on production technology, markets and so forth, and by advertising and marketing products. The service sector is part of the increasing division of labour occurring not only in the differentiation of specialist skills and technologies, but also in the growth of whole industries each concentrating on a specific service provision – welfare, information technology, advertising, finance, etc. (Bell 1976; Lash and Urry 1987, ch. 6; Offe 1985). Specialist services that were once provided by some individual firms – such as schools and health care for workers and their children in nineteenth-century Britain – are now provided by the state, quasi-state or private service industries.[3]

The growth of this sector has given rise to a large social group whose interests lie in service work. Several writers see this class identity as one which cannot be reduced to the interests of either capital or labour, and stress its positive attributes as a 'third force' contributing to the production and accumulation process and playing a significant role in shaping the poiitical and social structure of late capitalism. In this vein, Lash and Urry argue that 'Once attaining a certain threshold of development and mobilisation, this new class itself begins to have a dislocating effect on the relationship between capital and labour and an irredeemably disorganising effect on capitalist society in general' (Lash and Urry 1987, pp. 161–2; cf. Habermas 1976, p. 56; Offe 1985, p. 101).

Habermas and Offe see in the service sector the development of a new type of labour that is less subject to commodity production and its strategic rationality, and more committed to developing its own technology and knowledge base. Ideally, 'reflexive labour', like reflexive learning (see Habermas 1976, p. 15), entails a commitment to the communicative ethic of participants discursively and intersubjectively appraising the means employed in their labour and the ends to which their labour and its products are put. In its involvement with commodity production, this type of work is concerned with providing activities which operate outside the norms of economic and technological rationality, and which can exercise an influence over the production process, activities such as the education and training of future labour, and the diversion of capital from direct accumulation into various types of finance capital. Offe proposes that

> In industrial capitalist societies, the continuous and steady increase in the proportion of social labour employed in service production indicates that scarcity and efficiency problems, which determine the rationality of the production of industrial commodities, are supplemented with problems of order and normalisation which cannot be dealt with adequately by means of the technical and economic mastery of scarcity, but rather require a separate rationality of service labour. (1985, p. 137)

Of course, there are pressures on the service sector to conform to capitalist production that are bound to constrain its autonomy and compromise its communicative rationality. This may well prove problematic for Habermas who has consistently argued the distinction between communicative and strategic rationality – a distinction derived from his earlier critique of Marx's rendering of human interaction and self-formation to the single category of labour, with its determinist and reductionist connotations (see Habermas 1974, p. 142).[3]

However, notwithstanding this, Habermas and Offe stress the distinctive features of service work based on a 'reflexive' rationality that contributes to the formation of the normative sphere of society. By contrast with the controllable nature of work under commodity production, work in the service sector is characterised by a degree of heterogeneity and unpredictability, which cannot be made to conform to technological and economic standards of efficiency. The criteria governing service production are more concerned with producing concrete use values than with monetary profits, and depend on skills of interpersonal communication, empathy and consensus-building rather than technical and economic mastery – two sets of skills resting on different forms of rationality, Offe claims (1985, pp. 138–9). For example, welfare is often characterised as the provision of services for people with needs which cannot be met through the normal avenues of market exchange, and for which individuals cannot make straightforward preparation, as in the case of acute illness. The provision of medicine, social work, education and income maintenance will always entail elements that are personalised and unpredictable. In Freudian terms, Offe characterises the essential indefinability of service work as 'the return of the repressed' that inevitably follows in the wake of the routinisation and rationality of economic production.

However, it is arguable whether welfare and other forms of service work, which address needs and production-for-use, can be characterised by a communicative ethic devoid of strategic rationality. The changes welfare has been subject to in the 1980s have shown to a remarkable degree its submission to strategic considerations of budgeting, efficiency and bureaucratic administration. Offe acknowledges some of these problems such as the ever-present concern of service work to standardise its applications and maintain normality. In this he recognises the ambiguity surrounding the contrary objectives of attending to the particular contingencies of individual needs, whilst none the less ensuring that needs are treated in conformity with general rules. In this respect, Offe proposes the following dictum: 'It is always necessary to simultaneously standardise the case and individualise the norm' (1985, p. 106) – a dilemma also addressed by Habermas on the colonisation of the lifeworld, and by Foucault on modern disciplinary technologies.

Offe's and Habermas's accounts raise again the perennial problem in Marxist and non-Marxist theory of whether service labour can be categorised as either productive or unproductive. Offe is critical of the residual and negative connotations found in sociological accounts of the service sector as having *non*-material and *un*quantifiable outcomes and being *un*susceptible to technical rationalisation (1985, pp. 104–5, my emphasis). Thereby, service work, like welfare work, is characterised as unproductive. Habermas says further that

If one holds fast to a dogmatic conceptual strategy and conceives of reflexive labour as unproductive labour (in the Marxian sense), the specific function of this labour for the realisation process is overlooked. Reflexive labour is not productive in the sense of the direct production of surplus value. But it is also not unproductive; for then it would have no net effect on the production of surplus value. (1976, p. 56)

He refers to Marx's statement about the autonomy some means of production, such as 'labour power, science and land', possess within a given magnitude of capital, as an '*elastic power*' exercised as 'a field of action independent of its own magnitude' (Marx 1976, p. 758). The elasticity and autonomy of service work lies in its concern with interpersonal, symbolic and cognitive spheres of production. It has the power to mediate in communication problems to which commodity production is susceptible in adhering rigidly to the monological imperatives and disciplines of management hierarchies, which for the most part are not given to the pursuit of collaboration and dialogue. This collaboration is involved in satisfying welfare needs and in developing and disseminating knowledge. In contrast to the economic system with its finite resource limits and to the political with its legitimacy limited by its stock of credibility, the social system is seen by Habermas as characterised by its relative plasticity.

The elasticity and autonomy of the service components of production are all the more evident in the enlarged administrative systems of late capitalism, substantially modifying Marx's theorems about the realisation of value. For Habermas, 'the state has altered the determinants of the realisation process itself' (1976, p. 61). According to Marx's law of value, the production of surplus value can only operate in conditions of market capitalism. But today, instead, the existence of a relatively autonomous service sector that receives income for reflexive labour 'systematically alters the conditions under which surplus value can be appropriated from productive labour', and indirectly increases the production of surplus value. Habermas concludes that 'the classical fundamental categories of the theory of value are insufficient for the analysis of government policy in education, technology and science' (1976, p. 57), to which we would add welfare policy.

The intervention of the state in the labour market upsets market mechanisms for determining the price of labour power by setting prices according to political criteria. Consequently, this invalidates the value of labour power as a standard against which other value forms are measured, such as wage-, use- and surplus-value. For Habermas, the development of the state means that there is no standard for gauging the cost of reproducing labour that is independent of cultural norms, and so divorced from normative considerations (1976, p. 57). In this respect, his approach to the 'realisation' problem is a radical departure from Marxists generally.

Offe suggests further that standards for evaluating administrative production must be procedural as well as intrinsic – as in the case of value theories of classical and Marxist Political Economy – and should be determined by a consensus built between the administration and its public. It is this process that Habermas refers to when speaking of the 'discursive will-formation of need' (e.g. 1979, p. 84); a phrase suggesting that the determinants shaping need lie within the communicative structure of everyday life, producing social movements or crystallising public support for particular social policies. In this light, Offe sees that the value of the outcomes of administrative action are a 'co-production of the administration and its clients' (Offe 1985, p. 310). The 'product' the client receives from the service agency involves an act of collaboration: the producer identifies the individual needs of the client; and the client co-operates in interactive work with the provider, and only thereby completes the product, as in the case of students or social work clients. Although there can never be complete equality between service provider and client, a broadly shared sense of purpose informs their collaboration, which may not be possible under market exchange (Offe 1985, p. 311).[4] The emphasis shifts from the instrumental production of economic value to the intersubjective production of meaning (Habermas 1976, p. 73). Because of the growing service sector with its increasingly heterogeneous labour force producing a diversity of symbolic services and products, Offe claims that elements of the capitalist labour process such as the 'industrial reserve army' are losing their effectiveness.

However, against this claim, it should be noted that counter-tendencies are presently at work, to maximise surplus value by controlling and deskilling parts of the labour process – including those parts offering interpersonal skills in health and social work (Cousins 1987) – and to casualise a wide range of skilled manual tasks. For example, women returners and a new reserve army of young personnel are being trained on government schemes for a restructured labour market that enhances the role of a service sector of deskilled community and hospital carers overseen by a new managerial class of professional former-carers in social work and nursing (e.g. UKCC 1986).

The service, productive and administrative sectors are each driven by divergent logics that pose a potential for conflict in capitalist society: the logic of communication versus the logics of exchange and coercion. However much subject to ideological distortion, for Habermas, the communicative model of the service sector remains a distinct form of reasoning and an important source of validity. The question that remains for the politics of late twentieth-century capitalism, then, is how far the single-minded and strategic pursuit of surplus value, associated especially with the politics of the Right, can be followed before confronting a different set of values about human welfare based on universal criteria of need and communicative interaction.

Conclusion

Habermas and Offe's contribution to the theory of value represents a significant staging-post in an extensive itinerary that seeks to understand the nature of service work in the larger terrain of value production, and to advance the case for the superiority of communicative reasoning. At this stage in their endeavours they have achieved three objectives. First, they have constructed a model of reasoning relevant to the core concerns of service and – for our purposes – welfare work. Secondly, they have shown what components of Marxist realisation theory should be shed, for example, the distinctions between productive and unproductive labour and use- and exchange-value. Thirdly, they identify the previously ignored features of the labour process that positively contribute to the realisation of value: the symbolic, communicative and consensual processes specific to welfare but inherent in all forms of social organisation.

Against these insights, must be placed the limitations that characterise their approach. These stem from a tendency to explicate different logics and models of late capitalist society – communicative and strategic rationality – that represent pure types of social action whose explanatory utility has seemed limited when applied to recent developments, for example to Rightist policies and ideology. This is partly because these developments have far from exhausted themselves at this juncture, and partly because Habermas's faith in communicative rationality requires a commitment to the power of universal normative ideals that have been severely shaken by the politics of the Right – but a commitment none the less that may experience a revival after the setbacks suffered recently by the Right.

Modern Critical Theory has sought to understand the contradictions of the welfare state associated with the disorganisation and fragmentation of late capitalism. Yet more positively, the welfare state plays a key role in generating new means of interaction and communication that are necessary for the formation of social solidarity and economic production in late capitalism. To understand these processes requires a more developed theory of value realisation and the labour process that takes account of the production of use value in meeting human needs (as Leiss among others has suggested). For the nature of use value has changed in a disorganising environment. One of the significant features of the realisation process in the new – and some argue postmodern – world is the central role of symbolic production in economic and political life. The Marxist distinction between use- and exchange-value, with their respective material and symbolic connotations, breaks down in a context where the processes of communicative reasoning and material production increasingly overlap and intertwine. These significant retheorisations suggest a need to review the nature of ideology as the link between symbolic and material production. In this respect, the symbolic and real features of ideology come into their own in the discourse approach to understanding the welfare state, to which we turn in Part III.

Notes

1. Cf. Castells (1978) on 'collective consumption'.
2. Like Offe, Foucault also emphasises the dual aspects of capitalist technical production and social organisation, and the two aspects of discipline as coercion and enhancement (1979a, p. 221).
3. For an assessment of this distinction, see White (1988, p. 44).
4. Of course, New Right thinkers such as Hayek would claim that a higher order of universality governs market exchange. However, Hayek does not see this order as susceptible to conscious and rational interventions by participants. Rather, it arises from individuals pursuing their ends unimpeded by others.

PART 3

Discourse, ideology and welfare

In Part II we saw that Critical Theory in the hands of Habermas took a significant linguistic turn. In Part III we examine this theoretical shift further as it is executed in three different strands of social theory on ideology: Structural Marxism in Chapter 8; post-structuralism in Chapter 9; and structural psychoanalysis in Chapter 10. These strands are associated with the influential thought of three French thinkers, Louis Althusser, Michel Foucault and Jacques Lacan respectively. Chapters 8–10 examine the contribution each strand makes to understanding ideology, and in particular the resources offered in developing further insights into welfare ideology. Although these thinkers have not sought to apply their thought specifically to modern welfare states, their reception by other writers in sociology, politics and social policy in the 1970s and 1980s shows the extent to which their ideas have fomented a creative and wide-ranging series of studies on welfare ideology. Lacan is an exception in that he has attracted a limited and rather mixed response from social theorists (e.g. Giddens 1979, p. 122), though a more favourable response among philosophers, literary theorist and students of psychoanalysis. Yet I hope to show the value of his ideas in understanding the ideology of social need, and, drawing from Part II, to point to convergences between his thought and the Critical Theory of Habermas.

In comparison with Habermas's view of discourse – as propositions judged by their truth content – the approaches discussed in the next three chapters provide perspectives which are less propositional and more concrete in examining discourse in the form of text, books, reports, and other instances of representation; the material site in which ideology is present. Althusser defines ideology as 'a system . . . of representations (images, myths, ideas or concepts) endowed with a historical existence and role within a given society' (1969, p. 233). In this way he introduces the notion of the 'ideological state apparatuses' of modern society represented in a wide range of government texts in public policy, law, science and technology. More specifically, we can examine the particular ideological apparatus that constitutes the welfare state. This is seen in the many different texts – official reports, commissions, statutes, codes of practice and research – that contribute to the form and continuity of the policy process in the modern state, and bind its various levels and sectors into an administrative system. Ideology thus takes the form of an 'ideological formation' essential to the maintenance of modern society. Foucault's contribution (1972) has been to explore more single-mindedly the structure of specific historical 'discursive formations' that constitute a particular body of knowledge with its theoretical and normative assumptions; for example, eighteenth-century theories about mental illness, or the important changes in penal policy that separate modern from Victorian regimes (see Garland 1985). Drawing largely on the ideas of Lacan, Laclau and Mouffe trace the formation of a democratic discourse in the evolution of modern society over the last three hundred years, and in the 'hegemonic formation' of the modern welfare state, which, subject to concerted assaults recently, has shown signs of giving way to a less democratic hegemony – though the confrontation is far from settled.

8

Structural Marxism, ideology and the welfare state

From Structural Marxism and the work of Althusser, we gain a fresh perspective on ideology and the problems in theorising ideology left unresolved by the Marxist traditions discussed in Part II. Not without its own problems, however, this perspective none the less provides insights into the versatility that characterises the state's use of ideology in legitimating its policies, and into the relative autonomy of ideology in shaping the public's response to economic change – concerns downplayed by both Marxist Political Economy and Critical Theory. These insights are made possible by Althusser's proposal that ideology – and other parts of society or the social formation – is '*overdetermined*'. This aspect of ideology is central to the discursive turn in Marxist accounts of welfare ideology and especially Structural Marxism. This chapter examines three aspects of overdetermination central to Althusser's thinking and highlights the power of welfare as an ideological apparatus. The three aspects are: the overdetermination of a structure in dominance, i.e. the overendowment of key social structures empowered to determine others and to shape the overall structure of a social formation; the overdetermined relations individuals have with significant others, both individual and symbolic figures; and the ideological 'problematic' that structures the way people think about social problems. In the 1970s, when Althusser's influence was strongest, several studies of the politics of the welfare state utilised his ideas in areas including urban policy (e.g. Castells 1977; Cockburn 1977), education and training (David 1980), and social work (Corrigan and Leonard 1978). To begin with, however, Structural Marxism will be situated in its intellectual context.

In mainstream Marxism, the designation Structural Marxist would seem redundant, for Marxism is in essence an analysis of the social, economic and political structures comprising the overall structure of a social formation. However, in its French context, the influence of, *inter alia*, the structural linguistics of Saussure, the structural anthropology of Lévi-Strauss, the semiotics of Barthes and the psychoanalysis of Lacan imparted a nuance to intellectual life that encouraged a radical rereading of Marx.[1] Specifically, understanding social practices in terms of the patterns of signification they produce suggested a form of explanation more revealing and appropriate to social life than merely describing these practices and their causation. It implied that a social formation such as capitalist society could be examined in terms of its symbolic structures, its cultural signs and rituals, its political ideologies, and its academic and juridical discourses (Elliott 1987, pp. 332–5) – in other words, in terms of its superstructure, which would disclose a structural reality as interesting as studying the economic determinations of the infrastructure. It also permitted accounts of social processes in terms of supra-individual structures that operate independently of the will of individual or collective actors; the implication being – somewhat questionably – that structuralist analysis had a scientific and objective rigour absent from 'humanist' or 'existential' Marxisms that privileged the human subject of history (e.g. Lukács 1971; see Benton 1984, pp. 14–18).[2]

Thus, Structural Marxism represented a new departure in its close attention to – its 'symptomatic reading' of – the texts of Marx himself, the discourses of capitalist society, and elements of the superstructure. In this context Althusser attended closely to ideology as part of the superstructure exercising a particular form of influence over society. In contrast with the economic determinism of Marxist Political Economy, this approach accords an autonomy to the ideological domain, and opens the way for an account of social practices, including policy, involved in the ideological management of social crises. Further, Althusser's account of the 'relative autonomy' of ideology contrasts with the inbuilt limits that, for Habermas, are a formative feature of the ideological, political and economic systems, and which contribute to the crisis tendencies of late capitalism. It is therefore possible for ideology to exercise an influence over social beliefs with some degree of independence from economic and political determinations. Althusser's approach has paved the way for subsequent studies of ideology (Laclau 1977; Therborn 1980; Laclau and Mouffe 1985), postwar Britain (Hall *et al.* 1978), and late capitalism (Jameson 1984; O'Connor 1984), and suggests with considerable subtlety the complex role played by capitalist and welfare ideology.

Overdetermination as structure in dominance

By overdetermination, Althusser is referring to processes unifying a complex social formation where the relations between the parts – political, ideological, economic, legal, cultural – are prone to contradictions, but where none the less a particular order, such as bourgeois ideology, is dominant (1969, pp. 201–2). In Althusser's conception of overdetermination, the parts of a social formation are not only determined by the economic base, but also determine, however unevenly, each other, including the base. They stand in a complex of co-determined relations, a 'structure in dominance'. In this sense each part is overdetermined by being maintained by the others and in contributing towards their maintenance. Hence, the contradictions characterising each part are determined by contradictions in other parts, which in turn determine other contradictions. A revolutionary transition in society occurs when each of these contradictions fuses into a 'ruptural unity' (Althusser 1969, pp. 100–1; see Benton 1984, p. 68).

Given its complexity, the concept of structural causality – as more than the sum total of separate causal processes – raises problems when applied to the interpretation and analysis of a social formation. For one of the overdetermined elements is ideology itself, which overdetermines the *interpretations* of real relations of production and existence, the way we see and live real relations meaningfully. The phenomenon of overdetermination thus not only describes a complex pattern of causality (its scientific role of explanation in 'Marxist Theory'), but also refers to the role of ideology in misrecognising real relations (clearly its unscientific role of distortion). Althusser says that in ideology individuals express 'not the relation between them and their conditions of existence, but *the way* they live the relation between them and their conditions of existence' (1969, p. 233). Thus he distinguishes between 'both the real and an "*imaginary*", "*lived*" relation' (*ibid.*), so that ideology 'is the expression of the relation between men and their "world", that is the (overdetermined) unity of the real relation and the imaginary relation between them and their real conditions of existence' (*ibid.*). In this way, ideology can create a misconception of a single element or relation as if it were more dominant (or subordinate) than it in fact is. This instance of overdetermination in turn gives the appearance of uniting the totality of elements constituting society.

Marxism is vulnerable on this count – of furthering scientific understanding *and* ideological distortion – when seeking to understand, for example, relations between social class and ideology. However, it must be added that Marx takes seriously the role of ideology in the workings of society, and that Althusser acknowledges the existence of ideology in all social formations, including classless societies (1969, p. 235). In Marxist discourse, one of the functions of 'class', as a concept denoting the way real social relations of production are organised, is to explain the ideological unity informing the superstructure at different moments. At one moment, the ruling class establishes an ideology to justify its own dominance which is reflected in political and legal institutions, property relations and culture. At another moment, the emergence of working class solidarity in the face of ruling-class dominance challenges this unity and seeks to bring about its collapse, in the course of establishing a new unity organised around the dictatorship of the proletariat. Class relations are thus overdetermined in denoting, first, the ruling class as the 'natural' or 'rightfully' dominating subject, and, secondly, the working class as the oppressed subject who in time fulfils its 'ultimate destiny' of emancipation. The Marxist understanding of the role of class in the formation and dominance of bourgeois ideology supports an oppositional ideology of class struggle that overdetermines the role of the working classes. What serves to advance scientific understanding also serves the pursuit of ideological ends.

In *Policing the Crisis*, Hall *et al.* give several examples of the overdetermination of class relations occasioned by the increasing coercion wrought by successive governments since the 1960s. Class conflict is reflected in the formation of law and ideology which themselves overdetermine structures of class relations: 'the great constructions of crime and law . . . have emerged through the struggles between the dominant and subordinate classes at particular moments and stages in the development of capitalist social formations and their civil, juridical, political and ideological structures' (1978, p. 171). Likewise, feminist and anti-racist discourses have overdetermined the role of women and ethnic minorities respectively. However, this is not because of a structural blindness to other forms of subordination – a misrecognition alone – but because, being bound by a particular form of social consciousness and development, these discourses are able to articulate an awareness of the oppressive relations to which they are subject and against which they struggle (Laclau and Mouffe 1985, p. 154). It is important at this juncture to emphasise that such accounts of the overdetermination located in particular discourses retain some notion of the real relations each discourse refers to, and so retain a social scientific purchase on the real world.

In this 'discourse theoretic' approach, overdetermination is seen in the way ideological discourse represents a social formation. Real objects become subjects of an ideological discourse where they are drawn into a set of relations with other subjects, for example, class, gender and race. Discourse theory focuses on ideological discourse as a topic in its own right and seeks to explain how its subjects are overdetermined by overarching structures of state, dominant ideology and hegemony to form an ideological text. The infinite complexity of the real world may escape codification, but key elements are rendered accountable in terms of the ideological text. Certain constructs within the text play a central role in organising the different phenomena, focusing on particular patterns of social relations or structures. Notions of *unity* (e.g. society, state, community, class), *subordination* (class oppression, gender subordination, racial inferiority), and *dominance*, and the relations they form, are used to explain real events and problems. Rendering reality to forms of textual representation entails showing the symbolic importance given to certain elements over others, *condensing* some and *displacing* others. For example, Hall *et al.* contend that the ideological context surrounding the discovery of the problem of 'mugging' in the early 1970s entailed a process of condensing a wide range of fears and anxieties, conscious and subconscious, that afflicted different groups concerned with long-term trends in crime and social disorder, into a single symbolic object, the mugger as folk-devil. The problem 'arises in the middle of a general moral panic about the "rising rate of crime"; far from triggering into existence what does not previously exist, it clearly *focuses* what is already widespread and free-floating' (1978, p. 182).

Welfare state as discourse

An interest in the textual devices of ideology, specifically condensation and displacement, has given rise to several studies – drawing on Althusser – of the imagery of the welfare state in postwar politics. These studies serve as illustrations of the range of concerns prompting discourse theory: for example, the *stereotyping* of media mythologies of 'welfare scrounging' (Golding and Middleton 1982); the *ideological signification* of the collapse of the postwar consensus (Hall *et al.* 1978); and the *genealogy* of the democratic subjects of the welfare state (Laclau and Mouffe 1985).

On stereotyping, Golding and Middleton (1982) pay specific attention in welfare ideology to media and public attitudes on poverty and social security. They note the overdetermined use of welfare imagery by key institutions in filtering and amplifying popular stereotypes about the poor, especially in well-publicised cases of welfare scrounging in the mid-1970s. In one well-publicised court case, the judge and lawyers were found to share prevailing prejudices about the welfare state, which were further amplified in the media; prejudices that showed ignorance of the workings of welfare institutions, a mistaken sense of their wastage of public money and eagerness to hand out benefits, and a conviction that such events were 'the tip of a national scandal' (1982, p. 61). The courts and media are seen as giving shape and expression to public agenda and attitudes towards the poor (1982, pp. 236–7). Welfare imagery is created by those in positions of power and privilege, and reinforced by the media operating as 'secondary definers', reproducing and reinterpreting the values of the authors of policy, the politicians, civil servants, academic advisers and researchers. In the context of the disorders and dislocations of social change, a process of overdetermined meaning is produced as 'the media divert attention to a limited range of available metaphors and explanations' (1982, p. 237) and 'connect contemporary material expression and anxieties with particular cultural legacies' by resurrecting social types and characters (1982, p. 238) – an observation that reflects Hall *et al.*'s sightings of condensation.

These processes of overdetermination are examined in greater detail in Hall *et al.*'s aforementioned study *Policing the Crisis* (1978). They contend that gradually the mounting series of moral panics in the late 1960s and 1970s, of which scrounging was one instance, were interpreted by governments as evidence of an overall escalation in lawlessness, posing a growing threat to the state. Consequently, governments chose to sanction more coercive measures within the political framework of consent. The years 1968–70 were the turning point in the drift from 'consent to coercion' and towards the disciplining and 'augmented state'. The emergence of participatory and emancipatory politics during these years provoked a backlash from sections of civil society, which the state, with few exceptions, chose to support, thereby exacerbating new divisions. In this, 'the whole fulcrum of society turns' (1978, p. 251), requiring the installation of fundamental changes. In Althusserian terms – and in terms influenced by Gramsci (1971) – this amounts to a fusion in the relations of domination, a shift to a new 'structure in dominance'. Thus:

> any profound restructuring of the inner organisation and composition of capitalist relations – such as characterises the long transition from *laissez-faire* to monopoly . . . requires and precipitates a consequent recomposition of the whole social and ideological integument of the social formation. (1978, p. 255)

This recomposition is seen in the overdetermination of certain events, which became overlaid with a political significance threatening state hegemony and far outweighing their inherent importance. These processes of overdetermination are explored as examples of ideological signification, using the methods of discourse theory typical of Structural Marxism. By observing what Hall *et al.* term 'signification spirals', they suggest how issues such as drugs, student unrest and mugging gained significance in the context of the changing social and political climate of the 1960s and 1970s. This escalation is explained in terms of the representations each event receives within a grid of signification registering, first, the degree which a single issue converges with others, and, secondly, the degree it crosses various thresholds in a hierarchy of political concerns.[3] *Convergence* 'occurs when two or more activities are linked in the process of signification as to implicitly or explicitly draw parallels between them' (1978, p. 223). Thus politically charged meanings or labels concerning, for example, 'student hooliganism' can be produced by connecting the separate problems of 'student protest' and 'hooliganism' to impute a common denominator of 'mindless violence' or 'vandalism', and hence criminality, which would occlude reference to the politically legitimate nature of student protest. In semiotics theory, convergence operates on two levels of signification (see Barthes 1972, pp. 114–15). First, it works by displacing the meaning of a term into the context of another partially related term, so that 'student protest' and 'hooliganism' are related by their youthful challenge to authority, in order to reduce a complex of meanings to the partial meaning of 'mindless protest' (a single attribute from a complex whole transformed by metonymic elision). Secondly, convergence is achieved by condensing normally unrelated terms – 'student', with connotations of studiousness and rational learning, and 'mindless hooligan' – into a new fusion (a metaphorical construction) connoting 'student hooliganism', which underscores the mindlessness of the first level of meaning, and represses the rational aspects of student political dissent present in the second.

Secondly, an escalation in *thresholds* occurs when the limits to social toler- ance that an event breaches threaten to disrupt social, political or legal conventions. Certain events, such as acts of criminal violence, contravene thresholds right up a hierarchy of thresholds – social, legal and violence – by comparison with say acts of sexual permissiveness which transgress moral norms but remain legal and non-violent. However, escalating the significance of student unrest into student hooliganism suggests a threat to the social order that raises its threshold significance for the state and justifies a more coercive response. Hall *et al.* demonstrate the combined impact of shifts in meaning produced by convergence and by crossing thresholds in a statement on law and order given by Lord Hailsham (then Quintin Hogg) in 1969: 'when Unions, when University teachers and others, when students, when demonstrators of various kinds, when Labour and Liberal M.P.s announce their deliberate detes- tation of all forms of authority, how can you expect the police and the courts to enforce the law?' (1978, p. 249).[4]

In their study of processes of ideological overdetermination, Laclau and Mouffe depict a *genealogy* of the democratic subject reaching back to the eighteenth century and forward to the welfare state of the second half of the twentieth, a genealogy that has been radically redefined in the 1980s. At each turn the democratic subject acquires new rights and wider forms of equality which are part of a prevailing ideological and hegemonic formation, and which Laclau and Mouffe trace in the development of significatory 'chains of equivalence'. Their narrative draws extensively on Althusserian and post- Althusserian sources. The postwar welfare state has become the present point in the development of the long-term democratic revolution characterising politics for the last three hundred years. Laclau and Mouffe chart developments in hegemonic formations and democracy that have culminated in the welfare state of the second half of the twentieth century, and trace this development in the chain of equivalences linking democratic subjects since their inception in the French Revolution. At this moment a new notion of political legitimacy was introduced, 'the invention of a democratic culture', which affirmed the ideal of the absolute power of the people as citizens in general:

> Here lay the profound subversive power of the democratic discourse, which would allow the spread of equality and liberty into increasingly wider domains and therefore act as the fermenting agent upon the different forms of struggle against subordination. (Laclau and Mouffe 1985, p. 153)

The idea of universal equality gave rise to critiques of different types of inequality – monarchy, aristocracy, theocracy, patriarchy – and so to new political subjects each seeking equality with their betters. These political struggles focused on the concrete conditions of subordinate groups and gave voice to new and more substantive rights in law, politics and employment. Parallel to this shift, there developed from the liberal concern with political and legal rights a socialist critique of economic inequalities. Utilising the notion of the overdetermination of the political superstructure, Laclau and Mouffe reverse the conventional Marxist sequence which portrays socialist politics as determined by changes in the economic base. Instead, they contend that socialist demands were part of, and made possible by, the larger democratic revolution.

The present stage of democratic development is reached with the postwar welfare state. Somewhat more positively than Hall *et al.* and Golding and Middleton, Laclau and Mouffe see the welfare state as a social transformation which, though possessing the hegemonic means for dissolving resistance and antagonism, on balance has inaugurated political subjects with new needs, demands and rights. The welfare state provides an arena for articulating radical demands and engaging in new struggles against the arbitrary nature of power and inequality (1985, p. 158). It thus 'makes possible a new extension of egalitarian equivalences' that seeks to remove the differences between the deprived and well-endowed. The welfare state continues the spirit of 'one nationhood'. In particular, these new demands have given rise to new forms of political action and organisation, in the new social movements. Though recognising the welfare state as what Althusser termed an ideological state apparatus (ISA), Laclau and Mouffe stress that social subjects develop their own ideological project by extending the chain of equivalences between themselves and other subjects towards more democratic and egalitarian forms of political existence.

Before leaving discourse studies of the overdetermining structures of ideology, and passing on to a second notion of overdetermination, we should pause to consider important areas of difficulty in the discourse theoretic approach. Overdetermination creates ideological effects in discourse and social relations, each effect influencing the other. However, when the sole point of reference is the text to the exclusion of all else, several general problems arise. First, social relations outside discourse are in danger of being overlooked. To reply, as discourse theorists have done, that relations present themselves, and so become observable, only under the appearance of text is a reductionist fallacy that severely limits the variety of material available for study. Secondly, and more seriously, it raises problems about retaining a distinction between ideology and the real, and between ideological and scientific discourses. In discourse theory, this problem is highlighted by denying the difference between the two discourses: the ideological, whose symbolic constructs distort the real; and the theoretical, whose analysis of these constructs explains the real. It therefore follows that the idea that social science should explain reality and refute explanations which incorrectly account for reality is no longer tenable. Thirdly, it becomes difficult to differentiate the effectivity of different ideological texts – of, for example, media, official reports, ministerial speeches and informal discussions between individuals, all of which are implicated in the formation and propagation of ideology. On this basis, texts spawn other texts and become enmeshed in the Ideological Text from which there is no other explanatory point of reference. This problem can be significant in the context of competing ideologies, when, for example, an official governmental ideology conflicts with an emerging ideology amongst private individuals and groups.

However, for Laclau and Mouffe, the distinction between the symbolic and the real is removed altogether: 'The concept of overdetermination is constituted in the field of the symbolic, and has no meaning whatsoever outside it.' This leads to the conclusion that:

> the most profound *potential* meaning of Althusser's statement that everything existing in the social is overdetermined, is the assertion that the social constitutes itself as a symbolic order. The symbolic – i.e., overdetermined – character of social relations therefore implies that they lack an ultimate literality. (1985, pp. 97–8)

The radical consequence of conceiving of all social relations as symbolic and overdetermined is to subvert the 'literality' or facticity of every identity or element (1985, p. 104). However, this conclusion – the world as text – in the hands of post- Althusserians such as Laclau and Mouffe (and likewise Foucault discussed in Chapter 9), is powerful but questionable (and at variance with Althusser's position).[5] For it removes the need to explore connections between discourse and the real represented in discourse once the world is known only through discourse. Michèle Barrett (1980) has been critical of this post-Althusserian strand in feminist theory where, for example, the concept 'women' is seen as an ideological construct, an object created within the male-dominated texts of social theory, literature, state, welfare, media, and so forth, with no indisputable point of reference to women as real objects of oppression. For this strand sees reality itself as structured by sexual (and other) divisions, and refutes the suggestion that there is a domain of real objects – e.g. women – that precedes the structures of oppression and exploitation shaping the real world (e.g. Adams 1979). For Barrett, this approach has clear political consequences, for 'it is unclear that the project to deconstruct the category of women could ever provide a basis for a feminist politics. If there are no 'women' to be oppressed then on what criteria do we struggle, and against what?' (1980, p. 96). Similarly, Meiksin-Wood (1986) criticises the political implications of this kind of theory in leading to a politics that, in dispensing with the significance of material reality, abandons a politics founded in the struggles of working class people to re-appropriate material production and establish a more just social order. The consequence of this 'retreat from class' is an affirmation of pluralistic politics and a highly revisionist conception of 'true' socialism.

In addition to these political consequence, the post-Althusserian strand carries a significant theoretical implication. It leads to undermining the value of the concept of ideology itself, by removing the very notion of 'the real' that, however problematic and unknowable in its entirety, provides the purpose and object of human inquiry, and the rationale for designating false lines of inquiry and distorted knowledge as ideological. There is no point in considering the questions 'what is ideology?' and 'how can it be overcome?' unless it is considered in relation to its other, to knowledge of the real and objective problems, to science, reason, truth, and so forth – whether ideology is seen as deforming or prefiguring its other. In a similar vein, the notion of overdetermination loses its explanatory power without a standard of determination by which an overdetermined phenomenon is judged *over*determined. Althusser consistently retained the two distinct orders of discourse and the real, and argued that ideology gives way to scientific knowledge of the *real* means of existence only by way of Marxist theoretical practice, i.e. dialectical materialism (1969, p. 161). Althusser was not to clarify systematically his notion of a meta-science of 'Marxist Theory' or 'theoretical practice' – indeed he subsequently refuted some of his grander claims (Benton, 1984 p. 83). Instead, from the late 1960s, he developed in his theory of ideology the concept of the dialectical relationship of misrecognition that governs relations between an individual subject and the state – a relational rather than discursive notion of ideology – to which we now turn.

Overdetermination as ideological interpellation

The second aspect of Althusser's theory of overdetermination we have chosen to highlight concerns the relationships individuals have with significant others, which, in his later writings, he saw as playing a key role in the formation of ideology. For each individual, the relationship has a significance that is overendowed in comparison with its real significance, a discrepancy ideology denies the subject clear sight of. This occurs in relations with real persons, to whom an individual is dependent and subordinate (e.g. father, mother, teacher, policeman, priest), and in relations with symbolic figures who represent social ideals (state, society, nation, God, justice, law). The fact that individuals experience everyday life in concrete relations which are each endowed with specific meaning, enables this significance to be generalised to more symbolic relations. An individual's relationship with a concrete authority figure, such as in western culture a father, will induce an attitude towards general authority figures – normally one of respectful compliance – that is deeply felt in encounters with the state, the law and so forth. Yet, however symbolic the figure will be, it will be represented by a real person – such as the prime minister, a state official, a judge, policeman or priest – whose authority is heavily invested in the rituals, procedures and decor associated with their institutional settings. The normative significance associated with such figures is reinforced in encounters where they appeal to an audience directly and personally, through a televised prime ministerial broadcast, a judge's summing up – key parts of which are headlined and highlighted by the media – and a priest administering the sacraments. Ideology is implicated in the practices and interactions each individual engages in, which construct them as ideological subjects in each relation.

By overdetermination, Althusser suggests that ideology is 'interpellating individuals as subjects', addressing each person as subject to a specific relationship with another (1971, p. 170). By means of the relationship ideology installs between an individual and state authority (e.g. citizen and state, subject and sovereign, claimant and state official, student and teacher), the individual is drawn to see herself as a particular kind of subject in relation to a specific state apparatus (the state, monarchy, social security, education system), and to take on the subject-image as her status or role. A normative viewpoint is adopted. The overdetermined meaning inscribed in the individual's subjectivity entails misrecognising – and no doubt partially recognising – aspects of the real relations she engages in. The fact that each individual is '*always already*' an ideological subject, that she has since the first moments of life been in a relationship to a significant or ideal figure – at first mother and father, and later law, state, knowledge, God – underscores her susceptibility to ideology and her preparation for becoming an ideological subject.

For Althusser, the capitalist state has adapted its apparatus to provide more effective forms of control that replace brute coercion. The ISAs he instances are the church, school, family, law, political parties, trade unions, media and culture. These operate as a plurality of institutions, which extend the state's influence into every part of civil society. The traditional means of control, the 'repressive state apparatus' of the armed forces, courts and police, are kept in reserve. Each ISA draws the individual subject into a relationship the very practices of which underscore its ideological significance. Two examples show the significance of these practices for welfare. First, to take Althusser's example, the school and family are important ISAs because between them they provide virtually the full scope of socialisation twenty-four hours a day for the first sixteen years of life. Secondly, the welfare apparatus constitutes a set of practices which overdetermine the recipient's view of him or herself and lead to a misrecognition of self. For example, the routines for applying for means-tested benefits require that claimants account for their poverty according to a set of rigorous procedures conducted within welfare bureaucracy. The demeaning, stigmatising and self-disclosing actions demanded of claimants instil a *redoubled* sense of dependence which underscores the fact that the poor fall below the poverty line. Claimants experience themselves as poor before initiating the claim. Because of the means-test their experience is reinforced by ideology: not only are they deprived, they are now stigmatised and induced into passive dependence. For in performing a set of actions the individual comes to believe in the values that make sense of these actions. Ideology constitutes the individual as an ideological subject. Althusser says of such a subject that 'his ideas are his material actions inserted into material practices governed by material rituals which are themselves defined by the material ideological apparatus from which derive the ideas of that subject' (1971, p. 169). In this light, one can describe state welfare services as an ideological system which socialises dependants into attitudes of subservience, while providing them with the minimum means of subsistence, health and personal well-being – the makings of a contradiction which Habermas and others note.

However, this account of the absolute power of ideology to shape attitudes of dependence provides no room for resistance and self-determination by the claimant. Ironically, the critique of welfare tyranny voiced by the Left in the 1970s was echoed by the Right in the 1980s, when criticising welfare policy for encouraging a 'culture of dependency'.

The main concern prompting Althusser's account of the ISAs is to explain the central problem of how the means of production and especially labour power are reproduced, and how their reproduction sustains the flow of accumulation. It is this problem in particular that draws Althusser into the same orbit as other Marxists discussed in Part II. However, rather than treat this as an economic problem alone – the way resources are organised and technologically mastered in a complex chain of production – Althusser's approach is to examine the role of ideology in inculcating appropriate norms and developing technological knowledge within capitalist society. Political Economy and Critical Theory are fully aware of these processes, and acknowledge Althusser's important theoretical contribution, but do not explain sufficiently why individuals succumb to ideology, other than as subjects responding mechanically to economic forces; a position at variance with their belief in emancipatory class struggle or an ideal speech situation. For Althusser, it is the state, rather than economic forces alone, that disseminates a unified ideology through the plurality of relatively independent institutions constituting the ISAs, of which the welfare state forms a significant part. However, as we will see later, this account, though attending closely to ideological processes, also leaves little room for individual or collective volition.

Drawing on Althusser's work, feminist theory has paid close attention to the way state ideology in capitalist society reproduces gender divisions in the family, education system and work place, that reinforce the broader social division of labour within the relations of production. (Wolpe 1978; Barrett 1980). By means of ideology, beliefs in female subordination, acquired first in the family in the context of the biological and domestic division of labour, are reproduced at work. The education system reinforces the attitudes and practices of family and work, especially within the nexus of what Althusser terms the 'family-education couple' (1971, p. 157). This 'system is a key means of the production and reproduction of the ideological structure' (Wolpe 1978, pp. 2–3, quoted in Barrett 1980, p. 117). For example, David reports that even in 1860, before schools came under state control, the Victorian school curriculum was regulated by state Codes that, even if in a small way, explicitly required that the sexual division of labour, the gendered tasks of everyday life, be taught and understood (David 1980, p. 241). A hundred years later, the means of ideological reproduction had become more subtle and diffuse; in that 'sex differences were taught . . . through the hierarchical and patriarchal relations within schools and by the expectations made of girls' and boys' progress through schooling' (*ibid.*, p. 245).

More broadly, McIntosh examines the range of state roles in welfare, in reproducing the subordination of women, especially as part of a reserve army of labour, where 'the state itself carries out some of these functions of financial support and of servicing; yet it usually does so under such ideological conditions that it is seen as 'taking over' functions properly belonging to the family' (McIntosh 1978, p. 264). Even when the demands of accumulation for new sources of labour power threaten to disturb familial divisions of labour, by drawing from the reserve army of unemployed female labour, women continue to perform tasks consonant with this ideology. An example is the involvement of women in teaching in order to impart knowledge about wifehood, motherhood and domesticity (David 1980, p. 240).

Overdetermination as problematic

At the core of Althusser's account of ideology as overdetermined structures and relations is a conception of ideological knowledge produced by these relations and structures. What Althusser terms the 'problematic' structures our problem-conceptions of the world, including the inquiries that unravel these problems and the policies promulgated to solve them. Overdetermination determines the conceptual structures that shape the knowledge available to society at a particular moment in its history. The theoretical structure of the problematic governs our knowledge of – how we conceive – 'the means of existence' or means of production. In a structuralist vein, Althusser defines a problematic as 'the objective internal reference system of its particular themes, the system of questions commanding the answers given' (1969, p. 67n). This internal reference system is determined by the nature of the objective problems – social and economic rather than theoretical – operating outside ideology and posed for ideology by its time. Within an ideological framework objective problems are in some way deformed or misconceived, as ideology overdetermines the different objective elements in the real world, which a problematic addresses. Moreover, 'it is not the interiority of the problematic which constitutes its essence but its relation to real problems: *the problematic of an ideology* cannot be demonstrated without *relating* and *submitting* it to the real problems to which its deformed enunciation gives a false answer' (*ibid.*). Ideological distortion is revealed by a 'symptomatic reading', which lays bare the problematic operating within a text, and thereby confronts the problematic with the objective problems in the real world which it misconceives; problems that cannot be directly perceived independently of the problematic, but whose impact none the less affects everyday existence.[6]

Although posed in a highly theoretical manner, at home in French rationalist thought, the notion of problematic is not entirely alien to Anglo-Saxon thought. In social administration, for example, several writers have used similar notions, borrowed from different traditions, to convey the constructions defining social problems and policy: 'definition of reality' (Carrier and Kendall 1973), 'story-telling' (Rein 1976), 'models of relevance' (Rule 1978), 'policy readings' (Room 1979). Most explicitly, Donnison *et al.* (1975) have referred to an 'approach' in social policy in similar terms, with respect to the notion of a grammar that predicates 'characteristic' ways of formulating specific questions posed within social policy, and the characteristic explanations and policies they give rise to. He argues that to adopt an approach is to explore three kinds of 'disposition':

1. to pursue particular kinds of research, using characteristic methods to explore characteristic *questions*;
2. to adopt characteristic assumptions about society and its workings, refined and reinforced by research which produces characteristic *descriptions* of the world they study; and
3. to espouse particular attitudes and aspirations which lead to characteristic *prescriptions* for action. (Donnison *et al.* 1975, p. 14)

It is these dispositions which Donnison *et al.* explore in their collection of case studies of welfare services. Each disposition refers to an aspect of social policy informed by a particular type of assumption, assumptions which together identify the framework of a social policy problematic.[7]

A problematic exists not only as a structure of ideas about the world, but first and foremost in the concrete form of discourse, in reports, case notes, files, official reports of inquiry, Royal Commissions, judicial reviews, academic texts, research studies, etc. In policy studies, text is a medium that runs through all stages of the policy process, from problem identification, through policy formulation and implementation, to evaluation. Indeed, the practical framework for policy action – intervening in social conditions, changing social relations and restructuring infrastructures of human support – cannot be understood separately from this discursive framework. In passing, it should be said that until recently scant attention had been paid to the discursive medium of policy.[8]

It is principally as discourse that the many discrete operations of policy form a unity or continuous policy process. The convention that policy analysis as the study of the different stages of a policy process – formulation, implementation, evaluation, etc. – involves investing this process with an overdetermined discursive continuity, or narrative, which is ideologically determined. In Althusserian terms, this is because of the double function that ideology performs, both in imparting sufficiency and unity to discourse and in glossing its discontinuities. This complex process can be sketched as follows. On the one hand, given the limitations of knowledge in explaining phenomena, it is ideology which gives the impression of unity and sufficiency to explanatory knowledge. On the other hand, however, this sufficiency results from an imaginary sense of the totality conveyed by knowledge, an imaginary sense that overdetermines – and so distorts – the social relations occurring in society. Althusser captures this double function of ideology in referring to the *recognition-misrecognition* that a problematic imparts (1971, p. 172). We see a set of problems in a particular frame of reference, but by this very act fail to see other problems falling outside this frame. In this sense, the totality created in a discourse is an ideological effect of the problematic. Referring to a different order of policy-making, Hall *et al.*, in their aforementioned study of law and policy, consider the researcher's need to construct a 'map' of the dominant ideological problematic that governs the way 'the popular imagination "thinks" the problem of crime' (1978, p. 149). The purpose of this map is to make explicit in a problematic the complex structure of *recognition–misrecognition* shaping the images and attitudes which affect the way, for example, working class people see crime; by which specifically, for example, the ideology of law produces 'a misrecognition in the working class of its contradictions of interest . . . serving to split and divide sections of the class against each other', and by which this same ideology recognises none the less the fact that 'Certain kinds of crime are a real, objective problem for working people' (*ibid.*).

As Hall *et al.*'s and others' work shows, Althusser has influenced an important line of inquiry into textual practices, in explicating the ideological signification produced in newspapers, broadcasts and film, as well as in literature and art. This approach also offers departures for the study of policy texts and 'official discourse' (Burton and Carlen 1979). We can see how Althusser's notion of overdetermination helps to show the way a text works as ideology. Drawing imaginatively on the work of the French psychoanalyst, Jacques Lacan, Althusser argues that ideology works by means of an imaginary – or unconscious – process active in human thought that intrudes into the production of knowledge and overdetermines people's relations with the real world to render their perception of the world imaginary. It is the imaginary that imparts a sense of sufficiency to the problematic and gives it a semblance of total knowledge in conceptualising the real world. It is in this sense that Althusser defines ideology as a representation of 'the imaginary relationship of individuals to the real conditions of existence' (1971, p. 162).

Structural Marxism: an appraisal

The concept of overdetermination provides two kinds of leverage over some of the problems that characterise Marxist approaches to welfare ideology discussed in Part II. First, it overcomes the economic determinism characterising the Political Economy of Welfare approach, where the role of welfare is seen as largely supportive of capital's interests in reproducing and disciplining labour and in providing the necessary forms of social investment and infrastructure. Where the cultural and ideological functions of welfare are acknowledged in this approach, welfare represents values functional to the economic system. By contrast, for Althusser, welfare ideology is overdetermined by relations of production, so that it acts with a degree of relative autonomy in shaping attitudes and identities and in fostering forms of social practice among the population; practices that reproduce labour in the interests of the ruling class, or challenge these interests if class relations are changing.

Following this, a second type of leverage is provided by ideological over-determination. Both Structural Marxism and Critical Theory vouch the degree of relative autonomy in the socio-cultural or ideological sphere. However, Structural Marxism has a sharper sense of the way ideology mediates between economic forces and socio-cultural relations and practices. For here ideology simultaneously recognises and misrecognises real relations of existence and production, in imparting an imaginary perception that is not mere distortion but represents a partial view of the real means of existence. In addition, Structural Marxism recognises that ideology is installed in social practices. It is not a discrete domain or object of study, as it is for Habermas and Offe, but implicated in economic and political practices. This can lead to valuable insights about the ideological features of welfare in, for example, social work and social security.

Yet, despite these insights, Althusser's theory of ideological overdetermina-tion remains vulnerable on several counts. For example, by proposing that ideology produces an overdetermined unity between the *real* means of existence and the *imaginary* relations that are lived as if real (1969, pp. 233–4), Althusser introduced a fundamental distinction which requires clear specification. This clarity holds in so far as each category is defined in its own terms: the real as the conditions of existence; the imaginary as unconscious structures shaping conscious thoughts and actions. However, it is unclear precisely what are the relations that exist between the two. Of course, Althusser saw the real and imaginary as closely entwined, where ideology is implicated in the lived relations of social existence. Yet, because his theory of ideology depends on a categorical distinction between the real and imaginary, however intimate the relation, the real has to be specified as a basis for defining the imaginary. Moreover, as a Marxist and so realist, Althusser must specify the nature of the determination exercised by the real over the imaginary. This is specified as an overdetermined, complex structure in dominance, a suggestive metaphor that seeks to go beyond simple notions of causality, and which gives rise to the idea of the relative autonomy of ideology. For a Marxist realist, this must imply the determination of the real means of existence, or more strictly 'determination in the last instance by the economic' (1969, p. 113), and stand as a recognition of the *a priori* status of the real whatever the contingencies affecting a social formation and its various components, ideological and non-ideological. But Althusser specified neither what it is about the real that is *a priori* – a premiss problematised by his theory of ideology – nor the precise meaning of the relative autonomy of ideology; although others have attempted such a meaning (e.g. Barrett 1980).

More specifically, several commentators have argued that Althusser's discussion of the ISAs falls back on a functionalist account to explain their relations to the economy, in which they reproduce attitudes, skills and disciplines appropriate for capitalist production (e.g. Hirst 1979). The characterisation of ISAs as extensions of the state machinery for reproduction has the further effect of drawing elements of civil society under the all-pervasive umbrella of the state, in effect extinguishing civil society as a separate sphere from the state (as argued in the treatment of civil society by, e.g., Gramsci). The implications of Althusser's functionalist view of the state is that each of its apparatuses, in particular welfare, is limited to performing a regulative role alone, with no room left for autonomous action by ideological subjects that can be prefigured in ideology. Althusser's master-subject (i.e. the state, the law, God) interpellates a subordinate subject who has no powers of anticipation and self-determination. By contrast, as we have seen, Laclau and Mouffe, in drawing on Lacan's thought, provide a different conception of ideological interpellation which loosens the constraints in Althusser's notion of ideology, and describes a more prefigurative process. We will see in Chapter 9 how Foucault – on whom Laclau and Mouffe also draw – seeks to develop an account of welfare that escapes some (but not all) of Althusser's absolutism in these respects.

Notes

1. However, Althusser drew on various sources beside structuralism and denounced certain aspects of structuralism, as Elliott (1987) elaborates.
2. Althusser has been heavily criticised for his conception of 'history without a human subject', most notably by E. P. Thompson (1978).
3. These two moments correspond to the archetypal dimensions of structuralist analysis, the syntagmatic and paradigmatic respectively (see e.g. Jakobson 1971).
4. Parton (1986) applies a similar notion of signification in his analysis of media treatment of child abuse and the development of child care policy; as does Garland (1985) in his study of the emergence of modern penality.
5. See Althusser's conception of the real as 'the real object that exists independently of its knowledge' (1969, p. 246).
6. Althusser's conception of a problematic can be contrasted with Kuhn's term 'scientific paradigm'

employed in the philosophy of science (1970). The latter implies a self-contained theoretical system governing scientific research according to its own criteria of validity, and so assumes that truth is relative to the paradigm that dominates an area of scientific research – just as sentences are grammatically correct according to the rules of grammar governing them. By contrast, Althusser assumes the existence beyond the problematic of truth founded in reality, which it is the task of Marxist science to uncover in overcoming ideology.

7. Donnison's purpose in characterising a policy approach is less concerned to reveal the ideological underpinnings of policy than to explicate the nature of social policy reasoning.

8. See p. 11.

9

Welfare, power and knowledge: Foucault's account of welfare and ideology

Of all the writers who address the question of welfare ideology, Michel Foucault has devoted the most time and space to tracing its development through several centuries, and examining the many different forms of welfare that exist for the insane, the sick, the criminal, in a variety of different contexts, discourses and political regimes. His approach has inspired numerous studies by others who have applied his methods and insights to previously unexplored sites of welfare. This body of work represents a significant approach that has been developed throughout the 1970s and 1980s in France, Britain and North America into the ideological ramifications of welfare. Influenced in part by Structural Marxism, and sharing some of the concerns if not philosophical assumptions of Critical Theory, Foucault stands none the less in the post-structural stream that has repudiated central propositions of Marxism. In particular, this stream has rejected Marxism's historicist faith in the overthrow of capitalism; its belief in the ordained role of the proletariat in fulfilling this process; and, most import- antly, its claim to be a science of the totality that explains historical processes from an all-seeing vantage point whence the critique of capitalism is mounted and the case for socialism waged. It is on this last point, in particular, that Foucault even rejects the term ideology, as its revelation implies a superior position of truth from where ideology can be determined. In this respect Foucault differs from Althusser in rejecting the notion that ideology operates as a dominant delusion to which all are subject, except those armed with Marxist Theory, who are thereby privileged – and burdened with the responsibility – of being the sole force for political resistance and change. Instead of ideology- critique, Foucault has proposed the study of genealogies of discourse, 'regimes of truth' and 'power/knowledge', whose validity is an effect of their power rather than their intrinsic claims to higher reasoning. Whether the existence of ideology implies the existence of a truth it distorts, or the existence of an ideological power that constitutes truth – a contention we examine towards the end of the chapter – Foucault's studies of power and knowledge provide new insights into welfare practices and ideology.

Foucault's *Discipline and Punish* explores these aspects of ideology by providing 'a historical background to various studies of the power of normalisation and the function of knowledge in modern society' (1979a, p. 308). A programme of further studies on the formation of power, ideology and knowledge governing welfare and society has been developed by others on family policy and psychiatry, clinical psychology, child care, penal policy, education, social security and dietetics. [1] This work explores the role of welfare practices in the emergence of modern society. Welfare figures as a key apparatus for implementing power and knowledge. Specifically welfare plays a co-ordinating role in forming 'the social'. It organises ideology, knowledge, norms and social practices to regulate the quality of life of the population, its health, security and stability. For such statecraft, Foucault employs the terms 'the politics of life' and 'bio-power'; that is 'the proliferation of political technologies that invested the body, health, modes of subsistence and lodging – the entire space of existence in European countries from the eighteenth century onwards' (Donzelot 1980, p. 6). It is Foucault's contention that the body, individual and collective, has become the raw material for this undertaking. The study of the historical formation of welfare, its systems of regulation and knowledge, contributes to understanding their present formation and power, a 'history of the present'. Although Foucault's studies end in the nineteenth century, he has drawn out their lessons for late twentieth century society in several short essays and interviews (e.g. 1980, 1981, 1982, 1988).

The chapter begins by introducing Foucault's methods and concerns in studying the history of ideology and power in modern welfare society. In this respect the chapter highlights specific themes that have contributed to the formation of welfare ideology and practice. In this formation, the role of power and knowledge, conventionally termed ideology, is then examined. The remainder of the chapter discusses the contribution that the Foucauldian approach offers studies of modern welfare – studies inaugurated within social administration and developed in the Political Economy of Welfare – and highlights the difficulties attending all three approaches.

Foucault's method

It is perhaps helpful to say something – by way of warning as well as exposition – about Foucault's approach to the study of history. He discards many of its accepted precepts, including, for example, its insistence on tracing historical developments chronologically and establishing clear expositions of cause and effect. Instead, he examines ways in which the conception of a subject – such as sexuality, punishment or pathology – is constituted within knowledge as a central concern of a specific age, society or social strata. Subjects are not examined as factual givens or as the result of processes of causation. For Foucault, their facticity and causality are located at a deeper level. The subjects of social policy – e.g. dependency and social needs – are not produced by social forces and do not exist as pure facts. They are constructed within the discourse of social policy as categories, classification systems and forms of knowledge by individuals and groups working in political, administrative and economic areas. These constructions establish in a specific discourse (e.g. a Report, an academic text, a social work case-file) a relation between the conception of a subject (e.g. a social problem, a system of welfare, a client) and the forces which reputedly determine it. Through this process the subject is endowed with particular forms of facticity and causality. Foucault argues that these constructions of the subject, the ways they are constituted as knowledge within discourse, are made accessible by the methods of 'archaeology' and 'genealogy'. Such methods reveal an ordering of facts, concepts, norms and theories which he terms a 'discursive formation' (1972, p. 31).

By archaeology, Foucault is referring to a method of analysis which identifies a body of knowledge, its propositions and subjects, by discovering the rules of structure within the wider discourse that governs it. In anticipating his later work on genealogies of power, he sees these rules as more to do with strategy than scientific validity. Such rules establish both the boundaries dividing different discourses and the continuities traversing these boundaries, which together make up a discursive formation. It is broadly this approach, for example, that led him to argue that 'the [eighteenth century] theory of money and prices occupies the same position in the analysis of wealth as the theory of character does in natural history' (1970, p. 203), when referring, in a structuralist vein, to the homologous pattern of arguments informing theories developed in different discourses. Following the events in France in 1968, archaeology, with its structuralist supposition that social and political formations are determined by universal structures of language, gave way to the method of genealogy, more sensitive to the movements and contingencies affecting power and knowledge. Genealogy traces the development of knowledge from its conception within a particular socio-political regime of power, through its various stages of diversification and unification *vis-à-vis* other knowledges, to its present formation within new regimes. Thus, a 'regime of truth' is instituted where knowledge is deployed as an instrument of power promoting authoritative pronouncements and masking opposing truths.[2]

This development has important implications for understanding ideology. Foucault's archaeology examined discourse as the site wherein the structure of argumentation within and between different bodies of knowledge could be discovered. In particular, this involved explicating what he termed the rules of dispersion: the discursive arrangement governing the order of propositions, concepts and theories that constitutes a discourse. Thus an understanding of knowledge and ideology arose from an exclusive concern with discourse, as both the material gathered for research (e.g. medical treatises on insanity, diaries of mental patients, government reports on policy and so forth) and the object of study to be understood (e.g. medical knowledge about insanity). Although Foucault acknowledges the existence of an extra-discursive domain of social relations and institutions independent of discourse (1972, pp. 45–6), the archaeological period of his work mainly focused on discourse. However, with the development of a genealogical approach, Foucault widened his perspective to examine the activities and practices that produce, apply and develop knowledge. These activities are fundamentally about the exercise of power. It is the development of power relations and practices that constitutes history and whose constitution is traced by means of genealogy. From the point of view of providing an analysis of knowledge and power, Foucault saw that the scope of genealogy encompasses discourse *and* practice. It explores the development and structure of knowledge and the practices deploying knowledge. Power and knowledge are co-determining. Consequently, it is power/knowledge, rather than ideology as a separate entity produced by power relations, that becomes the focus of Foucault's studies. In this context, the rules of dispersion are concerned with the structure of power across a politico-discursive space rather than within discourse alone. We will see shortly the relevance of this development in his explorations of examples of welfare knowledge and practice.

Genealogical analysis has been applied to seemingly diverse topics such as punishment, psychiatry, sexuality and the family. For example, in *The History of Sexuality*, sexuality is presented as a 'scientific-legal discourse' in medicine, religion, law and social policy, which affects the workings of the entire social body. Its genealogy is traced in operations of the state, the church and other more dispersed centres of power which pronounce authoritatively on sexual knowledge and practice and which silence or reform departures from their codes. Discourses on sexuality have been conducted in a 'multiplicity of force relations' where 'man has been drawn for three centuries to the task of telling everything concerning his sex' in confessionals, novels, law, education and therapy (1979b, pp. 92, 23). In each instance a dialogic form of power exists between the penitent and confessor that penetrates to the utmost point of intimacy in a manner that is none the less carefully modulated (*ibid.*, p. 62). Moreover, the government of sexuality also gives rise to public controls that monitor the birth rate, the age of marriage, the legitimacy of births, the frequency of sexual relations, contraception, and so forth. Sex is a thing one administered. Its administrative effectiveness resides in the fact that it is both an intimately private and anonymously public form of regulation (*ibid.*, p. 24; 1980, p. 125). Through genealogy, the subject of sexuality is seen as central to the formation of policies which form the basis of the politics of life and are aimed at both the individual and social body. Other writers have provided genealogies of the politico-discursive strategies executed in the emergence of modern penality (Garland 1985), social administration (Rose 1979) and psychiatry (Miller and Rose 1986; 1988).

The formation of bio-politics

In his historical and sociological studies, Foucault has examined developments in bio-politics and welfare that have contributed to shaping the institutional, moral and intellectual order characteristic of modern capitalist society. The most important of these developments are what Foucault terms the objectification of the body and the subjectification of the human subject; the emergence of institutions of containment and techniques of normalisation; and the advent of the human sciences.

In his first major work, *Madness and Civilisation*, Foucault charts the emergence of institutions for containing the mentally ill, sick and indigent as the standard method of treatment in seventeenth- and eighteenth-century Europe. Prior to this 'classical age', as he calls it, the insane were not subject to containment alone, but allowed various modes of existence, some segregated in prisons or cared for in hospitals at public expense, some banished from the town or set adrift in 'Ships of Fools', and others, still, accorded a symbolic importance as madmen touched by divine folly or reflecting the truth of human existence surrounded by all its vicissitudes, in which 'madness is . . . linked . . . to man, to his weaknesses, dreams and illusions' (1971, p. 26). However, by the advent of the classical age, asylums excluded the insane from society in order to enforce a moral division between the rational and irrational, constitutive of a new politico-legal order that encouraged morality and spirituality through work, the power of labour 'to work redemption'. Thus confinement:

> organises into a complex unity a new sensibility to poverty and to the duties of assistance, new forms of reaction to the economic problems of unemployment and idleness, a new ethic of work, and also the dream of a city where moral obligation was joined to civil law, within the authoritarian forms of constraint. (1971, p. 46)

Already the lineaments of modern welfare were present. The confinement and segregation of patients provided a degree of physical concentration, so that by the end of the classical age their medical condition could be closely examined to reveal the nature of their insanity. From these examinations conducted in nineteenth-century institutions, the science and practice of psychiatric medicine evolved.

However, Foucault has been criticised over his periodisation of the 'great confinement' in Europe, and over the dominant rationalism he assumes in describing the marginalisation of the insane and other groups. On the former point, Porter reports that while France built institutions of confinement for its undesirables, the phenomenon 'was less concerted elsewhere' and did not get under way in England until the mid-nineteenth century (1987, pp. 7–8; see also Sedgwick 1981). On the question of rationalism, Porter argues that 'Foucault's notion that reason embarked upon a heroic "exorcism of madness" is . . . hyperbolic' (1987, p. 8). However, Porter does concede the otherness of madness, that 'history cannot understand the constitution of madness without first understanding what constituted it as madness . . . accepting how the progress of the subject, Reason, presupposes its own negation' (*ibid.* 1987, p. 279).

Fourteen years later, Foucault returned, in *Discipline and Punish*, to the themes of confinement, power and knowledge. However, by this time, his interest in forms of institutional and scientific control had shifted from the control of individual moral welfare to controlling the human body, upon which an extended repertoire of technologies were applied in addition to psychiatry. Interest in 'bio-power' emerges as a central preoccupation in Foucault's work of the 1970s. In this, the late eighteenth century is seen as the beginning of a period in which the body was endowed by various experts with a range of properties indicating types of crime, sexual aberrations and states of grace, health and mind. Each property was accorded a specific technology of control and form of corporeality. Correctional training, for example, was directed at 'the body, time, everyday gestures and articulation' of inmates to counter their economic and spiritual sloth with 'exercises, timetables, compulsory movements, regular activities, solitary meditation', and so forth (Foucault 1979a, p. 128). Medicine tended to individualise bodies, diseases, symptoms, lives and deaths within a disciplinary regime of architectural, administrative and therapeutic space so that 'out of discipline, a medically useful space was born' (*ibid.*, p. 144). Within hospitals, schools, prison workshops and military barracks, the practice of discipline was founded – forms of domination that extracted economic utility from the human body, whilst rendering it politically docile. In short, discipline dissociates power from the body (*ibid.*, p. 138).

The application of discipline to correct deviations of the body, its behaviour, timing, speech, sexuality and even thought, required attending to the norm. A 'swarm' of technicians, 'normative judges', namely teachers, psychologists, psychiatrists and social workers, would differentiate, quantify and rank individuals according to their ability to conform to the norms of disciplinary technology. These interventions reach beyond the judicial domain into one governed by norms affecting aspects of the body that cannot be inscribed with the exactitude of law (1979a, pp. 183–4, 304). Normalisation becomes one of the main instruments of power in modern society.

Normalisation distinguishes modern disciplinary power from pre-modern 'sovereign power', where the individual is subject to the sovereign's absolute and unmitigated power. A modern society that increasingly takes 'charge of life needs continuous regulatory and corrective mechanisms . . . it does not have to draw the line that separates the enemies of the sovereign from his obedient subjects' (1979b, p. 144). However, rather than fade into the background, the law operates increasingly as a norm, so that the judiciary is gradually incorporated into a continuum of apparatuses (medical, administrative, etc.) whose functions are regulatory: 'A normalising society is the historical outcome of a technology of power centred on life' (*ibid.*). Amidst these normalising activities, a new notion of rights arose, 'which the classical juridical system was utterly incapable of comprehending . . . . The "right" of life, to one's body, to health, to happiness, to the satisfaction of needs' (*ibid.*, p. 145). Bio-politics gave birth to the twin concerns central to modern welfare, to the notions of 'needs' and 'rights'.

These developments in disciplinary technology involved, for Foucault, new forms of knowledge and power. Clinical medicine, psychiatry, educational psychology and criminology were discourses that promulgated new technologies, targets and policies of intervention (1979a, p. 224). Within these human sciences, the individual was enthroned as though by humanitarian fiat (*ibid.*, pp. 189–91). In fact, this centring of the human subject was instrumental to the economic deployment of the disciplines. For Foucault, quoting a late-eighteenth century parliamentarian, ' "Humanity" is the respectable name given to this economy and to its meticulous calculations. "Where punishment is concerned, the minimum is ordered by humanity and counselled by policy". In such endeavours the notion of policy enters history' (*ibid.*, p. 92).

However, Foucault's dating of the break between old and modern regimes of discipline at around the close of the eighteenth century is questioned as far as it applies to penal policy. Garland, for example, contests the application of this periodisation to England, arguing that the modern 'penal-welfare complex' with its array of innovative technologies for transforming, and not merely punishing, the individual was not underway until the beginning of the twentieth century (Garland 1985). Prior to this moment, the nineteenth century was dominated by classical legal thought and maintained a punitive regime with limited scope for transformative methods.

Throughout, Foucault develops an analysis of the form of power that actualised disciplinary practices, norms and knowledges. Bio-power was defined by its corporeal nature; it was power over bodies by bodies. The body stood as both the raw material and the means of production. The health, welfare and productivity of bodies became the aim of bio-power. The social body itself was the engine of power, to produce and accumulate (cf. Bauman 1983). In an industrialising society power had to maximise human potential and not merely to threaten, punish or eliminate. Social policy in particular became one of the main apparatuses of the state for harnessing and circulating power. Welfare provisions would improve labour power, regulate the unproductive in disciplinary institutions, sanitise the living conditions of the general population, and order its living space in planned environments and partitioned dwellings. Yet, according to Foucault, the notions of order – the norms of medicine, education, public health, architecture, etc. – did not emerge as logically apparent solutions to the problems of capitalism, but had to be produced, their logic made clear, and applied as discourses and practices of normalisation.

However, the object of discipline was not the imposition of new forms of coercion, but the internalisation of self-restraint in freely constituted subjects. Foucault sees the beginnings of innovation in Samuel Tuke's moral treatment at the end of the eighteenth century, and a century later in Freud's 'talking cure', where the purpose in both was to encourage the insane into 'a dialogue with unreason', whereby the individual 'promised to restrain himself' (1971, pp. 198, 246). In principle, the optimisation of this process of normalisation is the fully internalised, self-regulation of mind and body. Donzelot describes the psychic space opened up for family life by psychoanalysis and counselling, so that old and new norms, prohibitions and ambitions – public and private – are allowed to float together to achieve an equilibrium that enhances the family's autonomy at the same time as preserving state regulation (1980, p. 199). These effects of normalisation are part of the deeper process of the detachment of meaning and values produced by commodification in all its forms, and by the floating of currency value, norms and meaning itself to find their 'own' level – a process proclaimed by two major instigators of modernist intellectual culture, Freud and Keynes (Donzelot 1980, pp. 231–3).

Normalisation became the principal means of discipline in democratic-welfare-capitalism, more appropriate to freely constituted subjects than repressive forms of coercion. Garland comments how 'In a democracy, where citizenship extended to all classes, discipline could no longer function through repression and exclusion'. The task of discipline was to reduce 'the "risk" that democracy entailed, ensuring that new citizens were good citizens' (Garland 1985, p. 247). Normalisation meant categorising different needs and partitioning different categories of individuals in a welfare state that confers right as well as enforces duties. Dean (1991) explores this 'partitioning of entitlement' in social security from the Poor Law through National Insurance to the social security reforms of the 1980s.

The idea of individuals freely discovering their own identity and level amidst the flux of social life points to one of the final themes Foucault developed before his death in 1984; the genealogy of the modern subject, 'the way a human being turns him or herself into a subject' (1982, p. 208). For example, the human sciences that evolved in the nineteenth century involved new methods of 'confessional technology'. Dreyfus and Rabinow argue that this new theme is not a departure from his earlier studies of disciplinary systems. Rather, his studies of the technologies of the subject and subjectification extend and complement his earlier analyses of the technologies of individual objectification (Dreyfus and Rabinow 1982, p. 169). Specifically, Foucault refers to the new methods of subjectification involved in state welfare provisions that exercise what he terms 'pastoral power'. In this respect, the state, in addition to attending to its subjects as a totality, attends to each individual's needs, serving material needs by means of secular 'salvation': 'In this context the word *salvation* takes on different meanings: health, well-being (that is, sufficient wealth, standard of living), security, protection against accidents' (Foucault 1982, p. 215). For Foucault, subjectification is one of the principal forces behind the emergence of the modern welfare state.

Welfare and bio-politics

Each of Foucault's studies marks a further step in his exploration of the nature of power, namely its capacity to form human subjects and their ostensible domains – madness, punishment and sexuality. For Foucault each subject is constituted by power.[3] Power is exercised upon, through and by the subject. For example, social policy constructs subjects upon whom power is inscribed (e.g. deprived individuals and neighbourhoods); it provides a capillary through which state power is circulated throughout the social body (administrative apparatuses affecting family life); and, by its own power, social policy establishes and preserves its interests (by legitimating governmental, professional, academic and research practices). To understand these disciplinary practices, we must first examine the conception of power that Foucault uses in his notion of bio-power.

Foucault contrasts his 'analytics of power' with other approaches that see power emanating from a particular source, an institution, a body of law, mode of repression or system of domination. Instead, it is inherent in all relations: 'Power is everywhere; not because it embraces everything, but because it comes from everywhere' (1979b, p. 93). Rather than conceiving of power as extending downwards from a central point, headquarters, ruling caste, economic elite or sovereignty, Foucault sees it immanently as originating from below in each instance of the machinery of production, in families, groups and institutions. It is this conception that informs his account of the development of bio-power, its embodiment (in 'force relations', 'the body' and 'social body') and its instruments of application (the disciplines and technologies of regulation, the 'Panopticon', the 'carceral' and the 'tutelary complex'). We will examine each of these figures.

While power is studied in ascending order from its local to its global formation – whether state, law or ideology – the analytical focus at each level remains the *force relation*. This relation is neither one of unchanging domination nor of total submission of one party to another. It is dialogic, exhibiting the never equal and yet ever mobile play of dialogue (1979b, p. 94). The force relation represents the energy of power by and upon the body. The *body* stands as a metaphor for both the anatomical focus and the embodiment of power; a materiality that acts as source and target of power, whether expressed politically, sexually, juridically or in discourse. It is not assigned a binary value as either active or passive, as the perpetrator or recipient of power. Rather, the body operates within the confines of force relations – whether between men and women, prisoner and warder, boss and worker or client and social worker, whether individually or collectively – which frame strategies of power ranging from constructive complicity to outright repression (1979a, p. 136; 1979b, pp. 95–6; 1980, p. 104). This guiding metaphor enables one to pay especial attention to the play and effects of power. At one historical moment the body asserts itself; at another it is subject to regulation. At one level in a social formation it is assertive; at another subject by a process of relays to a different layer of power. For example, Donzelot recounts how during the second half of the nineteenth century the French state gained access to working-class households, and in particular to the mother and child, by means of assistance schemes in housing, medicine and childcare. The mother was invested with new skills and in turn empowered to exercise a moral influence over husband and children. Neither the home nor its male head were directly dominated by the state. But the state via its agencies' links with the mother exercised moral influence over the patriarchal family at one remove – i.e. 'government through the family' – with the effect that relations between husband and wife were tactically reformed (1980, p. 36).

The *social body* is a metaphor for the collective embodiment of the targets of power, the body as 'species', whether in the form of an entire population or a specific group of prisoners, the insane, school children and so forth, who are subject to specific types of regulation. Foucault and others have described the administrative, judicial, penal and educational methods of discipline used from the seventeenth century onwards to preserve and regulate the life of the body, its health, sexuality, subsistence, accommodation, education, etc. The body was thus invested with a significance concerning its social well-being and required constant policing and detailed regulation. Power began to exercise a relative control over life and avert some of the imminent risks of death. It replaced the sovereign's absolute power over life and death, epitomised by the public execution and the just war. Henceforth, life entered history and 'For the first time . . . biological existence was reflected in political existence' (Foucault 1979b, p. 142). Foucault places the methods of bio-power under two categories. The *disciplines* are concerned with the anatomo-politics of the individual body, 'centred on the body as a machine: its disciplining, the optimisation of its capabilities, the exertion of its forces, the parallel increase of its usefulness and its docility, its integration into systems of efficient and economic controls'. The *regulatory controls* are concerned with the bio-politics of the entire population – the social body – 'serving as the basis of the biological processes: propagation, births and mortalities, the level of health, life expectancy and longevity, with all the conditions which cause these to vary' (1979b, p. 139). The economic and political functions of these disciplinary controls increase the productive forces of the body, and subject them to political obedience (1979a, p. 138). Armed with these two types of discipline, government is able to intervene in the private and public domains. Detailed examples of disciplinary power are given by Foucault and others which include school timetables, classroom organisation, clinical examinations, scholastic examinations, hygienic and sexual prohibitions, clinical symptomatologies, courtroom practices, prison organisation and army camps – each marked by hierarchical supervision, individual scrutiny and normative adjustments of behaviour.

From these many examples, Foucault *et al.* have constructed particular representations of disciplinary apparatuses: the 'Panopticon', the 'carceral' and the 'tutelary complex'. The Panopticon was Bentham's plan for a circular prison from the centre of which the warder, concealed in a turret, has clear visibility of each inmate in the surrounding cells. Unable to see the warder, nor know whether he is being watched, the inmate must assume constant observation, thereby internalising the 'gaze' and exerting self-discipline over his body. The Panopticon unifies the social organisation, architectural and administrative features of various punitive and corrective establishments into a perfect disciplinary institution for regulating the body and increasing its utility. At the close of the eighteenth century, it provided the idea for an instrument that informed the operation of different institutions thereafter, social and medical as well as penal. The dissemination of the Panopticon began with Bentham's idealised blueprint and its utilisation in various prison constructions. Later, compact methods of discipline were extracted from these institutions, broken down into flexible methods of control, and then regrouped and relocated throughout society. Philanthropic organisations, for example, were as disciplinary in securing their religious, economic and social policies as many other organisations. Throughout this process of dissemination, the state gradually gained control over the methods of discipline (Foucault 1979a, pp. 297–8).

The disciplines reached a further stage of development in what Foucault termed the carceral, which unites within a prison-like institution the disciplines of the family, army, workshop, school and judiciary (1979a, p. 293). However, unlike earlier institutions, the carceral domain no longer exercised its power in isolation from wider society. The realignment of disciplinary measures involved the reorientation of numerous penal and non-penal organisations towards a prison-like state in the wider community, which Foucault called the 'carceral archipelago'. The prison spread outwards to include agricultural prisons, almshouses, penal colonies, orphanages, apprentice workshops; and non-penal bodies employing carceral methods, such as charity societies, moral improvement associations, workers housing estates, hostels, and so forth. Even in areas of social life that remained relatively free of carceral discipline – e.g. the family and community – there developed a corresponding formation of normalising discipline, which Donzelot terms the 'tutelary complex'. This comprises the growing 'swarm' of social workers, benefits officers, psychiatrists, educators, and so forth who intervene in the plight of, for example, the deprived child and family, and today constitute the modern welfare state. The diversification of these specialists creates a new formation of authority: 'There is no longer two authorities facing one another: the family and the [state] apparatus, but a series of concentric circles around the child: the family circle, the circle of technicians [e.g. social workers], the circle of social guardians [e.g. magistrates] . . . . the more social rights are proclaimed, the more the stranglehold of tutelary authority tightens around the family' (1980, p. 103). In this way, judicial institutions are drawn into a continuum of apparatuses, alongside the 'judges of normality', to constitute the tutelary complex.

However, Foucault's assertion of the uni-directional process of carceral dissemination – 'the whole network that . . . spread[s] further and further outwards' (1979a, p. 297) – has not gone unchallenged. Other writers have suggested a complex of processes that coterminously move from the social to the penal and vice versa. In this way a diversified range of disciplines emerged outside the prison, transforming the prison within and the broader system of penality without; thus 'the prison was *decentred* . . . one institution among many in an extended grid of penal sanctions' (Garland 1985, p. 23). For example, Garland details four sites of innovation in late nineteenth-century England – criminology, social work, social security and eugenics – which contributed to the transformation of penality around the turn of the century and gave rise to a new 'penal-welfare complex'. Each of these sites produced new methods of intervention and policy discourses concerned to transform individuals into normalised subjects. Together they coalesced into 'a number of pragmatic formations of an eclectic nature wherein separate programmes and discourses are intertwined within a single set of recommendations' (1985, p. 203).

In developing the notion of bio-power, Foucault explicitly sought to define a form of power exclusive to modern society. Contrary to the view that describes the effects of power in negative terms which exclude, repress, abstract, conceal (labour, sexuality, knowledge, etc.), Foucault sees power as *productive*: 'it produces reality – it produces domains of objects and rituals of truth' (1979a, p. 194; 1980, p. 119). Bio-power constitutes the problems that call forth medical and administrative interventions. It engenders the forms of knowledge that structure these problems and interventions. Bio-power is essentially regulative. It extends the body's abilities and the population's capacities by manipulating and harnessing them for its own ends. Sex, for example, is seen as 'a thing not simply condemned or tolerated but managed, inserted into systems of utility, regulated for the greater good of all, made to function according to an optimum . . . it is a thing one administered' (1979b, p. 24). Foucault illustrates this 'deployment of sexuality' by way of the disciplinary interventions seen in four areas of nineteenth-century social life, where sex was problematised as an object of scientific intervention and discourse: the woman's body, child sexuality, birth control and homosexuality. The woman became an object of medical pathology ('the hysterical woman') and was subject to a wider corrective discipline of female responsibility for childbirth, the family and childcare. Child sexuality was more ambiguously cast as both a natural and unnatural activity ('the masturbating child'), posing physical, moral and social dangers which led to its control by the pedagogy of parents, educators, doctors and psychologists. Procreative activity became the target of economic inducements and restrictions, political concern for the growth or limitation of the population, and medical concern with health and unhealthy methods of contraception. Finally, a sexual instinct was isolated, its perversions identified and categorised ('the homosexual male'), its normal practices encouraged and its pathologies therapeutically regulated. The positive forces of power generated by these 'strategic unities' have advanced professional agents of intervention (social workers, doctors, teachers, etc.) with privileged bodies of knowledge that help decide which behaviour is problematic and by what norms. It is the distinctive features of bio-power and social policy that it generates positive and productive forces for the compliance and regulation of the body.

Welfare, needs and power/knowledge

Foucault's detailed studies of power entail an analysis of the nature of knowledge in disciplinary society. Power and knowledge are inextricably linked and established in specific relations, practices and sites comprising disciplinary society. This linkage offers further insight into the nature of ideology, or what Foucault – in rejecting assumptions implicit in the notion of ideology – prefers to call power/knowledge. The presence of this linkage in welfare policies is evidence of the pervasiveness of ideology in welfare practices.

The notion of power/knowledge rests on the premiss 'that there is no power relation without the correlative constitution of a field of knowledge, nor any knowledge that does not presuppose and constitute at the same time power relations' (1979a, p. 27). Hoy interprets this to mean 'that knowledge is not gained prior to and independently of the use to which it will be put in order to achieve power (whether over nature or over other people), but is already a function of human interests and power relations' (Hoy 1986, p. 129). This implies that ideology is present in the exercise of power and has no existence apart from the practical interests expressed in this exercise. As seen in the preceding examples of disciplinary practice, this approach means that ideology individuates specific power relations and groups of persons. The individual and material application of power/knowledge is seen in the corporeal force of ideology, inscribed on individual bodies by applying anatomical technologies of discipline. The concept of power/knowledge also has methodological implications. It involves passing from the study of single power relations, through networks of relations, to whole ensembles of structures such as governments and states. The ensemble of power practices characterising the welfare state creates 'the social': the hegemonic order of interests, attitudes and needs informing people's social lives, and creating institutions for the specific purpose of identifying, regulating and meeting social needs (cf. Smart 1986, p. 160; Squires 1990).

A society sensitive to the social elevates social over juridical concerns and undertakes to shift its centre of gravity from the rule of law to the rule of the norm. The juridical apparatus is gradually suffused with social norms. The process of normalisation extends throughout all parts of society. It secures at the same time the homogenisation of behavioural norms and the latitude of permissible deviations from the norm, so that most individuals achieve a sense of freedom within these limits commensurate with social functioning. The rule of law, with its tendency to subject human behaviour to the binary injunctions of permission and prohibition, is too rigid. By contrast, the power of the norm 'has to qualify, measure, appraise, and hierarchise . . . it effects distributions around the norm' (1979b, p. 144). Demarcating the normal and abnormal requires that judges accede to the recommendations of experts from numerous specialist fields who draw their criteria of truth from technologies evolved in the social sciences. In the field of punishment, for example:

> a quite different question of truth is inscribed in the course of the penal judgement. The question is no longer: 'Has the act been established and is it punishable?' But also: 'What *is* this act, what *is* this act of violence or this murder? To what level or to what field of reality does it belong? Is it a phantasy, a psychotic reaction, a delusional episode, a perverse action? . . . Another truth has penetrated the truth that was required by the legal machinery; a truth which, entangled with the first, has turned the assertion of guilt into a strange scientifico-juridical complex. (1979a, p. 19)

We can see here what distinguishes Foucault's notion of 'norm' from other notions used in the theories of ideology examined in earlier chapters. The norm is more than just a normative component within a system of values or an ideological system (as seen by the social administration school). It is active; it is practised, learnt and researched as knowledge. It is not totally dominant, a power imposed by one section of society on another (as seen by Marxists and the New Right). It is dispersed around different centres of expertise and practice, as in Donzelot's notion of the tutelary complex.

By comparing these different conceptions of the norm, we can begin to discern Foucault's critique of ideology. In earlier chapters, we saw that different Marxist approaches share a view of ideology as the obverse of truth; ideology either distorts truth or unifies a limited and fragmented knowledge into an imaginary unity that stands in for truth *pro tem*. In both senses a notion of truth is alluded to beyond ideology, whereby ultimately ideology is laid bare by the revelation of truth gained through scientific and philosophical exploration. The idea that truth is an absolute standard existing over and above, and in judgement of, the practices and discourses constituting knowledge and ideology is a metaphysical conceit which Foucault finds untenable. Instead, he seeks to determine how truth is constituted in the deployment of power and knowledge:

'the problem does not consist in drawing the line between that in a discourse which falls under the category of scientificity or truth, and that which comes under some other category, but in seeing historically how effects of truth are produced within discourses which in themselves are neither true nor false' (1980, p. 118). [4] Indeed, if, as we saw earlier, power 'produces reality', it can hardly be said to distort or conceal reality in the way that Marxists, for example, suggest in their characterisation of ideology.

However, Foucault's position on reality and ideology is itself problematic. For, by the same gesture, if power creates reality then there is no room left for other forces, beyond power and ideology, to create reality. Reality, as the basic ontological grounding – that which exists – is absorbed into the omnipotent force of power. The concept of reality loses its meaning without a counterfactual concept of ideological unreality – whether as distortion or an imaginary representation of truth – and so makes distinguishing between domains of reality and unreality impossible. This issue raises difficult questions about the status of reality which are not developed presently (see Dews 1987). [5] However, we will consider later whether the notion of truth can be banished so readily, as Foucault suggests, from the study of discourses and practices, including policy-making.

For Foucault, it follows that knowledge cannot exist independently of the political exercise of power, that there is no appeal to a true reality, and that any dividing line between true and false knowledge is no more than the outcome of the exercise of power. Using terms like truth, knowledge, ideology and even power/knowledge is a heuristic device of labelling a discourse or practice in order to examine and locate it in relation to other forms of knowledge that invest it with, or divest it of, validity. It is a nominalistic convenience, a naming device, adopted in the genealogical study of a particular form of power (Hoy 1986, pp. 134–5).

It follows that there can be nothing essential to the distinction between true and false, as seen, for example, in the notions of 'necessary' and 'surplus repression' used by Marcuse (1969), and of 'true' and 'false needs' used extensively by Marxists – a question returned to in Chapter 10. Foucault's critique of the 'very inadequate and possibly dangerous' notion that power only operates negatively as repression (1980, p. 59) ties in with his critique of these notions of truth. For they share the same essentialist assumptions by which power necessarily represses and by means of 'repressive desublimation' creates false needs.

In her study of theories of need, Patricia Springborg identifies further dangers lurking in Marcuse's and similar approaches. By invoking the notion of ideology or false consciousness to explain why an individual is in the grip of false needs, the theory of repressive desublimation denies the individual the authenticity of his or her experience in choosing to fulfil one set of needs rather than another (Springborg 1981, p. 9). However, though sharing with Foucault similar targets for criticism, Springborg mounts her criticism from a position based on a belief in truth criteria – e.g. authentic and inauthentic experience – which Foucault would not share. It is the post-structuralists, such as Foucault, who dispense with the core notion of truth, and related notions of authentic experience and the autonomous subject. From his position, Foucault no doubt would have pointed out that the truth-false needs distinction which Springborg criticises has been displaced in her system of thought to that of authentic and inauthentic experience which she wishes to preserve as a standard of true need. The question is not one of securing truth criteria for human experience, but rather one of understanding how the subject at a particular historical moment in the formation of needs comes to know him or herself as authentic or otherwise. By means of his genealogical approach to subjectivity, Foucault rejects teleological approaches, such as Marcuse's, based on the notion, implicit in theories of ideology, of a human subject whose struggle against ideology leads to emancipation and the discovery of true knowledge (see Hoy 1986, p. 138; cf. Dews 1987, ch. 6). But, in so doing, Foucault throws the baby out with the bath water, in dispensing with notions of truth that could provide a bulwark against the kinds of reasoning in theories of ideology and need that pose a threat to human freedom.

Knowledge, resistance and intervention

Foucault's ideas are clearly unsympathetic to the vocation of social policy pursued by mainstream analysts, [6] as they are to the belief held by Marxists that human welfare is about the possibility of universally fulfilling human needs (e.g. Heller 1976). Conventionally, the ethic of social policy demands that the advancement of welfare requires priority be given to individual and social needs, and a close relationship forged between theory and practice in pursuance of this priority. However, for Foucault these imperatives are no more than convenient myths created by prevailing systems of power and knowledge. As an anti-humanist, he sees the entrance of the human sciences into administration as guided not by humanitarian concern but by the advent of the disciplines with their normalising and individuating judgements.

However, despite the ubiquitous web of power entangling individual subjects, Foucault retains the hope that political resistance can emerge. He sees this located among the subjects on the receiving end of the disciplines that genealogy uncovers. In identifying new subjects and dispelling old myths, his studies provide knowledge of the successes and failures of previous forms of resistance and popular uprising, and of their relevance to present conflicts. By studying the histories of the disciplines, Foucault believes that it is possible to unearth 'subjected knowledges' buried and ignored by functionalist and other 'global' theories. From these discoveries – such as the hidden histories of struggle or disqualified accounts of low-ranking personnel – local criticisms surface as part of a wider and more dispersed offensive waged against various centres of power, such as hospitals, asylums, prisons, welfare organisations and so forth. These genealogies provide a basis for histories which throw light on present systems of discipline and promote tactical interventions of resistance (1980, p. 85). However, Foucault is not explicit about the mechanisms that kindle the spark of rebellion among some disciplined subjects and leave others in a state of perpetual submission. Nor is it clear by what political criteria a situation is judged to require resistance. Dews contends that by failing to answer these question, Foucault provided no more than an instrumental justification for his politics of resistance (1987, p. 215).

Foucault and Marxist Political Economy

The critical sweep of Foucault's work takes in Marxism as well as Liberal thought; indeed he contends that both traditions succumb to a 'sovereign' theory of power. What concerns Foucault is the global assumptions that stem from the functionalism and economism characterising these systems. In Chapter 5, we saw how Marxist Political Economy views welfare as determined by the mode of production and as a constituent feature of capitalism, so positing a relation of domination-subordination between economy and welfare. One outcome of functionalism is that the functions of welfare are cast in binary terms, for example, in producing either care or control, features that these writers put down to contradictions inherent in the capitalist welfare state. It follows that under certain conditions welfare becomes heavily involved in negative activities related to the repressive side of discipline (indeed, Marxists generally see discipline only in repressive terms). By contrast, Foucault accredits bio-power and the welfare apparatus with a positive and productive role in disciplining social subjects, one that fine-tunes specific areas of social life according to the designs of capitalism – a regulatory rather than repressive function.

However, not all Marxist analyses are functionalist and binary in their characterisations of social policy. In Chapters 6 and 7, we saw that Critical Theory overcomes some of these problems by developing a more wide-ranging theory of crisis that attends closely to functions in the political and ideological cultural spheres, as they absorb the impact of crises originating in the economic sphere. Within Critical Theory, Offe (1975), for example, provides an account sensitive to the productive features of policy arising from the transformation of the state under advanced capitalism. Social policy emerges as a distinctive feature of the capitalist state when capitalists are no longer able to co-ordinate production and further accumulation. At this moment, the traditional mode of state activity – the legitimate and neutral *allocation* of taxes and repression in accordance with the rule of law – is insufficient to guarantee capital accumulation and must be augmented by *productive* activities. However, unlike allocative activities, the state's productive activities need new forms of decision-making to produce what the state previously could not produce. Thus, public policy extends the repertoire of government in producing health, education, research and development. In the long run, however, the state has merely taken on the crisis of accumulation itself. For, as we saw in Chapter 6, the internal structure of the state – bureaucratic, oriented to strategic rationality, and earnestly seeking legitimation – cannot be reconciled with the tasks of accumulation. Though coming from different traditions, Offe and Foucault share interesting similarities (see Offe 1984, pp. 276–8). Specifically, they both credit state policy with positive capacities. Offe's distinction between state allocation (involving the political and judicial allocation of 'resources, taxation, state demand, tariffs, repression, subsidies, etc.') and state production (of 'education, skills, techno- logical change, control over raw materials, transportation, housing, a structure of cities, physical environment, energy and communication services' (1975, pp. 129, 134)) parallel Foucault's sovereign and disciplinary systems of power. However, this said, Offe retains a belief, that Foucault rejects, in the possibility of introducing principles of communicative rationality into public services that would in principle radically modify disciplinary statecraft.

We can better understand Foucault's challenge if we examine why he ascribes to Marxism and Liberalism a 'sovereign' notion of power, a term used in his history of the disciplines. Prior to the formation of the disciplines, the sovereign exercised power negatively according to laws that prohibit and sanctions that repress. Both the discursive and practical expressions of sovereignty involved a binary system of norms, the transgression of which required the imposition of a 'levy'. Thus, repression was exerted by taking the property, money and ultimately the body of the transgressor to restore social order, to right a wrong done to the sovereign or the social body. Foucault contends that remnants of this view remain in modern Marxist and Liberal thought where power in both cases is conceived of economically. In Liberalism – e.g. Marshall's notion of 'citizen- ship' and Titmuss's 'social policy' – it is a right which one possesses as a commodity. Its possession is maintained by contractual obligations of a legal or political kind which are universally binding and, if broken, remedied by the judiciary or the sovereign (i.e. parliament). Similarly, in Marxism, power involves a possession in the form of property which one class holds over another in controlling the relations of production for its own benefit, and which the other must expropriate if these relations are to be transformed. Economism is fun- damental to the Liberal and Marxist 'sovereign' suppositions of power, with their notions of levying and repression. Power is exercised through the medium of things (commodities, wealth and subjects) that are extracted, deducted, exchanged or expropriated. Moreover, the maintenance or transformation of power relations involves the use of repressive force in reallocating possessions, whether by the state's judicial apparatus or the revolutionary overthrow of the state.

The sovereign suppositions of the Political Economy of Welfare are revealed in its functionalism, its tendency to absolutism in ascribing binary concepts to the functions of welfare, and its assumption that welfare institutions are intrinsically neutral in reflecting whatever functions the state deems necessary to support its tasks of accumulation and legitimation. While Marxists see these suppositions as contradictions reflecting the nature of the capitalist state, Foucault saw that they are characteristic of a discourse that remains subject to a past era of thought. To use his oft-quoted metaphor, he claims that there are aspects of Marxist and Liberal thought where the king's head has yet to be toppled.

The ubiquity of power: a critique

In contrast to other conceptions of power, Foucault's is more ubiquitous and diffused. 'Power is neither given, nor exchanged, nor recovered, but exercised . . . it exists only in action' (1980, p. 89). Power in the welfare state is seen in the practices of the agents of bio-power, who strive to enhance the body's utility through the deployment of regulatory technologies that increase its manipulability. The body is made pliable and amenable to disciplinary norms that no longer operate according to binary injunctions, but to an increased register of dexterities, aptitudes, desires and needs geared to the requirements of economic productivity, family life, sexual conduct and so forth. The shift from sovereign- to bio-power involved, for example, the deployment of sexuality for enhancement rather than repression. In the development of the sexual disciplines, the bourgeoisie applied sexual strictures, whether as health-inducing practices of abstinence or as pathologies of sex, to themselves, and to their women and children, to secure their wider economic and political advancement. The extension of these sexual norms to the poorer classes came later (Foucault 1979b, p. 123).

However, there is a puzzling tension in Foucault's theory of power, between his conception of the ubiquity of power and his insistence on the specificity characterising the expression of power in particular practices and knowledges; the former a question of his theory of power, the latter his methodology. On the question, first, of methodology, power is analysed and described in multiple types of relations, each of which can be placed under ideal type categories such as the 'examination', 'confessional', 'Panopticon', 'tutelary complex', and so forth, and these in turn grouped under more general categories designating types of formation such as 'disciplinary' or 'carceral' society. The justification for each designation resides in the appropriateness of the observations Foucault makes in relation to each ideal typical category. On the question of theory, however, the conception of power is so general and ubiquitous as to limit theoretical conjecture about three kinds of relations: between power and other phenomena (e.g. economic and juridical), between different types of power, and between actual and potential regimes of power. The first of these relations raises the question of causality; the second the question of the dynamics of power, and the third the question of counterfactual argument. Without an articulation between the different contexts, types and potentialities of power, there can be no way of relating methodologically the conception of power to the different instances of power Foucault so painstakingly dissected, and thus no real theoretical advance.

In the first relation, the problem stems from the absence of any theoretical notion of causation between the different historical processes Foucault recounted. For example, why did bio-power emerge with the decline of medieval sovereignty and gain dominance throughout the nineteenth and twentieth centuries? Certainly, underlying his account of the development of discipline, power and knowledge are structural notions of change, of expanding, shifting and segmenting populations, and of transformed methods of production (1979a, p. 218). However, Foucault never elevated these material forces to an unequivocable determining status. Any hint, for example, of a base-superstructure compact between productive forces and power relations or ideology is avoided (1980, p. 118; cf. Beechey and Donald 1985, p. xvi). Indeed, he nullified all such causal connections. For example, two processes – the accumulation of men and the accumulation of capital – are inseparable; 'it would not have been possible to solve the problem of the accumulation of men without the growth of an apparatus of production capable of both sustaining them and using them; conversely, the techniques that made the cumulative multiplicity of men useful accelerated the accumulation of capital' (1979a, p. 221). Without an effective accumulation of persons, the sovereign methods of control, for example, were ineffective, creating numerous instances of 'bad political economy': ineffective or over-repressive punishments, sexual promiscuity, unregulated populations of the sick, vagrant, overcrowded, insane, and so forth (1979a, p. 219; cf. Donzelot 1980, pp. 40–5). The difficulty in discerning a clear process of causation in these accounts lies in the underlying vitalistic conception of power (cf. Donnelly 1982). This force is never defined, though it is everywhere 'made manifest' in all things. The enigmatic quality of power in itself led Foucault to attend to its manifestation in the way that his various subjects are constituted – rather than caused – and embodied in social practices and discourses.

The paucity of Foucault's theoretical conjecture about the second relation – between different kinds of power – stems from his ubiquitous conception of power, whereby power is the all-pervasive and essential driving force of social life. Power is not something one has or hasn't, it is 'everywhere'. It is not economic production but power which brings social organisation into being with its specific class formations and ideologies. As in economistic theory, such absolutism also leads to the limitations of functionalism and reductionism. Without a theory that differentiates between types of power, the phenomenon lacks a dynamic. For differentiation – e.g. between one class which exercises power over another – provides a leverage for alternative viewpoints on power, on its legitimacy or delegitimacy, and so forms a basis for its critique. Dews points out that:

> if objects of knowledge are always constituted within a specific form of power-knowledge, there cannot be 'other possible images', other points of view ... on the *same* historical and social processes. Foucault's doctrine that it is only within a form of power-knowledge that statements can be candidates for truth or falsity has the paradoxical consequence that any critique of a form of power-knowledge as misrepresention must already have accepted its fundamental assumptions. (1987, p. 189)

Given Foucault's rejection of power as a thing possessed or lacked, Hoy suggests that he would need a different 'contrast class' which would provide an essential dynamic for conceptualising power. Contrary to Dews, Hoy contends that the notion of contrasting classes *is* implied by the different configurations of power which Foucault contrasted with each other (Hoy 1986, p. 137). *Discipline and Punish*, for example, is about the shift from sovereign to disciplinary regimes of power. However, it must be said that within disciplinary power its various manifestations are no more than different species of the same genus.

For Foucault, the emergence of the disciplinary power of the bourgeois state is so total and far-reaching that it eclipses even the critical moment that a sovereign theory of subjectivity would provide. Dews contends that 'Foucault's argument is that any theory of the sovereign or self-determination must be abandoned, since the "free subject" upon which such theories rely is in fact intrinsically heteronomous, constituted by power'. For example, '*Discipline and Punish* repeatedly returns to the contrast between the illusion of a social order grounded in the will of all, and the grim reality of a technology of power which constantly enforces conformity to norms' (1987, p. 161). For Foucault's conception of the death of the self-conscious and determining subject also sounds the death-knell for critical judgement and the possibility of ideology critique. Without a critical subject, the contrast Foucault paints between the illusions of democracy, scientificity, justice and welfare in modern society, and the reality of an expanding and inescapable power cannot be used as an account of ideology which, by means of social critique, presages human emancipation – despite his claim to be unearthing the forgotten wisdom of oppressed subjects.

It is in this spirit that – concerning the third question of power – Foucault eschewed any reference to counterfactual possibilities within discourse and practice, on the ground that this would imply an orientation towards metaphysical criteria of truth. However, this restricts the scope of human potentiality and impoverishes the resources of discourse. On the one hand, human existence and history are predicated on the possibility of achieving or anticipating future ideals and utopias, or recovering lost states of community and contentment, that cannot be uttered in discourse in empirically referential terms, and straightaway enacted in political practice. On the other hand, however uncertain and even illusory, the hopes and desires for such ideals *are* proposed in discourse and strategically sought in practice. The human discourse of history is not read solely in the barren confines of a present bereft of possibilities, but with an anticipation of the fulfilment that only time can disclose. In contrast – at least in his early work – Foucault flattens the distinction between actuality and counterfactuality by treating all discourse as actual and contingent. For example, in pitting his positivist approach against hermeneutic inquiry, he urges that:

> we must grasp the statement in the exact specificity of its occurrence; determine its conditions of existence, fix at least the limits, establish its correlation with other statements that may be connected with it, and show what other forms of statement it excludes. We do not seek below what is manifest the half silent murmurs of another discourse; we should show why it could not be other than it was. (1972, p. 28)

It is in this context that we see his denial of the prefigurative function of ideology – the 'murmurs of another discourse'; that is, its ability to anticipate in its utterances other possible ideals of social existence that do not yet exist – except perhaps in certain very limited forms – but which could exist by political acts of collective will to engender change. One of the hallmarks of welfare statements and proposals is that they are instances of a discourse where ideals prefiguring future states of human betterment are enunciated in statements about present social and economic conditions from which society plans its release and by which it mounts its interventions and strategies of change.

This discussion of the prefigurative function of welfare ideology raises the important issue of the positivity that the various approaches so far discussed accord welfare. Fabian social administration points to the positive value of welfare in its contribution to social caring and cohesion. By contrast, both Marxist Political Economy and New Right deny these positive values by both seeing them as politically legitimating: for Marxists, as contributing to capital accumulation; for the New Right, as denuding capital of growth and enterprise. Foucault's analyses re-establish the positivity of welfare by seeing it as a productive and individually enhancing aspect of normalisation and discipline. But this is done with a certain cynicism, in so far as the productive nature of power is so extensive that little space is left for social critique by human subjects denied creativity. We will see in the next chapter how Lacan's and Habermas' restoration of a dialectic of need in social interaction clears a space for prefigurative possibility in welfare practice and ideology.

Notes

1. See for example on family policy (Donzelot 1980), psychiatry (Castel *et al.* 1982; Miller and Rose 1986), clinical psychology (Rose 1979), childcare and penal policy (Burchell 1980; Thorpe *et al.* 1980; Harris and Webb 1987), education (Jones and Williamson 1979), social security (Squires 1990) and dietetics (Turner 1991).

2. Dews has queried Foucault's claim about the political potential of genealogy. He argues that the intention behind Foucault's genealogy is to dissolve the philosophical link, stemming from the tradition of German Idealism and Marxism, between 'consciousness, self-reflection and freedom . . . and [therefore] to deny that there remains any progressive political potential in the ideal of the autonomous subject' (1987, p. 160; see, e.g. Foucault 1982, p. 210).

3. Towards the end of his life, Foucault restated the goal of his work: 'It has not been to analyse the phenomenon of power, nor to elaborate the foundations of such an analysis. My object, instead, has been to create a history of the different modes by which, in our culture, human beings are made subjects' (1982). He still maintained, however, the centrality of power in constituting the subject (see Dreyfus and Rabinow 1982, p. 169).

4. Beechey and Donald usefully unpack Foucault's pithy statement of his objections to theories of ideology (1985, p. xiv).

5. Broadly, Foucault can be contrasted with two traditions of philosophy: one which accepts that reality – the Kantian 'things-in-themselves' – lies beyond human experience and is only represented in the appearance of things; and the other – broadly positivist – which conflates reality with empirical experience and denies the division between things-in-themselves and phenomenal appearances. Foucault, like positivists, renders reality in the here and now, but, unlike them, accepts that its existence is problematic and must be traced in the genealogies of truth he seeks to unravel.

6. The implication of Foucault's work for welfare studies is developed, *inter alia*, in Hewitt (1991, p. 239).

10

Problems of human need: the real and ideological bases of welfare

In previous chapters *individual* need and its ideological construction make only brief appearances. Apart from a few exceptions ideology has been examined largely through structural and institutional perspectives that pay little attention to the impact of ideology on persons (cf. Leonard 1984). To redress this imbalance, this chapter studies personal need as an important factor in understanding welfare ideology.

In the welfare state, definitions of need perform an important service in disseminating ideology. A welfare state committed to meeting different types of need will define subjects who are welfare clients, recipients or claimants as lacking specific material and psychological requirements, as fulfilling certain criteria of desert, and so as worthy of state support. In short, this conjunction of material, mental and moral features presents the welfare dependant as an ideological subject in need. Different theories of welfare ideology point to this important feature of the ideological subject, who is cast variously as a fully-fledged citizen of a social democratic polity, a moral 'burden' or 'cost' on private wealth, or a unit of labour in the 'reserve army' to be reproduced in the interests of capital. More explicitly, for Althusser and Foucault, the welfare recipient is subject to, respectively, the ideological apparatuses of the welfare state and the individuating micro-technologies of disciplinary discourses. The different expressions of ideology – as political rights, coercion, exploitation, discourse – each focus on the subject of need. Society's constructions of need are saturated with ideological salience.

In this chapter, we will examine theories that explicitly refer to the construction of human subjects and provide accounts of welfare ideology in terms of the central concept of need. However, although social policy certainly recognises the importance of need, it has largely ignored its ideological construction. For example, the British tradition of social administration has taken as axiomatic that the main purpose of social policy is to meet need – as the many textbook

174

introductions to the subject testify (see Baker 1979). In adopting this welfare-meets-needs axiom, and making need central to the aims of welfare policy, policy-makers should strive to understand need in non-ideological ways. If social policy aims to meet need, then it should meet real need; it should maintain a realist stance towards need. This proposition is surely acceptable, and indeed imperative, as a normative view of the aims of policy. However, it presents problems as a statement of the kind of knowledge we can have about need, because, as this chapter will argue, it is based on a limited view of ideology as no more than a distortion of reality and as something that social science can and must eliminate. By contrast, recent theories of ideology – some of which have been discussed already in this book – suggest that needs are ideologically constructed and their reality knowable only through ideology. Hence, a realist theory of need must take ideology more seriously, as both a negative and positive force shaping our knowledge of need. However, this contention raises a serious question, relevant to both the practicalities of policy-making and the specula-tions of social theory, about how real needs are to be understood in this way, especially if human survival and welfare are to be assured.

A concern to safeguard need from ideological distortions has resurfaced in the context of the uncertainties faced by the welfare state since the 1970s. In different areas of policy – social, economic, penal, Third World development – analysts on the Left have advocated notions of basic needs (BN) and feasible policies that rest on realist premises, i.e. so called 'new realist' policy.[1] In each area, BN and realist standards are the best way to secure human interests against the threats posed by the 'new realists' of the Right.

Although a topical issue, the question of need has arisen throughout history as a problem concerning the kind of knowledge we can have about human desires, wants and needs. Broadly two approaches are followed: needs are defined either *intrinsically* or *procedurally* (cf. Leiss 1978, pp. 111–12). First, an understanding of needs *in themselves* provides criteria for allocating re-sources; so that by defining the nature, extent and intensity of need, one can arrive at prior claims on resources that secure an adequate level of human functioning (Galtung 1980; Plant *et al.* 1980, pp. 33–4). This is the BN approach, which has recently gained favour among policy-makers committed to new realist policies. In social and political thought, this tradition has a long and varied pedigree, indeed one that goes back to antiquity (Springborg 1981). In the 1920s, Malinowski's (1944) theory of social functioning posited a hierarchy of needs where BN are met prior to 'derived' and 'integrative' needs. A few decades earlier, Booth's (1971) and Rowntree's (1901) studies of nineteenth-century poverty assumed a similar notion of BN founded on, among other things, the minimal nutritional requirements for physical efficiency. Secondly, and some-times in opposition to the first, an ethic of rational and democratic decision-making is proposed as a prior condition for defining needs necessary for human functioning or flourishing (Leiss 1978, pp. 111–12; Habermas 1979, p.93).[2] Although the two approaches can be conjoined (Doyal and Gough 1984),[3] they are each based on different forms of universality. The BN approach posits a universal framework of needs shared by all and presupposed prior to understanding diverse forms of social existence, such as different states of dependency to be ameliorated, and varied cultural practices compared. By contrast, the procedural approach assumes that a consensus of understanding precedes the determination of need, and that this determination varies according to the culture giving voice to the consensus. This argument is seen in Habermas's discussion of 'discursive will formation' (1979, p. 93).

In this chapter, first we register doubts about the philosophical, empirical and ideological problems the BN thesis is supposed to overcome. These three doubts question attempts in social policy to offer clear accounts of BN that rest on a fundamental distinction between real and distorted needs. For each problem the BN thesis claims to have overcome, doubts emerge. We will see that these doubts arise from a particular view of ideology that requires reconstruction if the concept of need is to acquire greater validity in social science and policy. The following sections discuss the ideology of need by comparing distortional and imaginary accounts and by suggesting a 'precursory' or prefigurative function of ideology, whereby real needs are intimated despite the imaginary construction ideology imposes. This requirement is sought in the work of the French psychoanalyst Jacques Lacan, that the signification of imaginary needs and desires orients (or disorients) people towards their real needs. The final section concludes with a discussion of an unexpected convergence between Lacan and Habermas on the intersubjective foundations of need, pointing towards the role of ideology in orienting individuals towards real needs. Unlike previous chapters the present one is more programmatic, theoretical and speculative in seeking to look beyond the pointers given in this survey of theories of welfare ideology. As a speculative exercise it pursues a difficult and more complex argument than contained in the previous chapters.

Ideology and the basic needs thesis

First, in tackling the philosophical problem of determining a universally acknowledged realm of essential need, the BN thesis argues that there exists an order of 'basic need', natural or universal to humanity. This is distinguished from a second order of non-basic needs met by an extravagant use of resources. Plant *et al.* (1980), for example, suggest that the characteristic that distinguishes universal needs from subjective wants rests on the nature of the ends to which needs are put, such as the advancement of personal survival rather than indulgence. Ends concerned with the survival of all define a category of BN. All other ends define something non-essential such as subjective wants (1980, pp. 33–6, 38). Taylor-Gooby and Dale employ a materialist approach to argue a similar case (1981, p. 230). As the level of society's productive capacity is raised, needs above subsistence are met. They argue for two levels of need, 'basic' and 'higher' needs, before designating a level of wasteful need. In these discussions, the distinction between real and unreal needs is absolute: need belongs to one or other category – though, as we saw in the discussion of Marx's theory of need in Part II, to which category is a matter determined by historical circumstances. The implication is that ideological distortions of basic need can be remedied by direct appeal to the incontestable status of real need. Such a procedure confines the imaginary portrayal of need to a non-basic or ephemeral level and ignores the imaginary representation involved in all levels of need, basic and non-basic alike.

BN exponents see a second problem arising because welfare services often ignore empirical human need in pursuing unclear or alternative objectives (e.g. Bradshaw 1972; Walker 1982), such as the reproduction of labour for capital accumulation or some other non-welfare need. To counter this, the principle that welfare services should meet human needs is strengthened so that only needs accepted as *empirically* valid or real are used to secure appropriate forms of welfare. In order to satisfy need, the subject who needs (the client, patient, recipient) and not the object that meets need (welfare services) should determine welfare outcomes. This is a version of: 'to reason from the needs' (Galtung 1980, p. 104; Plant *et al.* 1980, p. 51). Again, the question of validity requires removing the ideological or normative distortions to which need is prone to uncover BN. The corollary of this view is the assumption of a hard and fast distinction between real or empirical need and distorted need.

Thirdly, an ideological problem arises because in making policy governments show little consistency in defining BN. In social policy discourse, the concept is treated with an elasticity that extends from seeing it as the basis of an ideal – a universal right of citizens and an absolute duty of government – to translating it into practical tasks bound by contingency, conditional on, for example, available resources and criteria for selecting dependency groups. For example, on the one hand, the National Health Service was envisaged in broad terms:

> to ensure that in future every man and woman and child can rely on getting all the advice and treatment and care which they may need in matters of personal health; that what they get shall be the best medical and other facilities available; that their getting these shall not depend on whether they can pay for them, or any other factor irrelevant to their real need. (HMSO 1944)

On the other hand, government provides numerous statements, marked by their specificity, describing the numbers of persons with particular needs who receive specific services. By shifting between the ideal and contingent registers, government can proclaim its aims and responsibilities, whilst in practice providing levels of welfare that fall short of its claims. Because we do not always espy this shift in argument, we may fail to see the contradictions between the rhetoric of a government's ideals and the reality of its actual achievements – a gap that ideology-critique has sought to uncover. In the face of this problem, policy analysts seek to discern the difference between empirical reality and ideals, practice and prescription, realism and idealism, the factual and counterfactual, and so forth (cf. Edelman 1977, p. 19). These requirements for analysing policy-making are again based on the real-ideology distinction. The first term is construed as a matter of contingency, where the practical imperatives of policy-making exert realistic constraint, and the second a matter of ideology, where political idealism nurtures the ideals of policy-making.

To summarise so far, the BN approach seeks to ground welfare policy on a theoretically sound footing that avoids ideological deception by adopting a position that assumes a categorical distinction between real and imaginary needs (see Heller 1980, pp. 214–25). In this position the nature of real needs can be grasped scientifically, and ideological distortion dispensed with, by some version of empiricist methodology. Real needs are the intrinsic properties of individuals and groups. Yet BN exponents fail to acknowledge the problematic nature of the distinction between real and distorted need, that it is culturally and ideologically drawn and in no sense absolute. As an alternative to this view, the chapter argues that *all* conceptions of need are ideological or imaginary representations of real need.

In seeking to resolve this dilemma, we look next at the distinction between distortional and imaginary accounts of ideology and introduce the idea that ideology plays a precursory role in articulating real needs. This alternative view sees needs as real phenomena whose nature, while open to scientific study, is ultimately ascertained by means of a process of consensus formation. Claims about the nature of real needs require not only scientific validation of their substance, but normative validation of their democratic acceptability to citizens of a welfare state. This position represents a particular view about the kind of knowledge appropriate for understanding need; an epistemology tied to the process of consensus formation in advancing truth claims. This opens up a second concern of the paper: to explore the pitfalls of the consensual approach and offer a development that does justice to its potential for taking the role of ideology in recognising needs seriously *and* in suggesting, none the less, a way to approach real needs.

Ideology and the imaginary

The distinction between distortional and imaginary conceptions of ideology suggests two accounts of need. In the distortional conception, false or imaginary needs are a distortion of basic or real needs. As we argued above, a theory of BN secures this distinction in the hope of offsetting ideological distortion. By contrast, an imaginary conception of ideology such as Althusser's would argue that all notions of need are constructions based on an imaginary or illusory view of the real relations between those with needs and those with resources to meet them. Our knowledge of need is imaginary to the extent that it is based on a misrecognition of real relations produced by ideology. Real needs cannot be addressed directly if they are conceived within an imaginary relation. Because, for example, Althusser contends that ideology is a representation of 'the imaginary relationship of individuals to their real conditions of existence' (1971, p. 162), the discovery of people's real relations to these conditions must precede any understanding of real need. This account disallows any notion, found in the distortional account, of BN or 'necessary consumption' running through all societies or specific to particular societies (e.g. Galtung 1980, p. 67; Doyal and Gough 1984, p. 17).

Yet, at the same time, such an imaginary account raises serious questions about how human satisfaction – and ultimately human survival – is possible where the meaning of need is determined by misperceived relations and there is no direct recourse to knowledge of real relations. From the perspective of public policy, the problem is all the more acute when one notes that such doubts undermine needs-based justifications for according rights to the deprived, whose survival is most at stake, and imposing duties on those whose survival is more assured.

This problem would be resolved if we could recognise a precursory function of ideology that guides the process of meeting needs. Here ideology misrecognises needs and yet, under certain conditions, recognises a truth about real needs and real means of fulfilment it cannot yet fully articulate. Marxist Critical Theory has described this precursory function of ideology in different spheres of social life. For example, for Marx, 'religious suffering is . . . an expression of real suffering and a protest against real suffering' (1963, p. 31); for Adorno, works of art, while conforming to some false sense of identity, none the less 'struggle against the repressive identification compulsion that rules the outside world' (1984, p. 6); and for Bloch, utopian writing at critical points of social transition portrays images of communal fulfilment, 'dream landscapes of a better world' (1971, p. 135). These insights imply that imaginary accounts of ideology and need involve none the less a truth-seeking task directed towards fulfilling real needs.

Indeed, an imaginary account of ideology without a sense of its precursory function would be at a severe disadvantage. Whereas the distortional account claims that imaginary distortions can be decoded back to the real world once the rules of encodement have been grasped, by contrast, an imaginary account cannot identify distortion of the real, because of the *totalising* effect of the imaginary in hampering the discovery of this code. This deficiency means that any code used would produce no more than a translation from one level of the imaginary to another, with no sense of the validity of one over the other. At best,

an imaginary account discloses 'old' ideological knowledge from a new ideological standpoint that '*overcomes*' the old.

However, the very notion of 'overcoming' implies criteria of delineation and
evaluation *beyond* and not just within an ideology (a 'problematic', 'discourse'
or 'power/knowledge'). What distinguishes new from earlier forms of ideology
is not merely the former's intrinsically different explanatory features ('the
system of questions' and 'answers given': Althusser 1969, p. 67n), but its
bearings on the question of truth and reality, which adherents to a new ideology
cannot claim. Such bearings lie transcendentally beyond ideology; that is, in the
conditions of knowledge that make it possible for knowledge to explain the real
world, to reveal ideological untruth and illuminate the path to human fulfilment.
However, because of the totalising effect of ideology, this is an approach that
can be made only via ideology. This requires discerning what content in
ideology acts as a precursor to human betterment, and what impedes such
precursory insight. One response to this question is to locate this precursory
function firmly in the development of scientific explanation. Thus, in the
philosophy of science, Roy Bhaskar has – in an approach he terms 'transcendental realism' or 'depth realism' – addressed the precursory impulse entailed in
needing that drives scientific inquiry in its concern to emancipate the human
condition from 'an unwanted and unneeded to a wanted and needed source of
determination'. This impulse, he contends, 'is both causally presaged and
logically entailed by explanatory theory' (Bhaskar 1986, p. 179). However,
because of the persisting effect of the imaginary upon such theory, further work
is required to understand the ways whereby ideology represents real needs
through its continuing articulation of imaginary needs, and whereby the unconscious influences the development of explanatory theory – a task that presently
we can only pursue in outline. This possibility is developed in relation to Lacan
and Habermas.

The dialectic of need and desire

Lacan's theory of desire and the unconscious provides a basis for theorising the
ideology of need beyond the limits posed by other accounts: for example, that
need is a biological prerequisite met prior to being culturally shaped (e.g.
Malinowski); is relative to regimes of power and truth (e.g. Foucault); is
symbolic (e.g. Leiss); is historically contingent (e.g. Marxism). Lacan's theory
of the real, imaginary and symbolic aspects of need contains all of these
conceptions whilst avoiding the reductionist tendencies of each. His major
contribution is to have foreseen that what the individual subject needs, formed
in its relations to these objects of need and desire (what psychoanalysts term
'object relations'), and transformed through language, sets the horizons for its
personal and political ideology:

[man's] dependence is maintained by a world of language, precisely because by and through language needs are diversified and reduced to a point at which their scope appears to be of a quite different order, whether in relation to the subject or to politics. (Lacan 1977, p. 309)

Lacan's writings are complex and deliberately obscure, for reasons we will not go into.[4] None the less, the following exposition seeks to show some of the fruitful insights into ideology and need that he furnishes, insights that have proved influential in the case of Althusser and his followers, and more recent analysts of postmodernity such as Jameson (1984) and Baudrillard (1983). Aspects of Lacan's theory are outlined in three steps each representing a process in the formulation of need: the tripartite system of the imaginary, symbolic and real; the 'dialectic of desire'; and the signification of need and desire. At each step, we will pause to consider the significance of these insights in understanding welfare needs.

1. The imaginary, symbolic and real realms of need

Lacan's theory of desire and need rests on a three-fold division of the realms of human experience. Lacan separates the imaginary and real by interposing the third realm of the symbolic – the realm of language and meaning – which, with its structure-conferring attributes, enables the real to be signified, albeit in an imaginary form, and understood by the human subject. It is at the juncture of the three realms that the human subject is placed – though in a manner profoundly fragmented by the vagaries governing this conjunction. The real, symbolic and imaginary each play a specific and indispensable role in mediating between the other two to produce the subject's knowledge of the world and its needs (see Schneiderman 1983). Being part of the real, the subject must strive to fulfil its organic needs by means of real resources – despite the problems of misrecognition posed by the imaginary. It is the symbolic universe of language and signification that, influenced by the subject's real and imaginary promptings towards fulfilment, arranges the real's content into a structured appearance of knowledge and potential satisfaction for the subject.

The dangers for the subject of being divorced from reality by ideology are avoided by the subject's entry into the social world of the symbolic and by the subject's grounding in the real. However, despite this grounding, it is the imaginary that directs (or misdirects) the subject's knowledge of the real. In this sense the problem of need remains ideological. This points to the dilemma posed by ideology, whereby the subject forever experiences its needs in the real world, while constructing an imaginary project of apparent fulfilment that none the less provides a cognitive basis for living in the real. In this sense, Lacan portrays the subject as a paradox split into its existential and cognitive being, while unified in its ideology.

This three-part conception of human experience presents a comprehensive but undoubtedly obscure account of how needs are ideologically shaped. This can be clarified by way of the following caricature – at the cost of some simplification. Lacan depicts an individual with her feet resting on a portion of the ground or real world, her vision obscured by the mists of ideology which is partially compensated for by her imaginary faculty, and possessing the further faculty of universal language with which to share her experience with others. The mist obscures her vision of the ground so that she must rely on her imaginary faculty to construct an ideological view of her position in relation to the ground. This imparts a sense of imaginary wholeness that compensates for the limitations of her restricted view of the real world. Any congruence between her experience and her imaginary view of the real is at best grasped intuitively, possibly arising from the sense of real physical forces acting on her, such as the pull of gravity and the impact of the perceptual field. However, the structure of the symbolic which shapes her speech and thought also provides a 'map' with vertical and horizontal axes (i.e. synchronic and diachronic); based, according to the tenets of structuralism, on the universal properties shaping the structure of language (e.g. metaphor and metonymy), and the pattern of cultural life communicated through language. With this map, she is able to organise her raw experience, gaining cognitive bearings in relation to the real, and sharing her knowledge with others.

On a political level, the ideological effect of the split between the real and imaginary can be seen in the Right's project. Here a new proto-hegemony has sought to replace the old hegemony of the postwar consensus surrounding the welfare state. The imaginary attractions of the market in optimising opportunities are expressed in a series of propositions about the relations individuals have to their means of existence and to each other. This is an ideology about market order, self-discipline, effort and incentives, which may bear some relationship to the real world of human need, but none the less remains fundamentally out of kilter with it. Inspired by these values, individuals produce commodities they need by co-operating with co-workers, competing with other firms to supply the market, and contributing towards satisfying a modicum of need. Real means of existence are utilised and real needs satisfied by dint of each individual's intuitive compulsion to survive; yet these real relations are expressed within the all-embracing imaginary project of market ideology, dominated by exchange rather than use value, by commodity fetishism and the marketing of need. In market ideology (and other ideologies), the real means of existence are present under the signified form of the imaginary relations of people to these means.

Rightist and other ideologies are effective to the extent that they gloss the split between the existential experience and the cognition of real need, permitting the individual only an illusory grasp of his or her needs in relation to their means of existence. However, this ideology becomes ineffective with the emergence of new ideology that both prefigures a state of greater well-being, and casts doubt on the utility of, say, market arrangements for meeting need. The new ideology casts suspicion on whether real needs after all are being met under the ideological regime of the Right.

This suspicion is seen in the ideological battle over the provision of the British National Health Service. On the one hand, the Right raises the imaginary possibility that real health needs could be met more effectively within the market or in public provision operating in near-market conditions. Needs remain unmet because bureaucracy, political intrigue and professional dominance inhibit the expression of patient choice and distort market relations between needs and resources, demand and supply. On the other hand, proponents of socialised medicine point to the modicum of real needs met within a universal state health service, recognising on largely utilitarian grounds the comparative advantage of a socialised system which meets the BN of the majority, rather than the select needs of the few. However, recourse to a BN justification also promotes an imaginary account of need – that there is a modicum of treatable health need – which discounts the reality of diverse health needs, and accepts the judgements of professional clinicians who identify ('interpellate') BN and bureaucrats who distribute resources on BN criteria of justice. Beveridge for example provided a narrative of progress founded on a notion of BN, whereby with the passing of time a NHS 'will diminish disease by prevention and cure' (1942, p. 162), so that more and more basic health needs would be met.

2. Need and the 'dialectic of desire'

Interwoven with the structure of the imaginary, real and symbolic is Hegel's account of the 'dialectic of desire', which informs the subject's relations with others in fulfilling need (Hegel 1977). For Lacan, this involves – in its simplest form – the unfolding of three dimensions of the psychoanalytic object relation: the subject and its objects of desire and need; the subject's objects and ego-ideals; and ego-ideals and the Other, in whose gift alone lies the satisfaction of need and desire.[5] In the *first* relation, the subject is directed to the objects it believes it needs, and thereby establishes an imaginary view of its needs and itself (the self having no direct cognition of the real); the subject comes to know itself in relation to these objects and simultaneously to invest them with values reflecting its ideals (not unlike Marx's commodity fetishism). From this relation unfolds the *second* between objects and ego-ideals, where the individual's desire for need satisfaction influences its imaginary view of itself, its needs, objects, and ideals.[6] However, because the objects of need are part of the real, the subject – however much it misrecognises itself, its objects and ideals – must submit to the exigencies of the real world, the subject's need for real resources stemming from the organic nature of human existence. The real appears in Lacan's scheme as an entirely distinct order, understood only indirectly because of the enfoldment of the symbolic and imaginary over it, though its presence is felt intuitively.[7] This is very different from proposing an unmediated categorical distinction between real and imaginary needs, as the BN thesis does. The real is that which would remain were it possible to remove the imaginary and symbolic from view.

The relations between subject and object and between object and ego-ideal give rise to the *third* and final relation between ego-ideal and 'the Other' ('l'Autre'). For Lacan, the Other is the crux of his theory of desire and the unconscious. The subject gains its objects of need only in interaction with another person who is seen as their bestower (in psychoanalysis, the mother figure of universal plenitude), an imaginary view that interacts with, to enhance or confound, the subject's ideal view of itself. From its particular standpoint of need, the subject demands of others, and especially of significant others, the satisfaction of all its needs, including of course its needs for recognition. From these many demands of the other, in turn, arises desire that over-reaches contingent needs and demands, and coalesces into the total and unconditional (or ideal) desire for the recognition of the Other. Directing the subject's desire, the unconscious surfaces at the point towards which the subject strives, the locus of 'the Other'. For Lacan, this is the point where the unconscious is governed by the symbolic order; hence, his oft-quoted 'the unconscious is the discourse of the Other' (1977, p. 193). This is because the Other is more then the other person in the subject's intersubjective project. It is also the totality of the subject's unconscious desires of others, which, in signifying potentially infinite demand (theoretically, implying a language designating the totality of objects demanded), places the unconscious under the symbolic order, and imparts relational and structural shape, direction and force to the real world. The subject imagines its desires in the substantive form of its objects of need, but unconsciously its desiring project is located at a different locus that shapes and directs needing. This is why it is important for ideology to create ego-unity for the fragmented subject. In Lacanian theory, the necessity of human satisfaction, despite the impossibility of complete fulfilment, means that the subject is formed through the ideological ramifications of desire, demand and need. The unconscious plays a formative role in the growth of knowledge of the real, presaging the possibility of need satisfaction and human emancipation (Bhaskar 1986, p. 127).

The relationship between the self in need and the other who proffers satisfaction offers an intersubjective framework for interpreting the structure and process of welfare ideology. The social worker–client relationship, for example, can be described in terms of this three-stage schema. The prospective client commences her career in welfare clientage only after having been driven by a sense of material and psychological helplessness. She enters into a welfare relationship *first* with a view – not always clearly formed – of her needs and the objects needed for satisfaction: material resources such as adequate income, housing and pre-school assistance, or symbolic esteem gained through education, training or therapy. These resources are identified according to the subject's imaginary view of her real needs (i.e. ego-ideals), a view already shaped by a complex history of past relationships with parents, relatives, friends and others.

Secondly, the social worker, in turn, will assess the clients needs in terms of the quality and type of resources available, categorising needs into typical cases (cf. Smith 1980). This relationship and the specification of needs involved convey to the client a view of herself as a particular type of client (possibly at variance with her own sense of need and ego-ideals).

At the *third* step, two options face the client. First, she may see a state of well-being that she presently lacks prefigured in the worker–client relationship and wider welfare provisions. Such a state will require work between client and social worker. This might involve, either, if the worker is amenable to her ideals and has resources to support them, a collaborative project between co-workers; or, if the worker is antipathetic to her, struggle between worker and client. Either way, the client is involved in work that opens up the opportunity for deepening self-knowledge, discovering real needs, reappraising ego-ideals, and even taking charge of her own history, however momentarily, through a dialectic of recognition between self and other. By contrast, the second option carries the possibility of the client accepting her clientage, reducing expectations and ego-ideals to conform with an alien view of herself. By means of these scenarios, we see in the dialectic of recognition the ambiguity that ideology confers on the subject's life. Its imaginary perspective can instil acquiescence with established norms, conventions of need and subjectivity; or it can incite a struggle to make new demands and gain new levels of personal fulfilment.

3. The signification of need and desire

Lacan – at least in his early work – adheres to the structuralist axiom that the system of differences signified in language (the order of 'signifiers') articulates the system of differences in thought (the order of 'signifieds') that conceptualises the world. However, in one crucial respect he departs from the tradition that stems from the Swiss linguist Saussure. Lacan asserts that in the production of meaning it is the signifier which structures the signified (rather than signifier and signified mutually reinforcing each other); that words instance objects in the world (1977, p. 65) and shape the form that the subject takes. For Lacan, the subject is ever at the mercy of the signifier. Thus a system of signifiers, words, and so forth signifying notions of desire and need, conditions the particular objects that form the subject's horizons, 'where the subject is subordinated, even suborned by the signifier' (1977, p. 233). The subject is thereby doubly alienated or 'suborned' by being the slave of its needs and necessarily construing these needs as demands that signify but do not satisfy, in making its 'need pass through the defiles of the signifier' (*ibid.*, p. 264). By virtue of the effect of language on human action the subject always signifies less than needs to be signified. Thus an important distinction is made between the subject who consciously states its needs (as part of its ego-ideal) and the 'true subject' whose real needs are often signified unconsciously outside such statements in slips of the tongue, figurative speech and so on (*ibid.*, pp. 298–9).

To apply this theory of language to the process of desire, Lacan proposes, following Jakobson (1971, pp. 49–73), that the two axes structuring meaning – metonymy and metaphor – are present in the discourse of the unconscious. In particular, desire is signified in the chain of need signifiers, or demands, moving towards (but never reaching) the total fulfilment of an unconscious point of fundamental lack (i.e. metonymy where each need is expressed as a part of desire); and in the substitution of repressed need by expressed need, shaping the horizons of conscious and unconscious longings (i.e. metaphor) (Lacan 1977, pp. 257–65). So a specific need is expressed as a demand – demand being expressed or signified need – by the available signifiers. The signification of need is articulated along the two axes. First, demand is displaced along a chain of signifiers if either a need remains unmet (in which case it shifts to a signifier for a demand that can be met), or, if met, new needs, and so new demands, replace those satisfied. This process of linear displacement in the representations of the unconscious conforms to the operations of metonymy. The ideological displacement of need signifiers is seen in the history of welfare; for example, in the changing definitions of poverty and mental handicap in the nineteenth and twentieth centuries, and in the changing specifications of welfare need expressed in official reports that respond to fluctuating levels of resources. Secondly, desire is repressed, in a metaphoric operation, to a level where its signification is confined to the unconscious, as a signified 'under the bar' of signification, and substituted by a demand representing a particular moment of desire, that is a need whose signifier stands in place of the repressed signified.

Conversely, unexpressed needs are brought to the surface and given expression as signifiers in new forms of welfare, whose ideological representation in policy statements relies on the deployment of metaphor and related figures. For example, these alternate uses of metaphor are exemplified in opposing accounts of the coming postwar welfare state with its prospects for liberty: portrayed by Hayek as *The Road to Serfdom* (1944), entailing the loss of individual freedoms and the encroachment of state control; and by Beveridge, in his moral allegory of welfare, as a 'The Way to Freedom from Want', part of the nation's postwar recovery, along which the 'giants' of 'want', 'disease', 'ignorance', 'squalor' and 'idleness' are slain (1942, p. 6). These processes of signification are seen also in Hall *et al.*'s account of the convergences and changing thresholds of meaning characteristic of postwar political rhetoric, discussed in Chapter 8.[8]

By shifting from one demand signifier to another, a chain emerges on which at each point the unsatisfied portion of demand indicates what remains unmet (for demand signifies but is not identical to need) and impels the subject to make fresh demands. Lacan locates desire, then, both at the moment when need is 'subtracted' from demand (i.e. the desire that remains unsatisfied when need is met in answer to demand) and in the sequence of object relations (between subject and objects desired and objects and ego-ideals) produced by the subject's 'lack of being' instilling a 'want-to-be' to assuage need:

> Desire is that which is manifested in the interval that demand hollows within itself, in as much as the subject, in articulating the signifying chain, brings to light the want-to-be, together with the appeal to receive the complement from the Other. (Lacan 1977, p. 263)

This process is described as '*asymptotic*', as the individual moves closer to the unreachable point of absolute fulfilment. For while language shapes the subject's world of need, by the same token it installs a fundamental 'gap', 'cut', 'split' or 'wall' between the subject and its real world, a plight of irrecoverable subjectivity that 'defiles' the individual.

These anticipatory and asymptotic features figure significantly in the formation of ideologies of need, either prefiguring or delimiting an individual's desire for welfare. The sense of simultaneously anticipating improved well-being, and yet encountering the elusiveness of fulfilment, leaves the welfare client in the dilemma of perpetually chasing the fading image of desire: a dot that is forever receding into the distance. Drawing on Lacan's thought, we can suggest two ways whereby ideology stabilises this elusive image. First, the weight and permanency of institutional and relational structures anchors down particular definitions of need (Lacan's 'points de capiton' (1977, p. 154)). For example, the material resources underlying welfare provisions sustain a particular regime of need by determining the institutional parameters that set the limits for how need can be defined and satisfied. Here, the function of ideology is to fix the elusive images of happiness and fulfilment within the stable, institutional welfare-relationship between benefactor and client, public resources and private needs. Secondly, the image of the subject's unique 'want-to-be' (Lacan's 'objet petit a' (1977, p. 313; see Green 1983a)), oscillating elusively between subject and other, can be replaced by a firmer image exercising a stronger purchase on concrete reality, such as a more realistic conception of need that can be satisfied from available resources.

When presenting new policies to the electorate, politicians frequently resort to this move, in seeking to impress a particular notion of need on the public mind by asserting that they know what the public really wants; a knowledge that bears less on the public's real needs, and more on government assumptions of the lowest common denominator of need among the population that can be met by a roughly equitable distribution of limited resources. Ideology in these instances fixes the complex of welfare-meeting-need by imposing a quotient of need (the least common denominator) on the processes of desire and needing. Here, the government's image of need will always represent less than the subject's self-image, in the hope of establishing a more realistic set of expectations and a modicum of satisfaction. The delimiting function of ideology in this instance is to close the gap between the subject's expectations and what government delivers, so removing the very incongruity that is the motive for struggle, work and greater understanding between self and other. By the same token, it flattens the anticipatory dimension of desire and needing, the belief in possibilities of future well-being (the 'want-to-be') that impels individuals in their political projects of needing.

Conclusion: lessons from Lacan and Habermas

From this outline of Lacan's account of need, three questions arise whose consideration points to a convergence between Lacan and Habermas, and offers an approach to a theory of need that gives sufficient attention to its real and imaginary characteristics. The first question concerns the way in which the three aspects of need – real, imaginary and symbolic – contribute to the subject's understanding of his or her needs. How does an individual, fragmented by the vagaries of selfhood – the particular conjunction of the real, imaginary and symbolic structuring the illusory ego – come to know his or her real needs? Lacan considers this question in the context of the dialectic of recognition.

This consideration poses a second question concerning the application of the dialectic in understanding the politics of need. This chapter has considered the question in relation to psychoanalysis and politics, especially to the politics of welfare. However, the relation between analyst and patient is not strictly parallel to, for example, relations between social classes or other political subjects. Further, for Lacan, there is no ordained historical subject who, like the proletariat, from the vantage of history is assured its destiny, as there was for Marx. There is only a subject who from its own vantage point of existence strives to understand its life's project and historic purpose. Yet, for understanding political ideology, Lacan's theory of the subject provides a seminal account of the formation of the subject and its ideology whatever the historical context.

However, for Lacan, the dialectic of recognition does not resolve the discrepancy between the real and imaginary – an impossible goal because of the lack of direct access to the real. Rather, it points to disagreements between two subjects, and refers to a third party – the analyst – standing apart from the ideologies of each, and offering the possibility of broader, consensual sources of validity in mediating between the two. The other as third party forms the basis for a widening sociality and collectivity.

The third question asks, if truth claims are consensually grounded, what additional guarantees exist to establish that the substantive claims around which a consensus forms are true and not ideologically distorted? There are two options here. Either a substantive truth claim – one, for example, that is empirically valid or intrinsically right – provides a way of verifying need claims *independently* of consensus, so that consensus is optional. Or consensual and substantive supports to a claim are contingent on each other – to use the earlier distinction, intrinsic and procedural approaches are conjoined in reasoning about needs, as Habermas concedes.

All three questions hinge on the validity of the consensual foundations for agreeing about real needs: foundations by which the fragmented subject can come to know its real needs; foundations which are only valid for a politics of welfare because they are collectively embedded in society's structures of meaning; and foundations which are fully valid when the needs appraised are substantively valid in themselves. To address these issues more fully, the chapter finally takes some tentative steps beyond the groundwork Lacan has laid towards Habermas's discourse theory of truth, with its linking of the dialectic of recognition and the formation of a truth consensus (his 'communicative ethics').

Both Lacan and Habermas describe the dialogic basis of needing and its signification. Lacan's dialectic of desire describes a process in which real and imaginary, and 'true' and 'false' needs, are assigned to objects in the dialogue between self and other. Agreement about real needs is sought either between individuals who share the same procedures for identifying needs and allocating resources, or who accept the immanent possibility of arriving at such procedures. Here, substantive agreement about needs is contingent on procedural agreement. For example, Lacan asserts that the substantive decision to terminate the treatment of a patient requires reaching a consensus, achieved, metaphorically, at 'the moment when the satisfaction of the subject finds a way to realise himself in the satisfaction of everyone' (1977, p. 105), a notion that elsewhere he terms 'full speech'(*ibid.*, p. 40). Here 'finding a way' can be taken as establishing a procedure for agreeing about substantive needs.

However, establishing consensus must guarantee that reason prevails throughout and is not distorted by ideology, an assumption problematic for Lacan's illusory ego. In this connection, Habermas has proposed a transcendental link between consensus and reason as the way to establish truth claims (e.g. about real needs) *at the outset* (1978, p. 359; 1979, pp. 24–5).[9] Habermas has suggested that immanent in all contingent relations between participants – even in dispute – who share the same point of reference (i.e. the same objects to be appropriated, equally or unequally, or understood according to shared or contrary beliefs or truth claims), there exists the desire to understand the other; a desire based on a potential agreement that prefigures actual agreement by posing the possibility of an ideal state of social, political and cognitive understanding. This, of course, is his notion of an ideal speech situation (e.g. 1976a, p. 110).

The implication is that individuals, even when lacking a basis for forming an actual consensus about their different needs, are bound by the search they unavoidably share in coming to terms with their real needs. This condition serves as the starting point when reasoning about substantive needs and differences. Individuals have a basis for reasoning together, but always in the context of an emerging shared ideal (or, to use a different term, an imaginary prefiguration) – a Lacanian twist to Habermas' arguments. It is because the struggle for just social arrangements can only be settled if underwritten by the *possibility* of agreement to collaborate in seeking these ends that hope exists.

Lacan's theory of the unconscious offers important insights for a realist theory of need and a necessary inflexion for Habermas' consensual theory of truth. Realism holds that the real world exists in the form of emergent events, structures and processes that are represented in the concepts and theoretical statements developed in science (cf. Bhaskar 1979). However, this leaves unstated the role of ideology. From a Lacanian perspective, ideology operates as the irreducable and ineluctable force of the imaginary in theoretical representations of the real. It is not – as some versions of realism would have it – an undetected residue in the theoretical representation of the real that distorts theory until corrected by a new theory that in one blow advances explanation and reveals ideological distortions.

In Lacan's theory of the unconscious, we can see the role of ideology in understanding needs in a more illuminating light. To do so we have to accept a particular view of needing. If the process of needing is purposive in seeking fulfilment (and not just functional to organic survival), and if there can be no direct and unmediated access to real needs, then, the construction of an ideal – or imaginary – source of total needs satisfaction (Lacan's 'Other') must be acknowledged, as it surfaces as the necessary moment of counterfactual thought required in planning all forms of human action. It is not sufficient merely to understand real needs and the deep social and psychic structures that cause them to be unmet. It is also necessary to have a vision of an ideal state where these needs are satisfied, an emancipatory form of realism. Of course, this counter-factual moment will be represented as an ideal and utopian state – Communist Society, the Welfare State, the Heavenly Kingdom, universal plenitude, etc. – shaped by individual preferences, prejudices and ideologies and far from what might be achievable in reality. However realistic or unrealistic is the pursuit of welfare, a *contrast relationship* must be construed between contingent and idealist conceptions of human needs. The unconscious is the locus of this articulation. In Lacan's theory of the unconscious, the Other is portrayed in several forms, including the totality of knowledge about human need,[10] and the source of 'full speech', of full communion with the Other (1977, p. 40).

We see here the conjunction between Habermas and Lacan, for Lacan's concept of full speech bears a close affinity with Habermas's 'ideal speech situation' and suggests that the unconscious is part of the transcendental grounds of real knowledge, that is, the structures of thought and reality that make knowledge possible. However, Lacan gives this concept a contingent inflexion.

Full or ideal speech signifies not only an ideal state, but also an intersubjective practice in the formation of knowledge; knowledge of the self sought in the psychoanalytic relationship, and cognitive and normative knowledge gained through scientific and political practice. We can explicate this practical aspect if we consider the role of the other/Other in consensus formation. The Other is the idealised representation of the third party who acts as judge of scientific and normative truth claims, and so plays a formative role in the broadening of consensus about truth beyond the confines of self and other (a triadic pattern replicated in numerous settings, in courts of law, in judgements of scientific dispute, in the alternative dispute resolution of industrial arbitrators, tribunals, divorce conciliation and so forth). The third party links the contingent other of everyday discourse with the ideal Other of democratic decision-making and rational discourse.

The notion of the third party links the process of consensual judgement with substantive truth claims, in that whoever occupies this position is accredited with the authority of a knowledgeable person whose experience is used to warrant or refute specific claims about science, justice or welfare. For both Lacan and Habermas, the signification of needs means that they are rendered communicable and thereby open to verification. Needs are subject to the hearer's assessment of their realistic basis, so that needs are determined and verified intersubjectively in relation to available resources. Any consensus reached between two persons is available to a third, and this consensus to a further person, and so on. The existence of the third person or party as other-in-perpetuity provides the basis for universal truth criteria concerning real needs and resources (Lacan 1977, pp. 9–10).

That this consensus is governed by an imaginary ideal necessitates that intersubjective determination of real needs is always at one remove. At the same time, the utility of the ideal itself is put under test as part of this determination. In effect, each person's attempt to formulate a statement of the real involves constructing a map which, however imaginary in its representation (in the sense in which, for example, cartography can never render an accurate account of the spherical in the form of a flat plane), is appraised pragmatically and opened to the universe of discursive validation.[11]

Thus the consensual and substantive grounds of truth claims are not independent but contingent. However, this contingency is not pre-given in the sense that substantive claims invariably provide the basis of a truth consensus. These claims are determined through the labours of political struggle, personal discovery and intellectual effort. In exercising this labour, individuals subject the authority of the Other to ongoing questioning.

There are, of course, important differences in tradition and substance separating Lacan and Habermas which make problematic a consistent move from the ideas of one to those of the other. In addition to their different theoretical affinities – with French Structuralism and German Critical Theory – each invests language with different functions. On the one hand, as we have seen, for Lacan, language institutes the irremediable alienation, 'cut' or 'bar' of the subject from the real, no longer guaranteeing reason, but acting in concert with the imaginary to produce misrecognition of the real and a potential source of irrationality. On the other hand, Habermas proposes a universal pragmatics of communication that provides the ground for the possibility of reasoning free of ideological distortion. Such fundamental differences leave further requirements to be met before appealing to a discourse theory of truth as a solution to the problems posed by an imaginary theory of need – requirements that are not settled in this chapter.

None the less, in the space which Lacan and Habermas allow between language and reality – wherein lies imaginary misrecognition and distorted communication respectively – a convergence is discernible. Both share the view that language is the universal basis for generating consensus in dialogue. Consequently, both are led to explore the relationship between the ideals of truth and the contingencies of illusion characterising such dialogue. A recurrent theme of Habermas counterposes the 'broken nature of all intersubjective relations' with an 'ideal speech situation' (Habermas 1986, p. 202). Similarly, Lacan has consistently contrasted the illusory ego 'responsible for the manifest disorder' between subject and Other with the truth-seeking subject (1977, p. 127). Further, whereas Lacan's pessimism stemming from the alienating function of language denies the subject the possibility of autonomous reason, there are elements of subject-determination in Lacan's account of the unconscious (at variance with his structuralist tenets) that are operative in the individual's search for his or her elusive want-of-being, and which can be taken as the basis for forming the truth-seeking subject of social consensus (see Dews 1987, p. 81).

Ideology performs a double function in the relation between subject and other (state, welfare agency, etc.). On the one hand, it depicts states of need representing the human subject's experience and knowledge – its function in representing the *contingent* world of need that the subject lives both existentially and cognitively. On the other hand, ideology depicts horizons of possibility for human fulfilment – its function in representing *ideal* prospects for the subject. Ideology gives voice both to social and material requirements through the medium of subjects' shared states of need, and, counterfactually, to goals towards which subjects strive. Ideologies of need simultaneously provide forms of subjectivity experienced in the face of the absence of resources, and ideal states whereby such lack would be fulfilled. The gap between present predicament and future fulfilment, between contingency and ideal, is sustained by ideology. At the same time, this gap designates a lack that ideology by itself cannot fill and which impels human activity – political, philosophical and scientific – towards achieving a fulfilment beyond that represented in ideology. No quest for basic needs in the formulation of policy can exorcise this process.[12]

Notes

1. For example Hopkins and van der Hoeven (1984); Lea and Young (1984).
2. See also Heller (1980, p. 215); Springborg (1981, p. 251); Ignatieff (1984, p. 17).
3. Indeed Veit-Wilson (1986) has argued that Rowntree's approach relies on a minimum income definition *and* a conventionalist, or 'relative', definition; the latter, in our terms, requiring agreed procedures for determining poverty prior to discovering what conventional view of poverty pertains.
4. Macey's recent book argues that Lacan's obscurantism conceals an inflated and eclectic philosophical system of doubtful value (1988). By contrast, Dews provides a more sympathetic exposition of Lacan's philosophical project in the context of French Post-Structuralism and German Critical Theory (1987).
5. Lacan summarises the object-relations comprising this structure in his 'L schema' and elaborates on their significance in Chapter 6 *et passim* of the *Écrits* (1977). See Green (1983a) for clarification of this schema and the 'objet a' contained within it.
6. Leiss's analysis (1978) of the commodification of human needs under capitalism encompasses many of these processes. However, his emphasis on increasingly manipulatable subjects governed by artificially created needs diminishes the role of human interaction and communication in determining real need.
7. For Lacan, the real, like Kant's 'things-in-themselves', is a cognitively inaccessible realm that must be accorded a heuristic and residual, if not referential, status in order that knowledge of reality can be delimited from and advanced beyond the limits of ideological (imaginary) interest or structured (symbolic) orderliness.
8. Green's analysis of the 1834 and 1909 Poor Law Reports provides more fully explored examples of the deployment of metonymy and metaphor in policy-making (1983b, pp. 25–6).
9. Habermas has proposed that this is a 'transformed' transcendentalism, where the distinction between *a priori* and empirical knowledge is not categorical. However, this contention has been criticised by among others McCarthy (1978) and Roderick (1986).
10. The Marxist notion of 'planning for needs' presents the possibility of raising total knowledge of human need in society to the level of conscious political action (see Deacon 1983).
11. From a Lacanian perspective, Frederic Jameson talks of 'cognitive mapping' (1984, p. 89). Here, he argues also for the 'methodological enrichments' of Althusser's thought gained from a return to its Lacanian underpinnings.
12. Readers may care to compare this account of the discourse of needs with Nancy Fraser's on the 'politics of need interpretation' which covers similar ground (1989, ch.s 7, 8).

11

Conclusion: policy, ideology and reason

Looking at the prospects for the 1990s, we see a welfare state that faces a degree of uncertainty unparalleled in recent decades. At a time of transition, it stands precariously on a serious of cusps dividing Thatcherism from post-Thatcherism; the end of the Settlement from the beginning of the new consensus on the welfare state; and, in the long term, modernity from postmodernity; the close of the twentieth century from the dawning of the twenty-first, and so on. No doubt any *fin de siècle* anxiety is intensified by the approaching new millenium. Yet it is the case that recent years have seen unprecedented changes on a global scale that encompass the demise of East European Communist systems and their lurching towards democratic capitalism, as well as the major assaults on western welfare states that have produced the deconstruction and now reconstruction of their edifices.

At the same time, the triumph of market-led policy has been achieved in the face of lamentable failures to reverse long-term trends in unemployment, poverty, homelessness, and widening inequalities in illness, mortality and access to health care. This suggests a degree of duplicity on the part of government in the presentation of its policy claims when compared with its achievements, a contrast caught most starkly in the difference between the public lifestyles of the rich and the hidden deprivations of a growing minority. The images of success that gloss the social realities of the 1980s point to the growing significance of ideology in the welfare state, a force that distorts the realities of late twentieth-century life and yet still has the power to augur new possibilities for the twenty-first. The unconscious forces underlying ideology discussed in Chapter 10 have taken on a palpable, if not readily discernible, shape in the restructuring of welfare state capitalism, projecting images that are both illusory and auspicious. Freud's dictum on the unconscious, *Wo es war soll Ich werden* – 'it' thinks in the space where 'I' has yet to appear – might roughly translate into societal terms as: ideology thinks what society has yet to become.

194

The proliferation of 'post-' prefixes – post-Thatcherism, post-modernity, post-capitalism, etc. – is a sign of the ideological uncertainty with which social and cultural commentators view the future: coining a name for an epoch that has yet to appear with an appellation that no longer applies; sensing a turning-point, but not knowing which way things will turn-out. In the face of this uncertainty, social analysis is – as it always was – fraught with difficulties.

This book did not set out to draw lessons for the future from the ideas and practices of the past. But it has been drawn into a number of engagements with the ideas of various writers who place different and conflicting values on state welfare – none of which is unequivocal about welfare's pros and cons. From these exchanges, the book has concluded that, despite the setbacks of recent years and the unclear prospect for the future, the welfare state will continue to play a strong role in societal cohesion and advancement, and specifically in the evolution of late capitalist society. This was basically the argument of Chapters 6 and 7. It is inconceivable that the major costs of capitalist development – some of which have grown particularly heavy of recent – will not be borne by government. The welfare state far more than the market possesses the potential to achieve social cohesion. One of the conditions for cohesion is government commitment to ensure the satisfaction of universal human needs – in a democracy, a condition also of government legitimation. For Habermas, we saw that consensus formation is a necessary condition for establishing the rational validity of the policy claims of government. A democratic welfare state of this kind allows ideology its prefigurative space and rational politics its critical edge. Social administration and Critical Theory, each with their own critical impulses, are two traditions that have recognised this.

We can summarise the arguments we have developed about the contributions that these and other strands of welfare studies have made to the development of social ideals and possibilities and to the mounting of rational critiques: two moments of ideology that can act to complement each other; but also that can mislead policy formation by misreading social needs and misjudging the outcomes of particular policies. This will lead to an appraisal of ideology and reason in policy debate.

The strong empirical tradition of Social-Democratic social administration has provided an important rational current in social policy, the foundation of critiques of social injustice and the means for corrective and potentially transformative policy. Yet in the postwar period Social Democratic ideals were stifled under the weight of its administrative apparatus; its democratic aspirations expendable in the service of rational policy-making and bureaucratic statecraft. It embraced a rationality that stood for the importance of substantive knowledge more than consensually grounded truth. It sought empirical findings that supported short-term policy objectives on the grounds of instrumentality, utility and efficiency. This was at the expense of political and educational work directed to forming a consensus among the variously aligned groups who formed the benefactors and beneficiaries of policy. It ignored the consensual basis of truth that has become increasingly pressing since the 1970s as disenchantment with aspects of public welfare set in across the political divide, and as social movements attacked perceived injustices in public policy.

Social Democracy's anti-democratic features were easily exploited in the politics of the 1970s and 1980s. However, rather than strengthen the democratic rights of citizens, the New Right set about dismantling welfare institutions that secured rights, and installing alternative means of distributing resources, using the social market rather than social policy (see Squires 1990), and restricting social provisions to residual groups unable to participate in the market. In sum, critical space has been curtailed, as we argued in Chapter 3. So much so that several writers on the Left – as well as the Right – have conceded that a new consensus has begun to transform the welfare state, its morality, theory and ideology (see Papadakis and Taylor-Gooby 1987, p. 19; Hall and Jacques 1989). Coupled with this have emerged arguments that universal values no longer receive the public support claimed for them. These views have given rise to a renewed interest in theories of democratic pluralism and welfare pluralism.

However, those who see convergence between Left and Right are in danger of making a premature judgement of the force of the Right's hegemonic project, and of overlooking universal ideals that, though shaken, have shown an ability to recuperate after more than a decade of assaults on Social Democratic welfare. These ideals stem from an understanding that the welfare of each is in part contingent on the welfare of all; that welfare services must guarantee basic levels of provision for all, and at the same time support a diversity of needs among individuals without weakening universal welfare. This problematic – with its idealist combination of equal and different provisions for all – has been at the centre of the Fabian tradition throughout this century, and has informed the relationship developed between the 'basic minimum' and the 'extension ladder'. More recently, this problematic is articulated in a different manner in the work of Critical Theorists like Habermas, whose arguments provide an important justification for a non-substantive, non-foundational and yet universal morality of politics; namely a morality that does not predefine the basic needs a welfare state should guarantee, but first provides the institutional forum to encourage consensus to form around such needs, around their identity and diversity. In seeking to build such a forum, this approach recognises the importance of both formal procedures of democracy and the informal, communicative under-standings that the lifeworld sustains in defining needs and in providing welfare. In a democratic welfare state, citizens ultimately judge the success of govern-ment policies by universal criteria of need fulfilment, of personal autonomy and social solidarity.

These speculations demand a far more detailed and critical consideration than I have given. However, the present encounter between two major traditions informing the intellectual culture of the 1970s and 1980s – namely post-structuralism and Critical Theory – with their divergent dispositions to relativism and rationality respectively, may prove significant in these considerations of politics and morality (see Dews 1987). This is especially so in so far as they both acknowledge something of the economic and cultural transformations affecting modernity during the last half-century, though they interpret them in different ways as symptomatic of postmodernity or of the developing crises of late modernity.

In conclusion, we will consider these two approaches to the problems of relativism and reason in political discourse and policy-making. The first strand, associated with Foucault, Lyotard and Rorty, argues that underlying the formal universality of liberal democracy are forces of power and cultural production that impose their own 'regimes of truth'. In this view universal criteria of truth are the product of, for Foucault, the pervasive technological order of the disciplines; for Lyotard, the profusion of language games played by the powerful who skilfully interpret universal sentiments and values to provide notions of 'performance' and 'outcomes' for their own ends; and for Rorty (1989), adventures in rhetoric that invent new vocabularies to articulate new social and political truths.

In Chapter 9 we saw that Foucault's analysis of the disciplinary apparatus construes the discovery of truth – the prime purpose of reason – as a product of power/knowledge. In this perspective the welfare state is an elaborate system of knowledge and social technology for individuating human souls under the expanding network of micro-powers that constitutes disciplinary society. By contrast with Marxists, Foucault does not acknowledge any one social, political or economic class that controls this process and uses ideology to dominate the rest of society. Instead, he sees a multitude of 'force relations' between individuals that each weave, and in turn are caught in, an invisible disciplinary web. For this reason the disciplines exist whatever the political regime in power. Whether society is democratic or not is less important than the existence of deeper forces in society that engender discipline.

Lyotard (1984), for his part, has also questioned the existence of rational foundations that supposedly underpin the grand designs for human progress that have characterised modern society. For him, these foundations are no more than ideological 'grand narratives' that institutions of higher learning have used to justify the contribution of their knowledge to emancipating humanity and nurturing an independent source of truth that legitimates scientific and philosophical values. His view can be targeted at the justifications Marxists give for the formation of socialist societies, and Fabian 'scientific administration' for the policies of the welfare state. However, for Lyotard, these narratives have now lost their legitimacy in a postmodern world where the rise of technological science since the Second World War has shifted the emphasis away from science as an activity pursuing valued ends to science as a means for achieving outcomes of a different order. In Lyotard's vision of a delegitimated world, knowledge is now no longer valued by universal criteria of truth, but by more immediate criteria of performance which proliferate with increasing technological complexity. Thus, 'in the context of delegitimation, universities . . . are called upon to create skills and no longer ideas – so many doctors, so many teachers in a given discipline, so many engineers, so many administrators, etc.' (1984, p. 48).

Borrowing from Wittgenstein, Lyotard suggests that this shift entails using the methods of reasoning as 'language games' that can translate universal truth criteria into a multitude of performance criteria, where successful moves are undertaken on pragmatic – even expedient – grounds. Although Lyotard concentrates mainly on the institutions of science and higher education, his arguments apply with equal force to the administrative institutions of society with their notions of rational planning. Like Foucault, with his conjunction of power/knowledge, Lyotard sees the emphasis on performance criteria as revealing a concern with power rather than truth; for 'in the discourse of today's financial backers of research, the only credible goal is power. Scientists, technicians, and instruments are purchased not to find truth, but to augment powers' (1984, p. 46). Legitimation becomes an effect of power and, *contra* Habermas, no longer the moral basis for a just society. Democratic consensus is reached not by agreement between individuals arrived at through dialogue, but by manipulating the system to improve its performance, so that 'administrative procedures should make individuals "want" what the system needs in order to perform well' (1984, p. 62). Hence, government defines its own standards of legitimacy. There is no universal warrant for these standards possessed by the public at large. Here we can detect Lyotard's objections to Habermas' project of determining the foundations of human action according to a 'universal pragmatics' of communicative reasoning (1979, ch. 1) – for Lyotard, an example of a more recent grand narrative.

In a not too dissimilar way, Rorty has recently used the notion of language games to describe the way liberal values can be revived in postmodern society, rather than used to describe the process of liberalism's subversion as Lyotard does. Instead of referring to a 'divine' moral foundation beyond the scope of human experience, liberal thinkers should develop 'self-descriptions' of the good society that acknowledge their status as 'contingent human artifacts'. This would mean 'giving up the idea that liberalism could be justified, and Nazi or Marxist enemies of Liberalism refuted, by driving the latter up against an argumentative wall' (Rorty 1989, p. 53). By means of this relativist argument, Rorty goes on to claim that, 'any attempt to drive one's opponents up against a wall in this way fails when the wall against which he is driven comes to be seen as one more vocabulary, one more way of describing things' (*ibid.*). Like Lyotard, Rorty depicts power politics – even the defence of democracy against totalitarian violence – as the deployment of rhetorical manoeuvre by skilful actors.

Against these strands of relativist thought, Habermas's writings represent an important source of continuity in modernity's quest for forms of reasoning that can sustain political and moral conduct, especially in the context of the social fragmentation that characterises recent developments in late capitalism and modernity. Within the tradition of Critical Theory, Habermas has examined the relationship between social purpose and reason in the context of what he terms 'discursive' or 'collective will formation', the way people discover and expedite in speech and action their common interests. In what is generally accepted as the most controversial of his theoretical proposals (see Thompson 1982), Habermas has sought to explore the development of moral thought at both personal and societal levels in the evolution of communicative action, in an approach that goes some way to recasting the problematic of universal ends and contingent differences.[1] For Habermas, developmental maturity is reached when the integration of individual and collective needs is achieved so that the fulfilment of neither is thwarted by the other. For individual functioning, this condition is fulfilled when individual needs can be expressed in the context of universal structures of communication and understanding; when 'ego-identity requires not only cognitive mastery of general levels of communication, but also the ability to give one's own needs their due in these communicative structures' (1979, p. 78). 'Collective will formation' must pass beyond the stage of 'culturally interpreted needs' to the point where 'the critique and justification of need interpretations acquire the power to orient action' (1979). This represents an exercise in the *precursory* function of reason and ideology in the quest for human emancipation and welfare. We can see in this evolutionary account how Habermas's theory is drawing on the emancipatory impulse which characterises much of Critical Theory, and which Structural Marxism, for example, lost. This is an approach to the study of social and political action – and therefore of policy – that holds out the possibility of restoring to reason some degree of universal status and emancipatory force, and that deserves the further consideration of policy studies.

It is in the context of public democratic debate that we see the explication of reasoning in policy-making. For here the universal interests of individual citizens are expressed as part of the public discourse on truth claims established or refuted by communicative reasoning. On this point, Habermas has concluded that 'Only at the level of a universal ethic of speech can need interpretations themselves – that is, what each individual thinks he should understand and represent as his "true" interests – also become the object of practical discourse' (1979, p. 90). While such needs cannot be categorically defined for all, in the way that the basic needs theorists assume (see Chapter 10), universal interests concerning social needs can emerge in democratic society. The unswerving nature of the British public's support for the National Health Service bears testimony to this, as does opposition to the perceived iniquities of the ill-fated poll tax. The *raison d'etre* of a welfare state is the provision of policies that secure universal needs and security as culturally and politically defined. Thus moral truth claims secured by communicative reason are expressed in the ideals of a democratic welfare state that seeks to advance universal interests in meeting social needs.

This argument has again become influential after more than a decade of Thatcherism and its aftermath, at a time when an awareness of universal needs has begun to emerge as a strong political motive in the public mind. It can be seen in several areas of policy where universal services have been under threat: the National Health Services, community care, public water and environmental services and public broadcasting. New Right policies of selectivity and privatisation have yet to demonstrate their widespread credibility. By contrast, the establishment of universal policies that underwrite citizenship rights in the framework of British public policy has provided a political culture of expectations that cannot be easily displaced into the private market, and that will resist forces promoting private interests alone (see King 1987, p. 167). Of course, the framework of public and private aspirations in a welfare state will develop over time new social relations of solidarity and autonomy, of universality and selectivity, as universalists such as Titmuss have long acknowledged and as more recent studies of public opinion demonstrate (e.g. Taylor-Gooby 1985). Yet, ultimately, the impact of policy is borne by the public at large and tested against the private and collective interests of its members in social betterment, interests that have established deep roots in the welfare state. For this practical reason – let alone for philosophical ones – we should not dismiss too readily universality as a continuing force in the formation of the welfare state.

An awareness of the significance of such universal rights has emerged in recent approaches to conceptualising needs, especially in relation to the concept of poverty. Several studies in the 1980s have sought to develop a consensual definition of needs based on what a representative sample of individuals in the population would consider the minimum income necessary to attain certain minimum standards or the minimum set of necessities for life (see Veit-Wilson 1987). The best known study, *Poor Britain* (1985), was conducted by Mack and Lansley for London Weekend Television. They established a consensual definition of the minimum necessities required by households in 1983 and found how many households fell below this minimum. This approach can be compared with Townsend's study (1979), which used a deprivation index based, not on a consensus of opinion, but on the objective findings of social scientists of a common lifestyle that the poor in 1968/9 were unable to participate in. Both Townsend's objective approach and Mack and Lansley's consensual approach identified a threshold level below which the poor's index of deprivation increased disproportionately: a cut-off point demarcating real poverty. Desai notes a marked degree of similarity between the two thresholds (1986, p. 18). Townsend's objective threshold and Mack and Lansley's consensus measures were about 50 per cent and 33 per cent respectively above the Supplementary Benefit level for a two-parent, two-child family. Further, in Townsend's more recent study of poverty in London (1987) a degree of agreement was also found between his own consensual and objective measures of poverty, prompting him to observe that 'People's judgements of the minimum income required to fulfil basic family living standards and meet their minimum social obligations seem to correspond closely with the results obtained by more objective observations of the relationship between income and deprivation' (*Guardian* 29 November 1989). More speculatively he suggests that 'it may be possible to "objectively" calculate a "poverty line" for most household types that would correspond with the judgements of the majority of the population' (1989, p. 54).

The symmetry found between recent scientific and consensually determined standards of need supports Habermas's idea of a discursive ethics (discussed in Chapters 6 and 10), according to which the validity of truth claims requires substantive *and* consensual warrants, and only such fully warranted claims provide sufficient grounds for accepting the legitimacy of government policies and countering official untruths. The recent work on poverty in principle provides a powerful basis grounded on a discursive politics for advancing policy in a democratic society (see Dryzek 1990).

Following a period when the political climate has dampened our sense of optimism towards the welfare state – a climate that itself nurtured a renewed interest in the study of ideology – and has implanted instead a sense of retrenchment, pessimism and new realism towards social progress, it is perhaps possible to end on a more hopeful note. A culture of solidarity cannot easily be ignored or subverted by ideology in a democratic society where moral claims concerning human needs are subjected to rational discourse.

Notes

1. Habermas, however, is extremely circumspect in following through this line of thought, stating explicitly the pitfalls standing in the way of this programme, and laying down the theoretical conditions required to bring it to conclusion (see 1979, pp. 102, 110).

Bibliography

Abercrombie, Nicholas, Hill, Stephen and Turner, Bryan S. (1980) *The Dominant Ideology Thesis*, London: Allen & Unwin.

Adams, Parveen (1979) 'A Note on the Distinction between Sexual Division and Sexual Differences', *m/f*, no. 3.

Adorno, Theodor W. (1984) *Aesthetic Theory*, trans. C. Lenhardt, London: Routledge & Kegan Paul.

Althusser, Louis (1969) *For Marx*, trans. Ben Brewster, Harmonsworth: Penguin Books.

Althusser, Louis (1971) *Lenin & Philosophy and Other Essays*, trans. Ben Brewster, New York: Monthly Review Press.

Althusser, Louis and Balibar, Etienne (1970) *Reading Capital*, trans. Ben Brewster, London: New Left Books.

Baker, John (1979) 'Social Conscience and Social Policy', *Journal of Social Policy*, vol. 8, no. 2, pp. 177–206.

Banton, Ragnild *et al.* (1985) *The Politics of Mental Health*, Basingstoke: Macmillan.

Barrett, Michèle (1980) *Women's Oppression Today*, London: Verso.

Barry, Norman P. (1987) *The New Right*, London: Croom Helm.

Barthes, Roland (1972) *Mythologies*, trans. Annette Lavers, London: Cape.

Baudrillard, Jean (1983) *In the Shadow of the Silent Majority*, trans. P. Foss, J. Johnston and P. Paton, New York: Semiotext.

Bauman, Zygmunt (1983) 'Industrialism, Consumerism and Power', *Theory, Culture and Society*, vol. 1, no. 3.

Bauman, Zygmunt (1988a), 'Britain's Exit from Politics', *New Statesman and Society*, 29 July 1988.

Bauman, Zygmunt (1988b) *Freedom*, Milton Keynes: Open University.

Beechey, Victoria and Donald, James (eds.) (1985) *Subjectivity and Social Relations: a reader*, Milton Keynes: Open University.

Bell, Daniel (1962) *The End of Ideology: on the exhaustion of political ideals in the fifties*, New York: Free Press.

Bell, Daniel (1976) *The Cultural Contradictions of Capitalism*, London: Heinemann.

Bennett, Fran (1987) 'What future for Social Security', in A. Walker and C. Walker (eds.) *The Growing Divide: a social audit 1979–87*, London: Child Poverty Action Group.

Benton, Ted (1984) *The Rise and Fall of Structural Marxism: Althusser and his influence*, London: Macmillan.

Beresford, Peter and Croft, Suzy (1984) 'Welfare Pluralism: the new face of Fabianism', *Critical Social Policy*, no. 9, pp. 19–39.

Beveridge, William H. (1942) *Social Insurance and Allied Services*, (Cmd. 6404) London: HMSO.

Bhaskar, Roy (1979) *The Possibility of Naturalism: a philosophical critique of the contemporary human sciences*, Hemel Hempstead: Harvester Wheatsheaf.

Bhaskar, Roy (1986) *Scientific Realism and Human Emancipation*, London: Verso.

Birch, Anthony H. (1984) 'Overload, Ungovernability and Delegitimation: The Theories and the British Case', *British Journal of Political Science*, vol. 14, pp. 135–60.

Bittner, Egon (1974) 'The Concept of Organisation', in R. Turner (ed.), *Ethnomethodology: selected readings*, Harmondsworth: Penguin Books.

Bloch, Ernst (1971) *On Karl Marx*, New York: Herder.

Booth, Charles (1971) *Charles Booth's London*, eds. A. Fried and R. M. Elman, Harmondsworth: Penguin Books.

Bradshaw, Jonathon (1972) 'The Concept of Social Need', *New Society*, 30 March 1972.

Brenton, Maria (1985) *The Voluntary Sector in British Social Services*, London: Longman.

Burchell, Ian (1980) 'Putting the Child in its Place', *Ideology and Consciousness*, no. 8.

Burton, Frank and Carlen, Pat (1979) *Official Discourse: on discourse analysis, government publications, ideology and the state*, London: Routledge & Kegan Paul.

Carrier, John and Kendall, Ian (1973) 'Social Policy and Social Change', *Journal of Social Policy*, vol. 2, no. 3, pp. 209–24.

Castel, Richard, Castel, Françoise and Lovell, Anne (1982) *The Psychiatric Society*, trans. Arthur Goldhammer, New York: Columbia University.

Castells, Manuel (1977) *The Urban Question: a Marxist approach*, trans. Alan Sheridan, London: Edward Arnold.

Castells, Manuel (1978) *City, Class and Power*, trans. Elizabeth Lebas, London: Macmillan.

Catephores, George (1989) *An Introduction to Marxist Economics*, Basingstoke: Macmillan.

Chapman, Tom and Cook, Juliet (1988) 'Marginality, Youth and Government Policy in the 1980s', *Critical Social Policy*, no. 22.

Clarke, John, Cochrane, Allen and Smart, Carol (1987) *Ideologies of Welfare: from dreams to disillusion*, London: Hutchinson.

Cockburn, Cynthia (1977) *The Local State: management of cities and people*, London: Pluto.

Corrigan, Paul and Leonard, Peter (1978) *Social Work Practice under Capitalism: a Marxist approach*, London: Macmillan.

Cousins, Christine (1987) *Controlling Social Welfare: a sociology of state welfare and organisations*, Hemel Hempstead: Harvester Wheatsheaf.

Crosland, Charles A. R. (1956) *The Future of Socialism*, London: Cape.

Cutler, Tony, Williams, Karel and Williams, John (1986) *Keynes, Beveridge and Beyond*, London: Routledge & Kegan Paul.

Daudi, Phillipe (1986) *Power in the Organisation: the discourse of power in managerial praxis*, Oxford: Basil Blackwell.

David, Miriam E. (1980) *The State, the Family, and Education*, London: Routledge & Kegan Paul.

Deacon, Alan (1984) 'Was There a Welfare Consensus', in C. Jones and J. Stevenson, *The Year Book of Social Policy in Britain*, London: Routledge & Kegan Paul.

Deacon, Alan and Bradshaw, Jonathon (1983) *Reserved for the Poor: the means test in British social policy*, Oxford: Martin Robertson.

Deacon, Bob (1983) *Social Policy and Socialism: the struggle for socialist relations in welfare*, London: Pluto.

Dean, Hartley (1991) *Social Security and Social Control*, London: Routledge.

Desai, Meghnad (1986) 'Drawing the Line: on defining the poverty threshold', in P. Golding, *Excluding the Poor*, London: Child Poverty Action Group.

Dews, Peter (1987) *Logics of Disintegration: post-structuralist thought and the claims of critical theory*, London: Verso.

Donnelly, Michael (1982) 'Foucault's Genealogy of the Human Sciences', *Economy and Society*, vol. 11, no. 4.

Donnison, David V. *et al.* (1975) *Social Policy and Administration Revisited: studies in the development of social services at the local level*, London: Allen & Unwin.

Donzelot, Jacques (1980) *The Policing of the Family*, London: Hutchinson.

Doyal, Len and Gough, Ian (1984) 'A Theory of Human Needs', *Critical Social Policy*, no. 10, pp. 6–38.

Dreyfus, Hubert L. and Rabinow, Paul (1982) *Michel Foucault: beyond structuralism and hermeneutics*, Hemel Hempstead: Harvester Wheatsheaf.

Dryzek, John S. (1990) *Discursive Democracy: politics, policy and political science*, Cambridge: Cambridge University Press.

Eagleton, Terry (1991) *Ideology: an introduction*, London: Verso.

Edelman, Jacob M. (1977) *Political Language: words that succeed and policies that fail*, New York: Academic Press.

Elliott, Gregory (1987) *Althusser: The Detour of Theory*, London: Verso.

Etzioni, Amitai (1961) *Comparative Analysis of Complex Organisations*, New York: Free Press.

Feher, Ferenc (1978) 'The Dictatorship Over Needs', *Telos*, no. 32, pp. 31–42.

Field, Frank (1989) *Losing Out: the emergence of Britain's underclass*, Oxford: Basil Blackwell.

Finch, Janet (1989) *Family Obligations and Social Change*, Cambridge: Polity Press.

Foucault, Michel (1967) *Madness and Civilisation: a history of insanity in the Age of Reason*, trans. Richard Howard, London: Tavistock.

Foucault, Michel (1970) *The Order of Things: an archaeology of the human sciences*, London: Tavistock.

Foucault, Michel (1972) *The Archaeology of Knowledge*, trans. A. M. Sheridan Smith, London: Tavistock.

Foucault, Michel (1979a) *Discipline and Punish: the birth of the prison*, trans. Alan Sheridan, Harmondsworth: Penguin Books.

Foucault, Michel (1979b) *The History of Sexuality, Volume I, an Introduction*, trans. Robert Hurley, London: Allen Lane.

Foucault, Michel (1980) *Power-Knowledge: selected interviews and other writings*, ed. Colin Gordon, Hemel Hempstead: Harvester Wheatsheaf.

Foucault, Michel (1981) 'Omnes et Singulatim: towards a criticism of political reason', in S. M. McMurrin (ed.), *The Tanner Lectures on Human Values, Volume II*, Cambridge: Cambridge University Press.

Foucault, Michel (1982) 'The Subject and Power', in H. L. Dreyfus and P. Rabinow, *Michel Foucault: beyond structuralism and hermeneutics*, Hemel Hempstead: Harvester Wheatsheaf.

Foucault, Michel (1988) *Politics, Philosophy, Culture; interviews and other writings*, ed. L. Kritzman, London: Routledge.

Fraser, Derek (1973) *The Evolution of the British Welfare State: a history of social policy since the Industrial Revolution*, London: Macmillan.

Fraser, Nancy (1985) 'What's Critical About Critical Theory?', *New German Critique*, vol. 35, pp. 97–131.

Fraser, Nancy (1989) *Unruly Practices: power, discourse and gender in contemporary social theory*, Cambridge: Polity Press.

Fukuyama, Francis (1989) 'The End of History?', *The National Interest*, Summer, pp. 1–18.

Galtung, Johan (1980) 'The Basic Needs Approach', in K. Lederer (ed.) *Human Needs: a contribution to the current debate*, Cambridge, Mass: Oelgeschlager, Gunn & Hain.

Gamble, Andrew (1979) 'The Free Economy and the Strong State: The rise of the social market economy', in R. Miliband and J. Saville (eds.) *The Socialist Register, 1979*, London: Merlin.

Gamble, Andrew (1988) *The Free Market and the Strong State: the politics of Thatcherism*, Basingstoke: Macmillan.

Garland, David (1985) *Punishment and Welfare: a history of penal strategies*, Aldershot: Gower.

George, Vic and Wilding, Paul (1976) *Ideology and Social Welfare*, London: Routledge & Kegan Paul.

George, Vic and Wilding, Paul (1984) *The Impact of Social Policy*, London: Routledge & Kegan Paul.

Giddens, Antony (1979) *Central Problems in Social Theory: action, structure and contradiction in social analysis*, London: Macmillan.

Ginsburg, Norman (1979) *Class, Capital and Social Policy*, London: Macmillan.

Glennerster, Howard (1987) 'Goodbye Mr Chips', *New Society*, 9 October 1987.

Golding, Paul and Middleton, Sarah (1982) *Images of Welfare: press and public attitudes to poverty*, Oxford: Martin Robertson.

Goodrich, Peter (1986) *Reading the Law: a critical introduction to legal methods and techniques*, Oxford: Basil Blackwell.

Gough, Ian (1972) 'Marx's Theory of Productive and Unproductive Labour', *New Left Review*, no. 76, pp. 47–72.

Gough, Ian (1979) *The Political Economy of the Welfare State*, London: Macmillan.

Gough, Ian (1983) 'Thatcherism and the Welfare State', in S. Hall and M. Jacques (eds.) *The Politics of Thatcherism*, London: Lawrence and Wishart.

Gough, Ian *et al.* (1984) 'Thatcherism and Social Policy: the first four years', in *Year Book of Social Policy in Britain*, eds. C. Jones and J. Stevenson, London: Routledge & Kegan Paul.

Gramsci, Antonio (1971) *Selections from the Prison Notebooks of Antonio Gramsci*, eds. Q. Hoare and G. Nowell-Smith, London: Lawrence and Wishart.

Green, André (1983a) 'Logic of Objet (A) and Freudian Theory', in J. H. Smith and W. Kerrigan (eds.) *Interpreting Lacan*, London: Yale University Press.

Green, Bryan S. (1983b) *Knowing the Poor: a case-study in textual reality construction*, London: Routledge & Kegan Paul.

Habermas, Jürgen (1970) 'Towards a Theory of Communicative Competence', *Inquiry*, vol. 13, pp. 360–75.

Habermas, Jürgen (1974) *Theory and Practice*, trans. J. Viertal, London: Heinemann.

Habermas, Jürgen (1976a) *The Legitimation Crisis*, trans. T. McCarthy, London: Heinemann.

Habermas, Jürgen (1976b) 'Systematically Distorted Communication', in P. Connerton (ed.) *Critical Theory*, Harmondsworth: Penguin Books.

Habermas, Jürgen (1978) *Knowledge and Human Interest*, trans. J. J. Shapiro, London: Heinemann.

Habermas, Jürgen (1979) *Communication and the Evolution of Society*, trans. T. McCarthy, London: Heinemann.

Habermas, Jürgen (1984) *The Theory of Communicative Action, Volume I: Reason and Rationalisation in Society*, trans. T. McCarthy, London: Heinemann.

Habermas, Jürgen (1985/6) 'The New Obscurity: the crisis of the welfare state and the exhaustion of utopian energies', *Philosophy and Social Criticism*, vol. 11, Winter, pp. 1–18.

Habermas, Jürgen (1986) *Habermas: Autonomy and Solidarity – interviews with Jürgen Habermas*, ed. P. Dews, London: Verso.

Habermas, Jürgen (1987) *The Theory of Communicative Action, Volume II: Lifeworld and System*, trans. T. McCarthy, Cambridge: Polity Press.

Hadley, Richard and Hatch, Stephen (1981) *Social Welfare and the Failure of the State: centralized social services and participatory alternatives*, London: Allen & Unwin.

Hall, Stuart (1983) 'The Great Moving Right Show', in S. Hall and M. Jacques (eds.) *The Politics of Thatcherism*, London: Lawrence & Wishart.

Hall, Stuart (1984) 'Authoritarian Populism: A Reply to Jessop *et al.*', *New Left Review*, no. 151, pp. 115–24.

Hall, Stuart *et al.* (1978) *Policing the Crisis: mugging, the state and law and order*, London: Macmillan.

Hall, Stuart and Jacques, Martin (eds.) (1989) *New Times: the changing face of politics in the 1990s*, London: Verso.

Harris, David (1987) *Justifying State Welfare: the New Right versus the Old Left*, Oxford: Basil Blackwell.

Harris, Ralph (1988) *Beyond the Welfare State*, London: Institute of Economic Affairs.

Harris, Robert and Webb, David (1987) *Welfare, Power and Juvenile Justice: the social control of delinquent youth*, London: Tavistock.

Hayek, Friedrich A. (1944) *The Road to Serfdom*, London: Routledge.

Hayek, Friedrich A. (1976) *Law, Legislation and Liberty, Volume II: The Mirage of Social Justice*, London: Routledge & Kegan Paul.

Hegel, Georg W. F. (1977) *Phenomenology of Spirit*, trans. A. V. Miller, Oxford: Clarendon Press.

Held, David (1979) *Introduction to Critical Theory*, London: Hutchinson.

Heller, Agnes (1976) *The Theory of Need in Marx*, London: Allison & Busby.

Heller, Agnes (1980) 'Can "True" and "False" Needs be Posited?' in K. Lederer (ed.), *Human Needs*, Cambridge, Mass: Oelgeschlager, Gunn & Hain.

Hewitt, Martin (1991) 'Bio-politics and Social Policy', in M. Featherstone, M. Hepworth and B. S Turner (eds.) *The Body: social processes and cultural theory*, London: Sage.

Hindess, Barry (1987) *Freedom, Equality and the Market: arguments on social policy*, London: Tavistock.

Hirst, Paul Q. (1979) *On Law and Ideology*, London: Macmillan.

HMSO (1944) *Employment Policy* (Cmd. 6523), London: HMSO.

HMSO (1944) *A National Health Services* (Cmd. 6502), Ministry of Health, London: HMSO.

HMSO (1954) *Report of the Committee on the Economic and Financial Problems for the Provision of Old Age* (Phillips) (Cmd. 9333), London: HMSO.

HMSO (1956) *Report of the Committee of Enquiry into the Cost of the NHS* (Guillebaud) (Cmd. 9663), London: HMSO.

HMSO (1981) *Care in Action*, Department of Health & Social Security (DHSS), London: HMSO.

HMSO (1985) *Reform of Social Security: Volume 1* (Cmnd. 9517), DHSS, London: HMSO.

HMSO (1988) *Community Care: Agenda for Action*, a report to the Secretary of State for Social Services by Sir Roy Griffiths, London: HMSO.

HMSO (1989a) *Working for Patients* (Cm. 555), London: HMSO.

HMSO (1989b) *Caring for People: community care in the 1990s and beyond* (Cm. 849), London: HMSO.

HMSO (1990) *Children Come First* (Cm. 1264), London: HMSO.

HMSO (1991) *The Citizen's Charter: raising the standard* (Cm. 1599), London: HMSO.

Hoggett, Paul (1990) *Modernisation, Political Strategy and the Welfare State: an organizational perspective*, Bristol: School of Advanced Urban Studies.

Hopkins, Michael and van der Hoeven, Rolph (1984) *Basic Needs in Development Planning*, Aldershot: Gower.

Horkheimer, Max (1972) 'Traditional and Critical Theory', in M. J. O'Connell *et al.* (eds.) *Critical Theory*, New York: Seabury.

Hoy, David C. (1986) 'Power, Repression, Progress: Foucault, Lukes and the Frankfurt School', in D. C. Hoy (ed.) *Foucault: a critical reader*, Oxford: Basil Blackwell.

Ignatieff, Michael (1984) *The Needs of Strangers*, London: Chatto & Windus.

Illife, Steve (1985/6) 'The Politics of Health Care: the N.H.S. under Thatcher', *Critical Social Policy*, no. 14, pp. 57–72.

Jakobson, Roland (1971) *Studies in Child Language and Aphasia*, The Hague: Mouton.

Jameson, Frederic (1984) 'Postmodernism, or The Cultural Logic of Late Capitalism', *New Left Review*, no. 146, pp. 54–92.

Jessop, Bob, Bonnett, Kevin, Bromley, Simon and Ling Tom (1984) 'Authoritarian Populism, Two Nations and Thatcherism', *New Left Review*, no. 147, pp. 32–60.

Jessop, Bob, Bonnett, Kevin, Bromley, Simon and Ling Tom (1988) *Thatcherism: a tale of two nations*, Cambridge: Polity Press.

Johnson, Norman (1987) *The Welfare State in Transition: the theory and practice of welfare pluralism*, Hemel Hempstead: Harvester Wheatsheaf.

Jones, K and Williamson, K (1979) 'The Birth of the Schoolroom', *Ideology and Consciousness*, no. 6.

Jowell, Roger, Witherspoon, Sharon and Brook, Lindsey (1990) *British Social Attitudes*, Aldershot: Gower.

Kaye, H (1987) 'Our Island Story Retold', in *Guardian*, 3 August 1987.

Keane, John (1988) *Democracy and Civil Society*, London: Verso.

Keane, John and Owens, John (1986) *After Full Employment*, London: Hutchinson.

King, Desmond (1987) *The New Right: politics, markets and citizenship*, London: Tavistock.

Kuhn, Thomas S. (1970) *The Structure of Scientific Revolutions*, Chicago: Chicago University.

Labour Party, The (1990) *Citizen's Charter*, London: The Labour party.

Lacan, Jacques (1977) *Écrits*, trans. Alan Sheridan, London: Tavistock.

Laclau, Ernesto (1977) *Politics and Ideology in Marxist Theory: capitalism, fascism, populism*, London: New Left Books.

Laclau, Ernesto and Mouffe, Chantal (1985) *Hegemony and Socialist Strategy: towards a socialist strategy*, London: Verso.

Larrain, Jorge (1979) *The Concept of Ideology*, London: Hutchinson.

Lash, Scott and Urry, John (1987) *The End of Organised Capitalism*, Cambridge: Polity.

Laurance, Jeremy (1988) 'Wanted: a Super Social Worker', *New Society*, 15 April 1988.

Lea, John and Young, Jock (1984) *What is to be Done about Law and Order?*, Harmondsworth: Penguin Books.

Lee, Phil and Raban, Colin (1988) *Welfare Theory and Social Policy: reform or revolution*, London: Sage.

Le Grand, Julian (1982) *The Strategy of Equality*, London: Allen & Unwin.

Leiss, William (1978) *The Limits of Satisfaction*, London: Calder.

Leonard, Peter (1984) *Personality and Ideology*, London: Macmillan.

Levitas, Ruth (ed.) (1986) *The Ideology of the New Right*, Cambridge: Polity Press.

Lindblom, Charles E. (1959) 'The Science of "Muddling Through"', *Public Administration*, vol. 19, pp. 79–88.

Lukács, Georg (1971) *History and Class Consciousness*, London: Merlin.

Lukes, Steven (1982) 'Of Gods and Demons: Habermas and practical reason', in J. B. Thompson and D. Held (eds.) *Habermas: Critical Debates*, London: Macmillan.

Lyotard, Jean-François (1984) *The Postmodern Condition: a report on knowledge*, Manchester: Manchester University.

McCarney, Joseph (1986) 'What Makes Critical Theory Critical?', *Radical Philosophy*, no. 42, pp. 11–23.

McCarthy, Thomas (1978) *The Critical Theory of Jürgen Habermas*, Cambridge, Mass.: MIT.

Macey, David (1988) *Lacan in Contexts*, London: Verso.

McIntosh, Mary (1978) 'The State and the Oppression of Women', in A. Kuhn and A. Wolpe (eds.) *Feminism and Materialism*, London: Routledge & Kegan Paul.

Mack, Joanna and Lansley, Stewart (1985) *Poor Britain*, London: Allen & Unwin.

Magee, Bryan (1973) *Popper*, London: Fontana.

Malinowski, Bronislaw (1944) *A Scientific Theory of Culture and Other Essays*, Chapel Hill: University of North Carolina.

Mann, Michael (1987) 'Ruling Class Strategy and Citizenship', *Sociology*, vol. 21, no. 3, pp. 339–54.

Marcuse, Herbert (1964) *One Dimensional Man: studies in the ideologies of advanced industrial society*, London: Routledge & Kegan Paul.

Marcuse, Herbert (1969) *Eros & Civilisation: a philosophical inquiry into Freud*, London: Allen Lane.

Marshall, Thomas H. (1963) 'Citizenship and Social Class', *Sociology at the Crossroads and Other Essays*, London: Heinemann.

Marshall, Thomas H. (1981) *The Right to Welfare and Other Essays*, ed. R. Pinker, London: Heinemann.

Marx, Karl (1963) *Karl Marx: selected writings in sociology and social philosophy*, ed. T. Bottomore and M. Rubel, Harmondsworth: Penguin Books.

Marx, Karl (1976) *Capital: A Critique of Political Economy*, trans. B. Foukes, Harmondsworth: Penguin Books.

Meiksin-Wood, Ellen (1986) *The Retreat from Class: a new 'true' socialism*, London: Verso.

Miller, Peter and Rose, Nikolas (eds.) (1986) *The Power of Psychiatry*, Oxford: Basil Blackwell.

Miller, Peter and Rose, Nikolas (1988) 'The Tavistock Programme, the Government of Subjectivity and Social Life', *Sociology*, vol. 22, no. 2, pp. 171–92.

Mishra, Ramish (1981) *Society and Social Policy: theories and practice of welfare*, 2nd edn., London: Macmillan.

Mishra, Ramish (1984) *The Welfare State in Crisis: social thought and social change*, Hemel Hempstead: Harvester Wheatsheaf.

Murray, Charles (1984) *Losing Ground: American social policy 1950–1980*, New York: Basic Books.

Murray, Charles (1990) *The Emerging British Underclass*, London: Institute of Economic Affairs.

Murray, Robin (1989) 'Fordism and Post-Fordism', in S. Hall and M. Jacques, *New Times: the changing face of politics in the 1990s*, London: Verso.

Norris, Christopher (1982) *Deconstruction: theory and practice*, London: Methuen.

O'Connor, James (1973) *The Fiscal Crisis of the State*, New York: St Martin's.

O'Connor, James (1984) *Accumulation Crisis*, New York: Basil Blackwell.

Offe, Claus (1975) 'The Theory of the Capitalist State and the Problem of Policy Formation', in L. Lindberg *et al.* (eds.) *Stress and Contradiction in Modern Capitalism*, Massachusetts: Lexington.

Offe, Claus (1982) 'Some Contradictions of the Modern Welfare State', *Critical Social Policy*, vol. 2, no. 2, pp. 7–16.

Offe, Claus (1984) *Contradictions of the Welfare State*, ed. J. Keane, London: Hutchinson.

Offe, Claus (1985) *Disorganised Capitalism: contemporary transformations of work and politics*, trans. J. Keane, Cambridge: Polity Press.

Olsonn, S (1987) 'Towards the Transformation of the Swedish Welfare State', in R. R. Friedmann, N. Gilbert and M. Sherer (eds.) *Modern Welfare States: a comparative view of trends and prospects*, Hemel Hempstead: Harvester Wheatsheaf.

Oppenheim, Cary (1990) *Poverty: the Facts*, London: Child Poverty Action Group.

Papadakis, Elim and Taylor-Gooby, Peter (1987) *The Private Provision of Public Welfare*, Hemel Hempstead: Harvester Wheatsheaf.

Parton, Nigel (1986) *The Politics of Child Abuse*, Basingstoke: Macmillan.

Pinker, Robert (1971) *Social Theory and Social Policy*, London: Heinemann.

Plant, Raymond, Lesser, Harry and Taylor-Gooby, Peter (1980) *Political Philosophy and Social Welfare: essays on the normative basis of welfare provision*, London: Routledge & Kegan Paul.

Popper, Karl (1966) *Open Society and its Enemies, Volume II: Hegel and Marx*, London: Routledge & Kegan Paul.

Porter, Roy (1987) *Mind Forg'd Manacles: a history of madness in England from the Restoration to the Regency*, London: Athlone.

Quam, Lois (1989) 'Post-American Health Care', *Oxford Review of Economic Policy*, vol. 5, no. 1.

Rein, Martin (1976) *Social Science and Public Policy*, Harmondsworth: Penguin Books.

Reisman, David (1977) *Richard Titmuss: welfare and society*, London: Heinemann.

Riddell, Peter (1983) *The Thatcher Government*, Oxford: Martin Robertson.

Riddell, Peter (1989) *The Thatcher Decade: how Britian has changed during the 1980s*, Oxford: Basil Blackwell.

Robinson, Ray (1986) 'Restructuring the Welfare State', *Journal of Social Policy*, vol. 15, no. 1, pp. 1–21.

Robson, William A. (1976) *Welfare State and Welfare Society: illusion and reality*, London: Allen & Unwin.

Roderick, Rick (1986) *Habermas and the Foundations of Critical Theory*, Basingstoke: Macmillan.

Rojek, Chris, Peacock, Geraldine and Collins, Stewart (1988) *Social Work and Received Ideas*, London: Routledge.

Room, Graham (1979) *The Sociology of Welfare: social policy, social stratification and political order*, Oxford: Martin Robertson.

Rorty, Richard (1989) *Contingency, Irony and Solidarity*, Cambridge: Cambridge University Press.

Rose, Nikolas (1979) 'The Psychological Complex: Mental Measurement and Social Administration', *Ideology and Consciousness*, no. 5.

Rowntree, B. Seebohm (1901) *Poverty: a study of town life*, London: Nelson.

Rule, John B. (1978) *Insight and Social Betterment: a preface to applied social science*, New York: Oxford University.

Runciman, Walter G. (1966) *Relative Deprivation and Social Justice: a study of attitudes to social inequality in twentieth-century England*, London: Routledge & Kegan Paul.

Rustin, Michael (1989) 'The Politics of Post-Fordism', *New Left Review*, no. 175, pp. 54–77.

Saussure, Ferdinand de (1974) *Course in General Linguistics*, trans. Wade Baskin, intro. Jonathon Culler, London: Fontana.

Schneiderman, Stuart (1983) *Jacques Lacan: death of an intellectual hero*, Cambridge, Mass.: Harvard University Press.

Searle, John (1969) *Speech Acts: an essay in the philosophy of language*, London: Cambridge University Press.

Sedgwick, Peter (1981) *Psychopolitics*, London: Pluto.

Smart, Barry (1986) 'The Politics of Truth and the Problem of Hegemony' in D. C. Hoy (ed.) *Foucault: a critical reader*. Oxford: Basil Blackwell.

Smith, Gilbert (1980) *Social Need: policy, practice and research*, London: Routledge & Kegan Paul.

Springborg, Patricia (1981) *The Problem of Human Needs and the Critique of Civilisation*, London: Allen & Unwin.

Squires, Peter (1990) *Anti-Social Policy: welfare ideology and the disciplinary state*, Hemel Hempstead: Harvester Wheatsheaf.

Tawney, Richard H. (1964) *Equality*, London: Allen & Unwin.

Taylor-Gooby, Peter (1981) 'The New Right and Social Policy', *Critical Social Policy*, vol. 1, no. 1, pp. 18–31.

Taylor-Gooby, Peter (1985) *Public Opinion, Ideology and State Welfare*, London: Routledge & Kegan Paul.

Taylor-Gooby, Peter and Dale, Jennifer (1981) *Social Theory and Social Welfare*, London: Edward Arnold.

Therborn, Göran (1980) *The Ideology of Power and the Power of Ideology*, London: New Left Books.

Thompson, Edward P. (1978) *The Poverty of Theory & Other Essays*, London: Merlin.

Thompson, John B. (1982) 'Universal Pragmatics', in J. B. Thompson and D. Held, *Habermas: critical debates*, London: Macmillan.

Thompson, John B. (1984) *Studies in the Theory of Ideology*, Cambridge: Polity Press.

Thorpe, David H. *et al.* (1980) *Out of Care: the community support of juvenile offenders*, London: Allen & Unwin.

Timmins, Nicholas (1989) 'Is the N.H.S. safe in their hands?', *The Independent*, 9 February 1989.

Titmuss, Richard M. (1963) *Essays on 'the Welfare State'*, 2nd edn., London: Allen & Unwin.

Titmuss, Richard M. (1968) *Commitment to Welfare*, London: Allen & Unwin.

Titmuss, Richard M. (1974) *Social Policy: an Introduction*, London: Allen & Unwin.

Townsend, Peter (1975) *Sociology and Social Policy*, Harmondsworth: Allen Lane.

Townsend, Peter (1979) *Poverty in the United Kingdom: household resources and standards of living*, Harmondsworth: Penguin Books.

Townsend, Peter (1987) *Poverty and Labour in London: interim report of a centenary survey*, London: Low Pay Unit.

Townsend, Peter (1991) 'Tales of Future Past', *New Statesman & Society*, 1 February 1991.

Townsend, Peter and Gordon, David (1989) Memorandum submitted to the House of Commons Select Committee on Social Services report on *Minimum Income* (HC 579), London: HMSO.

Trevillian, Steven (1988) 'Griffiths or Wagner: which future for community care?', *Critical Social Policy*, no. 24, pp. 65–73.

Turner, Bryan S. (1986) *Citizenship and Capitalism: the debate over reformism*, London: Allen & Unwin.

Turner, Bryan S. (1990) 'Outline of a Theory of Citizenship', *Sociology*, vol. 24, no. 2, pp. 189–217.

Turner, Bryan S. (1991) 'The Discourse of Diet', in M. Featherstone, M. Hepworth and B. S. Turner (eds.), *The Body: social processes and cultural theory*, London: Sage.

UKCC (1986) *Project 2000: a new preparation for practice*, London: United Kingdom Central Council for Nursing.

Veit-Wilson, John (1986) 'Paradigms of Poverty: a rehabilitation of B. S. Rowntree', *Journal of Social Policy*, vol. 15, no. 1, pp. 69–99.

Veit-Wilson, John (1987) 'Consensual Approaches to Poverty Lines and Social Security', *Journal of Social Policy*, vol. 16, no. 2, pp. 183–211.

Walker, Alan (1982) 'Dependency and Old Age', *Social Policy & Administration*, vol. 16, no. 2, pp. 115–35.

Wallerstein, Immanuel (1990) 'Culture as the Ideological Battleground', *Theory, Culture & Society*, vol. 7, nos. 2–3, pp. 31–55.

Webb, Sidney (1911) *The Necessary Basis of Society* London: Fabian Society.

Webb, Sidney and Webb, Beatrice (1911) *The Prevention of Destitution*, London: Longman Green.

White, Stephen K. (1988) *The Recent Work of Jürgen Habermas: reason, justice and modernity*, Cambridge: Cambridge University Press.

Williams, Karel (1981) *From Pauperism to Poverty*, London: Routledge & Kegan Paul.

Williams, Karel and Williams, John (1987) *A Beveridge Reader*, London: Allen & Unwin.

Wolpe, AnnMarie (1978) 'Education and the Sexual Division of Labour', in A. Kuhn and A. Wolpe (eds.) *Feminism and Materialism: women and modes of production*, London: Routledge & Kegan Paul.

Index